Language and Chronology

Language and Computers

STUDIES IN DIGITAL LINGUISTICS

VOLUME 84

The titles published in this series are listed at *brill.com/lc*

Language and Chronology

Text Dating by Machine Learning

By

Gregory Toner
Xiwu Han

TUTA SUB AEGIDE PALLAS · 1683 ·

BRILL

LEIDEN | BOSTON

This work was supported by a Research Project Grant from the Leverhulme Trust [grant number RPG-2015-089]. We gratefully acknowledge the permission of CELT (https://celt.ucc.ie/) to use their digital editions.

Library of Congress Cataloging-in-Publication Data

Names: Toner, Gregory, editor. | Han, Xiwu, editor.
Title: Language and chronology : text dating by machine learning / Gregory Toner, Xiwu Han.
Description: Leiden ; Boston : Brill | Rodopi, 2019. | Series: Language and computers, 09215034 ; 84 | Includes bibliographical references and index.
Identifiers: LCCN 2019023891 (print) | LCCN 2019023892 (ebook) | ISBN 9789004410039 (hardback) | ISBN 9789004410046 (e-book)
Subjects: LCSH: Irish literature–Middle Irish, 1100-1550–Dating. | Irish literature–Middle Irish, 1100-1550–Criticism, Textual. | Manuscript dating–Methodology. | Machine learning–Technique.
Classification: LCC PB1322 .L36 2019 (print) | LCC PB1322 (ebook) | DDC 891.6/2002–dc23
LC record available at https://lccn.loc.gov/2019023891
LC ebook record available at https://lccn.loc.gov/2019023892

Typeface for the Latin, Greek, and Cyrillic scripts: "Brill". See and download: brill.com/brill-typeface.

ISSN 0921-5034
ISBN 978-90-04-41003-9 (hardback)
ISBN 978-90-04-41004-6 (e-book)

Printed by Printforce, the Netherlands

Contents

List of Figures, Tables and Algorithms IX
Abbreviations XII

Introduction 1
0.1 Automated Dating Methods 3
0.2 How to Read This Book 7

1 **Dating Texts: Principles and Methods** 11
1.1 Introduction 11
1.2 Texts by Known Authors 11
1.3 Internal Evidence 13
1.4 Manuscripts 16
1.5 Intertextuality 17
1.6 Metrics 19
1.7 Linguistic Dating 21
1.7.1 *Linguistic Strata and Scribal Revision* 23
1.7.2 *Dialect* 26
1.7.3 *Register* 27
1.7.4 *Archaism* 29
1.7.5 *Lexical Dating* 33
1.7.6 *Methodology* 36
1.8 Conclusion 39

2 **Computational Approaches to Text Dating** 41
2.1 A Brief History 41
2.1.1 *Early Research* 42
2.1.2 *Recent Research* 42
2.1.3 *DTE Task* 43
2.1.4 *Features for Dating* 43
2.1.5 *Lazy Method* 44
2.2 The Problem Stated 44
2.2.1 *Problem Formulation* 44
2.2.2 *Evaluation Methods* 46
2.3 Previous Solutions 47
2.3.1 *Language Modelling* 48
2.3.2 *Ordinal Regression/Ranking* 48
2.3.3 *Classification* 49

2.3.4 *Feature Selection Methods* 50
2.3.5 *Regression vs Classification* 50
2.4 New Solutions 52
2.4.1 *Flexible Time Interval* (FTI) 52
2.4.2 *Sliding Time Interval* (STI) 53
2.4.3 *Greedy Grouping* (GG) 56
2.4.4 *Temporal Landmark Selection* (TLS) 57
2.4.5 *Compound Solution of* FTI&TLS 63
2.5 Datability 64
2.6 Conclusion 65

3 **Trials in English and Medieval Irish Texts** 67
3.1 Dating English Texts 67
3.1.1 *Data and Features* 68
3.1.2 *Choosing Basic Classifiers* 69
3.1.3 *Experiments and Results* 70
3.2 Dating Medieval Irish Texts 75
3.2.1 *The Corpus: the Irish Annals* 77
3.3 Implementation 80
3.3.1 *Data Pre-Processing and Features for Classification* 80
3.3.2 *Experiments and Results* 81
3.4 Temporal Parameters 83
3.5 Datability 90
3.6 Conclusion 92

4 **Dating Long Documents** 94
4.0 Introduction 94
4.1 Building a Datable Medieval Irish Corpus 95
4.2 Dating Long Documents 98
4.2.1 *Test Data and Pre-Processing* 98
4.2.2 *Dating Long Documents with the Most Frequent Predict* 100
4.2.3 *Dating Long Documents with Multiple Choices* 100
4.2.4 *Evaluation of Bias Compensation* 106
4.3 Establishing the Date of Composition 109
4.3.1 *Correlation between the Results and the Accepted Date of Composition* 110
4.3.2 *Extending the Range of Texts* 113
4.3.3 *Conclusion* 116
4.4 Transmission and Manuscript Dates 117
4.5 Focussed Dating Predictions 119

4.5.1 *Overall Performance* 124
4.6 Periodisation 125
4.7 Stratification 127
4.8 Conclusion 129

5 **Conclusion** 132
5.1 A Temporal Model 133
5.2 Towards a Tool: Computational Chronometrics 137
5.3 Applicability to Other Literatures 140

Appendix A: Conventional Dating of Texts Used in This Study 143
A.0.1 *Book of the Dun Cow* 143
A.0.2 *Rawlinson B 502* 144
A.0.3 *The Book of Leinster* 144
A.1 Texts 145
A.1.1 *Acallam na Senórach* 145
A.1.2 *Aided Derbforgaill* 146
A.1.3 *Aided Echach mac Maireda* 146
A.1.4 *Aided Guill maic Carbada* 147
A.1.5 *Aided Nath Í* 147
A.1.6 *Aislinge Óengusso* 148
A.1.7 *Aislinge Meic Conglinne* 148
A.1.8 *Bethadh Bibuis* 148
A.1.9 *Betha Adamnáin* 149
A.1.10 *Betha Colmáin* 149
A.1.11 *Bethu Brigtc* 150
A.1.12 *Bórama Laigen* 150
A.1.13 *Bruiden Da Choca* 150
A.1.14 *Caithréim Thoirdhealbhaigh* 150
A.1.15 *Cath Almaine* 151
A.1.16 *In Cath Catharda* 151
A.1.17 *Cath Maighe Léna* 151
A.1.18 *Cath Ruis na Ríg* 152
A.1.19 *Cogadh Gaedel re Gallaib* 152
A.1.20 *De Dosibus Medicarum* 153
A.1.21 *Echtra Láegaire* 153
A.1.22 *Fingal Rónáin* 153
A.1.23 *Guy of Warwick* 154
A.1.24 *Genemain Áeda Sláine* 154
A.1.25 *Maundeville* 154

A.1.26 *Mesca Ulad* 154
A.1.27 *Merugud Uilix* 155
A.1.28 *Monastery of Tallaght* 155
A.1.29 *Regimen na Sláinte* 156
A.1.30 *Saltair na Rann* 156
A.1.31 *Scél Mucce Maic Dathó* 157
A.1.32 *Táin Bó Cúailnge* 157
A.1.33 *Táin Bó Fraích* 158
A.1.34 *Tochmarc Emire* 160
A.1.35 *Treatise on the Psalter* 160
A.1.36 *Tucait Indarba na nDéssi* 160
Appendix B: Machine Learning 162
B.1 Classification, Regression and Clustering 162
B.1.1 *Text Classification* 162
B.1.2 *Feature Selection* 163
B.1.3 *Training* 163
B.1.4 *Evaluation* 163
B.2 Other Relevant Statistics 164
Bibliography 165
Index 181

Figures, Tables and Algorithms

Figures

2.1 Examples of data format and class labels in *Y* 45
2.2 Fixed (a) and flexible (b) time intervals for multi-class classification 53
2.3 Fixed and sliding time intervals for multi-class classification 54
2.4 Per-class dating precisions of three NBM classifiers trained on texts labeled with time intervals from three different segmentations 55
2.5 Greedy grouping according to the similarities among temporally adjacent texts 57
2.6 Reformat the time intervals by selecting a landmark 59
2.7 Example of binary format for timestamps with $\delta = 3$ 59
3.1 Classifying accuracy comparison of different classification models on DTE2 70
3.2 Tuning results of FTI δ' 90
3.3 Tuning results of STI *w* and *s* 90
3.4 Tuning results of GG *i* 91
3.5 Tuning results of GG_{MI} *i* and *c* 91
3.6 Tuning results of *K* and *k* in TLS and TLS&FTI 91
3.7 Estimated datability for dating our six corpora with $\delta = 10$ 92
4.1 Accuracy rates by time for annals with $\delta = 25$ 97
4.2 Number of entries in the annals by half century 97
4.3 Chunk dating results and multiple choices for dating *Aislinge Óengusso* 102
4.4 Example for providing improved multiple choices for dating Aislinge Óengusso 107, 108
4.5 Uncorrected datings for Mesca Ulad A and Mesca Ulad B (texts 25 and 30) 114
4.6 Uncorrected datings for Bruiden Da Choca (32) 115
4.7 Top dating features in Bruiden Da Choca (32) over time 115
4.8 Dating by traditional method v. our method (without bias reduction). Texts are arranged by the conventional date. With thanks to Tom Toner for producing this graph 122
4.9 Mesca Ulad version B (chunks 1-92) and A (chunks 93-109) in narrative order. Box indicates extent of version A 128
5.1 Dating of the translations of the Annals of Ulster with $\delta = 50$ 135

Tables

2.1 Loss function on off intervals (Popescu and Strapparava, 2015) 47
2.2 State-of-the-art dating performances on DTE Subtask 2 (Popescu and Strapparava, 2015) 51
3.1 English corpora and relevant information 68
3.2 Computing time (in seconds) comparison of different classification models on DTE2 69
3.3 FTI tuning results of δ' values on the training set of DTE2 70
3.4 Dating accuracies (%) of FTI and UCD SVM on the test set of DTE2 71
3.5 Tuning results of STI parameters on the training set of DTE2 71
3.6 Dating accuracies (%) of basic STI classifiers on the training set of DTE2 72
3.7 Dating accuracies (%) of STI and UCD SVM on the test set of DTE2 72
3.8 GG and GGMI training results and dating performances (%) on DTE2 73
3.9 TLS training results of 10-fold cross-validation and dating performance (%) on the test set of DTE2 74
3.10 TLS&FTI training results of 10-fold cross-validation and dating performance (%) on the test set of DTE2 75
3.11 Training results of 10-fold cross-validation for all solutions on Freecycle 76
3.12 Dating accuracy (%) for all solutions on freecycle test set 77
3.13 Our medieval Irish corpora 81
3.14 Numbers of feature types for our text dating experiments on medieval Irish corpora 81
3.15 Training results of 10-fold cross-validation for all solutions on Inisfallen 82
3.16 Dating accuracy (%) for all solutions on Inisfallen test set 83
3.17 Training results of 10-fold cross-validation for all solutions on Ulster 84
3.18 Dating accuracy (%) for all solutions on Ulster test set 85
3.19 Training results of 10-fold cross-validation for all solutions on Loch Cé 86
3.20 Dating accuracy (%) for all solutions on Loch Cé test set 87
3.21 Training results of 10-fold cross-validation for all solutions on combination 88
3.22 Dating accuracy (%) for all solutions on combination test set 89
3.23 Temporal parameters for each of our solutions 89
3.24 *H*, the history period covered by the training corpus 91
4.1 Dating performance (%) estimated by 10-fold cross-validation on the extended large medieval Irish corpus 97
4.2 Accuracy of dating 700-999 relative to size of training corpus annals with $\delta = 25$ 98
4.3 Test data of long medieval Irish texts 99
4.4 Dating long medieval Irish texts by estimation with the most frequent predict 101

4.5 Top-3 most frequently predicted dates as multiple choices 103
4.6 Possibly biased dates 105
4.7 Improved top-3 multiple dating choices 106
4.8 Long-text dating with bias compensation ±50 years. Bold = date within dating tolerance = 50 years; bold italic = within the given date range 110
4.9 Long-text dating with bias compensation ±50 years. Bold = date within dating tolerance = 50 years; bold italic = within the given date range 113
4.10 Texts sorted by date of manuscript 118
4.11 Dates adjusted to ±10-year tolerances before bias adjustment; texts sorted by given date 120
4.12 Dates adjusted to ±10-year tolerances with bias reduction; texts sorted by given date 121
4.13 Accuracy of focussed dating by century using D1 only 124
4.14 Accuracy of focussed dating by century using D2 only 125
4.15a Focussed dates from Table 4.11 sorted by D1 (before bias reduction) 126
4.15b Focussed dates from Table 4.12 sorted by D1 (after bias reduction) 126

Algorithms

2.1 Dating texts by classification with flexible time intervals 54
2.2 Dating texts by classification with sliding time intervals 57
2.3 Dating texts by classification with greedy grouping 58
2.4 Dating texts by classification with greedy grouping via mutual information 58
2.5.1 Temporal landmark selection via Column Subset Selection 61
2.5.2 Merging timestamps into class labels 62
2.5.3 Classification and prediction with merged class labels 63
2.6 Dating texts by classification with FTI&TLS 64
4.1 Building a larger and more datable medieval Irish corpus 96
4.2 Improving the multiple choices by reinforcement and adaptive learning 104

Abbreviations

AU	Annals of Ulster, ed. Mac Airt & Mac Niocaill (1983) to 1131 CE and Hennessy & Mac Carthy (1887-1901) for the remainder
Brus.	Bibliothèque Royale de Belgique, Brussels
CELT	Corpus of Electronic Texts
CSS	Column Subset Selection
d.	died
DIAS	Dublin Institute for Advanced Studies
DTE	Diachronic Text Evaluation
eDIL	electronic Dictionary of the Irish Language (www.dil.ie)
f./ff.	folio(s)
FTI	Flexible Time Intervals
GG	Greedy Grouping
GG_{MI}	Greedy Grouping via Mutual Information
MS(S)	manuscript(s)
NB	Naïve Bayes
NBM	Naïve Bayes Multinomial
NLLR	normalised log-likelihood ration
NLP	Natural Language Processing
NM	normal distribution matrix
RIA	Royal Irish Academy
SMO	Sequential Minimal Optimization
STI	Sliding Time Intervals
SVD	Singular Value Decomposition
SVM	Support Vector Machine
TEI	Text Encoding Initiative
tf-idf	term frequency-inverse document frequency
TLS	Temporal Landmark Selection
TM	Trained Distribution Matrix
TNM	Trained Normal Distribution Matrix
UM	Uniform Distribution Matrix

Introduction

The dating of texts is essential to a historical understanding of the intellectual and social environment in which they were produced. As Lévi-Strauss (1966, 258) observed, 'There is no history without dates… history's entire originality and distinctive nature lie in apprehending the relation between *before* and *after*'. It is axiomatic that historians must arrange and interrogate events chronologically: to do otherwise would not be history. We take for granted in the modern world that important documents are dated closely – letters, newspapers, diaries, witness statements, parliamentary bills, journals and books are all supplied with exact dates of writing or issue. Electronic communications and transactions are dated yet more precisely to the hour, minute and even second. Explicit dating is not universal, however, particularly in the pre-Modern, pre-print period and many written cultures have little by way of securely dating the documents that they produced. It is true that charters and laws in the medieval period are often given a year of writing, or at the very least they may be dated to the reign of a particular king, but this does not extend to all texts.

In the absence of explicit dates, the floruit of the author, if known, can be used to locate a text in time, assuming of course that the attribution is secure. However, it is often the case in many antique and medieval literatures that, as well as lacking explicit dates, texts also lack a reliable attribution. In their absence, we may be able to identify datable events such as a reference to a battle or a king in the text. The Book of Haggai, for example, claims that it was written in the second year of the Persian king, Darius the Great, which would place it in 520 BCE (Nelson 2014: 214). More often than not, however, such references are to events in the past, in which case they provide evidence for a terminus post quem ('a limit after which') – the text cannot have been written before the date of a named event. In practice, multiple dating methods are employed to secure dates for unattributed texts but ultimately such dates are more often than not provisional and approximate. Further research may lead to a revised view as new facts are brought to light but texts may only ever remain dated to within a range rather than a specific year. The fundamental fact of the date of a text may, therefore, remain contentious.

An important distinction must be made between the date of a document and the date of the text(s) that it contains. We use 'text' here as a generic term for a written work 'regarded in terms of its content rather than its physical form' (see OED), such as a story, a religious treatise, a legal tract etc. It is independent of its physical instantiation, whether that be in a manuscript,

 | DOI:10.1163/9789004410046_002

papyrus or printed book for which we use the term 'document'. We may think of the document, therefore, as the individual physical occurrence of a text. Consequently, a single text may appear in multiple documents, and a single document may contain many texts. In terms of chronology, the document and text may be of the same date, as for example the original copies of charters or letters. However, in ancient and medieval literatures, the earliest manuscript may well postdate the composition of a text by many centuries or even millennia, so that the date of the manuscript, if that can be ascertained, may provide nothing more than a terminus ante quem, a 'limit before which' the text must have been composed. To date a manuscript, therefore, is not the same as dating the texts that it contains, and while manuscripts are susceptible to a range of dating techniques, including codicological and palaeographic analysis and, in extremis, radio-carbon dating, these methods cannot be used directly on the texts themselves.

If internal evidence for the date of a text is not forthcoming, we must turn to other methods, and the one most commonly used is linguistic dating. Linguistic dating seeks to fix the time of writing of a text relative to other texts in the same language based on a thorough analysis of their syntax, morphology and orthography. Languages tend to change over time so that, in principle, we should be able to track those developments and use them to date other texts. The method relies on significant changes in speech, but such variations are not always evenly and predictably represented in written texts. At the most basic level, changes in speech patterns may not occur evenly across a language area or even a dialect, and so may appear irregularly in written texts. Written texts may be conservative or knowingly archaising, so that linguistic changes may be only partially reflected in documents for several centuries after they begin to occur in the spoken language. A further complication is that the texts that we are interested in here were often copied and recopied over successive centuries. Revisions and corrections by later copyists can complicate the picture by adding different linguistic strata to a text that can be impossible to disentangle at a sufficiently granular level. The method works best when we have a large corpus of already dated or attributed material existing in contemporary or near-contemporary copies. The development of the language can thus be traced from generation to generation, securely anchored to the dates and dialects of known authors. However, where authorship is not generally attributed in a literature, we may be denied two key pieces of information – the dates of a representative sample of texts and the place of writing which could point towards variation due to regional dialects. Without attribution, it can be difficult or impossible to know whether a particular linguistic feature is a result of chronological developments or of dialect.

We may compare this situation to attempts to understand an archaeological site without radio-carbon dating and dendrochronology. Tools such as these have revolutionised archaeology which was previously reliant on the typology of artefacts and stratification – objects belonging to the same soil layer could be assigned to the same period and the further down the archaeologist dug the older the material must have been. A closely datable object found in one layer – such as coin minted in the year of a particular emperor or king of known date – enabled archaeologists to place all objects in that stratum in that period, but otherwise dating was relative – object X is older than object Y because it is in a lower layer. The introduction of externally calibrated technological measures of dating facilitated the establishment of absolute, calendrical dates more widely, albeit with certain margins of error. For literatures, linguistic dating is, by definition, relative, although texts can be fixed approximately to absolute dates by comparison with others of known date. However, linguistic dating is necessarily more ambiguous than the tools available to archaeologists and, as we shall see, despite a rigorous methodology diligently applied, almost always comprises some element of subjective judgement. Indeed, the level of complexity is such that dating has been abandoned by some in favour of an ahistorical approach (see Neidorf 2013, 167).

0.1 Automated Dating Methods

In this book, we describe the development of new dating techniques using machine learning methods. Machine learning is a branch of Artificial Intelligence in the field of computer science that often uses statistical and/or mathematic techniques to give computers the ability to 'learn' (i.e., progressively improve performance on a specific task) from supplied data without being explicitly programmed (Samuel, 1959; Koza et al, 1996). The name 'machine learning' was coined in 1959 by Arthur Samuel (1959). Evolved from the study of pattern recognition and computational learning theory in artificial intelligence, machine learning explores the study and construction of algorithms that can learn from and make predictions on data (Kohavi and Provost, 1998). What is generally understood as a computer program consists of series of instructions, sometimes amounting to millions of lines of code, that tell the computer how to perform particular functions, whether that be displaying the time or guiding a rocket into space. These programs, however complex and sophisticated they may become, are essentially static. The programmers must foresee every eventuality and provide mechanisms for dealing with them. Machine learning algorithms overcome strictly static program instructions by making data-driven predictions or decisions through building a model from sample inputs. Machine learning is closely related to (and often overlaps with) computational statistics, which also focuses on prediction-making through the use of computers and it has strong ties to mathematical optimisation, which provides the field with methods, theory and application domains.

Within the field of machine learning, there are two main types of task: supervised and unsupervised. Algorithms used in the research covered in this book belong mostly to the former. Both methods use a training set from which the computer learns particular patterns. In unsupervised learning, the algorithm infers its own structure from an unmarked data set. In supervised learning, however, the training data is labelled for the desired feature and the algorithm must learn a function that describes the patterns associated with each label. When that function is then applied to unknown data sets, it should be able to apply the appropriate label to its contents. For example, in visual identification software, the algorithm seeks patterns in the pixels of a picture of an object such as a cancerous cell and builds a virtual model of that object that can then be used to identify other similar objects in previously unseen images. In the dating of documents, we assemble a corpus of texts that are labelled by date and the algorithm constructs a model of the changing profile of those texts over time.

A successful method applicable to pre-Modern texts must solve certain problems not normally associated with modern languages. Firstly, it must work with non-standardised and perhaps highly inflected languages. The standardisation of languages and their orthography as we would understand it today is largely a product in the West of nineteenth-century nation building and codification. One of the unintended consequences of standardisation is that it has facilitated the digital age – standardised orthographies greatly simplify the processes of machine sorting and searching. Even relatively straightforward procedures such as concordance building, and more complex areas such as topic modelling, are much more difficult in a non-standardised language due to a lack of correspondence between written forms that allow them to be easily grouped under a single lemma or headword, and this may be further compounded by high degrees of linguistic inflection. English is a largely uninflected language, making the connection between the various forms of a word and their lemma relatively straightforward. For example, it generally forms the plural of nouns by adding an *s* or *es* (lights, houses, birds, foxes) with only a small number of inflected forms which require a more radical change to the stem (oxen, mice, geese). Inflected forms are used in the past tense (fight – fought, run – ran) but they do not vary according to number or person (I, she, we, they thought) and are relatively limited. Other languages show a much greater degree of inflection, as in Latin which commonly has six cases of nouns and has a synthetic verbal system in which the person and number are indicated in the form of the verb rather than being expressed by an independent pronoun as in English. The practical solution most frequently adopted to deal with such variation is to parse and lemmatise the texts but this is labour-intensive and, as a result, expensive. The more formally complex the language is the more difficult this becomes. Fortunately, non-standardised languages can be an advantage in chronological machine learning. If the language is standardised, there will be little variation in the surface representation of the language over time, even though the spoken language may be changing. A digital dating technique for English may rely to a large extent on an examination of key words and phrases that vary over time – the five-word string 'case of the Cistercian buildings' is an effective indicator of a nineteenth-century date when found among Google's collection of nineteenth- and twentieth-century books (Josund, Rampuria and Shroff (n.d.): 10). Non-standardised languages are more amenable to a more general linguistic examination as changes in the oral language are more likely to be represented in the written word. Variation in spelling and linguistic form can be a more important indicator of age, therefore.

A further problem that automated dating techniques need to address is that they may be dealing with comparatively small, incomplete or lacunose collections of texts. Modern corpora of major languages tend to be large, securely dated and well documented. All machine learning methods require a reasonable set of training texts in order to learn patterns relevant to their chronology, but many literatures are quite small and may lack a large enough corpus of time-stamped texts for training. Machine-learning methods, therefore, should, where possible, allow for training and testing on one type of text for which dates are available and from which a general language model that is applicable to other genres can be constructed. This is not a trivial problem and it is preferable to train an algorithm on texts of a similar nature, but this is not always going to be possible.

As we have already noted, the long transmission of texts in a manuscript culture is an added complication for the dating of texts as it can lead to the corruption and modernisation of the language and contents of a text. If this is superficial, scholars can detect earlier forms of the language but scribes were often engaged in much more than the mere transmission of a fixed text. They frequently corrected the content, introduced new material, reworked the telling, or completely rewrote all or parts of the text to suit a contemporary audience. Fortunately, their rewriting is not always entirely thorough and earlier strata can be distinguished but the practice of revision raises fundamental questions about the nature of a text. Depending on the extent of the later reworking we may legitimately ask what is the date of such a text? Indeed, does it have 'a date' or do we need to think of it as having multiple dates? There is a wide recognition among textual scholars that they have to read the texts as they are found in the manuscript, but this does not mean that they accept that the date of the text is the same as that of the manuscript. Clearly it would make no sense to apply the date of the manuscript to the Iliad, the earliest extant copy of which was written some two millennia after Homer composed his epic poem. As scholars, we are more interested in the authorship of the text than its transcription, but if there are effectively multiple authors, on account of later revisions, which text are we reading and dating? In short, we should not expect a dating algorithm to supply a single date of composition. Yes, we would hope that it could detect the work of the original author, but it should also encapsulate the possibility of later revisions.

Digital dating methods have been developed in the last decade for application to modern literary and non-literary texts but so far they have remained largely within the realm of Computing Science, and have not been applied to the more difficult and pressing problem of dating ancient and medieval documents. Some progress has been made in the area of automated document dating – that is, the dating of physical copies by analysis of their palaeography (e.g. He, Sheng, Samara, Burgers & Schomaker (2016), Christlein, Gropp & Maier (2017), Adam, Kalthoum, Asim Baig, Al-Maadeed, Bouridane, and El-Menshawy (2018)) and by a mixture of palaeographic, orthographic and expert supervision (Wahlberg, Mårtensson, and Brun 2016). Tilahun, Feuerverger and Gervers (2012) use recurrence of word n-grams ('shingles') of one, two and three words in English charters to determine closeness of documents, but admit that the method is effective only in this narrow domain. Belinkov, Magidow, Romanov, Shmidman, and Koppel (2016) use a 5-gram model for Arabic using a much broader training corpus spanning 1400 years, thereby enabling them to date texts from unspecified genres. What we try to develop here is a method which can learn on one genre (annals) and apply the model that it builds to others. As medieval Irish is a highly inflected language with little by way of standardisation for most of its history, our method must look beyond word patterns and work with only a minimal degree of textual markup. We borrow the term 'chronometrics' from archaeology to describe this approach as it attempts to provide absolute dates, with a defined margin of error, for texts rather than dating them relative to one another. The dating is, of course, relative to the annalistic texts, but as these are annual records they have the benefit of offering a series of precise dates against which other texts can be ranked, provided of course that we can circumvent the problem of non-contemporary recording that besets the annals (see below).

0.2 How to Read This Book

There has arisen something of a division in digital humanities between the makers and interpreters – between those who code and those who seek to use digital tools to further their own research (see e.g. Fitzpatrick 2012: 13-14). This divide is unhealthy and can only lead to the isolation of digital humanities research from traditional modes and methods and so hinder the kind of collaboration that we need if the new technologies are to be most productive. Digital humanities cannot exist outside and separate from the humanities but must enter into dialogue with traditional methods and scholars. A more important question than programming skill is whether humanities scholars need to be able to understand the workings of the algorithms through which code functions. As Le Deuff (2018: 93) remarks, 'digital humanists do not necessarily need to become computer specialists, but rather encoders and decoders'. In other words, they need to know how to prepare data for a program and then interpret the results. Ramsay and Rockwell (2012: 80) hold that we don't have to understand how particular tools work, rather '[t]heir theoretical assumptions have to be inferred through use or else explained through the very stand-in documentation that we are trying to avoid treating as a necessary part of the tool.' That is to say, it might be sufficient to understand what a program does by examining its output. It is probably not important to know how a concordance works on the programming level – the output is itself transparent, and it is left to the user to evaluate the significance of the statistics that it generates. However, for more complex programs, the relation between the input and out put is not as straightforward, and in machine learning it may not even be clear from an examination of the algorithms how the output has been generated. Uricchio (2017: 127) observes that current machine learning techniques 'have enabled algorithms to self-optimise and generate their own improvements. They can now self-author and self-create.' A machine-learning program, therefore, is no longer a static set of instructions relentlessly followed by a computer but an evolving, malleable algorithm which is different at the end of the process of learning. The learning transforms the algorithm. Understanding what a program is doing in that context is far less straightforward.

The opacity of complex machine learning algorithms has been termed 'black boxing' (Rieder and Röhle 2012). This stems from engineering uses in which a complex mechanism could be represented graphically by an empty box which signified all its features. With the increasing complexity of machine learning algorithms, the real test of the functionality of a piece of software is in the evaluation of its input and output. This places the domain expert at the heart of the process of design and critical enquiry for it is she who is best placed to assess the performance. But even this is not uncontroversial. Humanities research proceeds by way of argumentation – the presentation and weighing of the evidence in an explicit way. Other scholars can evaluate the evidence, produce counter-evidence and agree, and ultimately reject or modify the conclusions. With machine learning, the computer gives us a result but does not provide a rationale, or even an array of evidence that we, as humans, can access or assess. A different kind of evaluation is called for. Computing experts can assess the functionality of the algorithm on one hand, and both computing expert and domain expert can be involved in evaluating the results. By testing the algorithm on objects with known properties, such as dates in this case, we can ascertain how frequently it gets the right answer and how much variance there is in the responses (i.e. how far wrong it may be). As we shall see, we can determine which data sets it works well for and which ones it performs poorly on. Where it performs poorly, we can seek to improve the results by a combination of innovations in the learning method (the algorithm) and improvements in the training data. The need for collaboration between computing and humanities experts extends, therefore, from design through to evaluation.

The centrality of the humanities scholar is further highlighted in recent epistemological research which questions the use of data by machines. Drucker (2012: 89) warns us that 'Graphs and charts reify statistical information. They give it a look of certainty.' Rieder and Röhle (2012: 70) caution that 'while the results may be visually impressive and intuitively convincing, the methodological and epistemological status of their output is still unclear'. Moreover, we have become increasingly aware that the selection of the input data can be just as important as the algorithm. Kitchin (2014: n.p.) observes that data provides 'oligoptic views of the world: views from certain vantage points, using particular tools, rather than an all-seeing, infallible God's eye view'. In other words, data sets do not have an objective reality in and of themselves but are human constructs. While this is especially true of social science research, in which data is generated from the real world, it also applies to literary and historical research in which the data is harvested from written sources. This places the humanities scholar back at the core of digital process. Van Es, López Coombs & Boeschoten (2017: 174) advocate a reflexive approach to digital humanities tools. They argue that researchers need to adopt an open and transparent approach to their work, allowing readers and users to see how the results have been arrived at. They identify three stages in digital data analysis in which the researcher must be 'reflexive': the acquisition of the data, cleaning and preparing the data, and analysis and presentation.

We have attempted, therefore, in this book to address the problem from both angles – that of the nuts and bolts of machine learning and the issues of input and output. We lay out the workings of the algorithms used for those with sufficient expertise to evaluate and critique. The computing researcher will be able to assess how we have approached the problem of dating and see how our methods attempt to tackle it. However, we also adopt an evaluative approach advocated by digital humanists. We lay bare the nature of the dating problem and we discuss the sources used for training and explain how they have been prepared for training and testing. Finally, the results are evaluated both quantitatively and qualitatively from both a statistical and humanistic perspective. The examination of the algorithms can assure the reader that the approach is rigorous and scientific, but it is the results, we believe, that demonstrate the efficacy, and limitations, of the methods.

Different audiences may approach the book in different ways and the following is only a recommendation. Chapter 1 frames the problem and is important to both audiences. It is written in an accessible way so that no prior knowledge is required. It is focused on the dating of the Irish Gaelic corpus of c.700-c.1600, but the issues are similar to those encountered in ancient and medieval texts in general. It provides an overview of the problems of traditional methods of dating medieval texts, including author attribution, internal evidence, linguistic dating and metrics, and through this attempts to identify the theoretical, textual and linguistic issues that face both textual scholars and machine learning algorithms. What do we mean when we assign a date to a medieval text which may have been generations in the making? How secure and precise are traditional methods and is the endeavour feasible at all? How is language change reflected in written texts, and how do we allow for dialect differentiation, conservatism and archaisation? This discussion explains the methods by which accepted dates have been established. It is meant to remind the Humanities reader of the fragility of current methods and to inform the computing specialist of the complexity of the problem that any algorithm must address. A simplistic view based on our own understanding of modern texts will lead to errors in implementation and interpretation.

Chapters 2 and 3 provide the technical discussion of the problem and possible solutions. Humanities scholars may find these daunting and may wish to read only the introduction and conclusion to each. Chapter 2 reviews current computational approaches to dating documents and formulates the problem from a computational perspective. It describes existing language modelling methods including ordinal regression (ranking), classification and feature selection, and presents new solutions to some of the problems associated with these methods. Finally, it suggests a way of measuring the datability of a particular corpus. The solutions developed in this chapter are tested and evaluated in Chapter 3 using various corpora in English and Irish.

The ultimate aim is to be able to date narrative texts of unknown dates but testing of the effectiveness of a particular model requires the use of texts of known dates, and this is tackled in Chapter 4. This should be readily accessible to all. The accuracy of the machine-generated predictions is evaluated against dates agreed among scholars in the field, and the robustness of the model along its entire timeline is examined. Unsurprisingly, the model is at its strongest where there is the most training data, so it is important to identify its weaknesses before applying it to texts of unknown date. Various biases appear to be present and we develop here a method for bias correction that proves most effective where the model is weak.

A brief history of scholarly analysis of the dates of the individual texts studied in Chapter 4 is given in Appendix A. This should alert readers to the nature of the evidence for the dates generally agreed – or sometimes merely accepted – among scholars in the field, and to the composite or stratified nature of others. In order to help humanities scholars understand the principles of machine learning, a brief outline of the main terms and their use is given in Appendix B, along with references to further reading.

CHAPTER 1

Dating Texts: Principles and Methods

1.1 Introduction

We have seen that the problem facing scholars engaging with ancient and medieval texts is one of providing an historical context for the works that they are studying. In this chapter, we will examine conventional dating methods used in the field. We will use examples primarily from medieval Gaelic Ireland which produced a substantial and more or less continuous corpus of material in a wide variety of genres. Although confined primarily to this one language, the methods described are comparable to those applied elsewhere and the discussion will reveal some of the problems with current approaches, as well as some of the issues facing any kind of dating methodology such as the digital methods proposed in Chapter 2. We turn to other traditions, notably biblical and Anglo-Saxon, in the discussion of lexical dating (1.7.5) as this method has not been widely employed for Irish texts.

We will begin the chapter with a discussion of dating by means of author attribution and through the use of internal evidence (reference to known historical events), and then proceed to an extensive analysis of linguistic dating methods and the issues that it must grapple with. This is especially relevant to the machine learning method being explored later in the book as computers must confront many of the same issues as faced by humans performing the same task, such as distinguishing between different historical strata within a text, or the irregular and uncertain pace of adoption of linguistic changes by different writers. As we shall see, scholars are rarely faced with a pristine copy of a text written by the author or a contemporary scribe, but rather must struggle with palimpsest texts that in some cases have passed through generations of scribes. Importantly, in the case of Ireland, texts are rarely treated as canonical, to be transmitted accurately without variation. Rather, they were copied by scholars with an active interest in the content who felt free to insert, rearrange, update and delete where they felt appropriate. Disentangling these phases is a major challenge that probably can only ever be partially achieved.

1.2 Texts by Known Authors

The most secure texts historically are those that are found in autograph manuscripts with a known author of acknowledged date, and failing that, texts

 | DOI:10.1163/9789004410046_003

in which an anonymous work is contemporary with the time of writing of the manuscript. Unfortunately, in the Irish tradition, named authors are extremely rare for prose texts before the fifteenth century. We have several works in Latin with known authors who also include a small amount of material in Irish, chiefly names of people and places, for example, Muirchú and Tírechán's Lives of St Patrick (Bieler 1979) and Adomnán's Life of St Columba (Anderson and Anderson 1961), but nothing in Gaelic.

Verse texts differ from prose in that an author is frequently named, although there is frequently serious doubt about the validity of the ascription. It seems that verse was used for the preservation of knowledge, even within a largely literate environment, and, within this context, poems could provide authority to texts which cited them (see Toner 2005; Ní Mhaonaigh 2014). The fathering of poems on influential, established poets, therefore, was a method of imbuing a text with his authority, and a great many poems were falsely attributed as a result (see below). This reduces the reliability of dating through ascription, and the usual approach is to conduct further tests, whether linguistic, contextual or stylistic, to confirm the authenticity of the ascription. The 'Hymn to Columcille' (*Amra Coluim Chille*) is ascribed to a sixth-century poet, Dallán Forgaill, and it was thought to have been written shortly after the death of the saint in 597. However, Bisagni (2009) argues that there is no trace of Early Old Irish and he would now place its composition as late as the ninth century. Another early poem, 'The Hymn of Senán' (*Amra Senáin*) is attributed to the same Dallán, but it is likely to have been composed c.900 by the bishop and king of Cashel, Cormac mac Cuilennáin (†908), to whom it is also ascribed (L. Breatnach 1989).

In addition, a large number of poems are put in the mouths of early Irish saints, even though the language of the poems clearly indicates a later date of composition. Equally fanciful are the numerous attributions to mythical or pseudo-historical poets, such as Fintan mac Bóchra, one of the putative early invaders of Ireland who survived the Flood and lived for five millennia, taking on many different forms. Revenants such as Fintan play an important historiographical function in providing an authoritative conduit for the transmission of history (see Nagy 1997). As supposedly one of the first men to arrive in Ireland, he lived through each successive wave of invaders and was an eye witness to the unfolding events. By creating or appropriating characters such as Fintan, medieval Irish historians were able to explain how they had access to knowledge of ancient events and so validate their own histories.

Nevertheless, poets of the tenth, eleventh and subsequent centuries did leave a body of poetry, much of which can be safely attributed to a known historical person. For example, the poem 'All the annal-writing heretofore' (*Annálad anall uile*) is dated twice within the poem to 1072 (Smith 2007: 190,

210), and the ascription to Gilla Cóemáin can be accepted as genuine. However, even correctly attributed poems suffer from some of the same problems as prose texts, notably the intervention of later scribes or scholars. The poem 'Champions who dwelt in Emain' (*Fianna bátar in Emain*, Stokes 1902) is ascribed to the poet Cináed úa hArtacáin who died c.975. The work is preserved in several manuscripts including the twelfth-century Book of Leinster where we find a number of additional verses ascribed to Finn, a bishop of Kildare, who was associated with the writing of the manuscript. It is rare to find insertions attributed in this way, however. Much more frequently, accretions must be detected by other means.

Irish verse exhibits a characteristic ornamentation that marks the possibility of later additions. Almost invariably, the first syllable, word or series of words is repeated in the last line of the poem, a feature known as 'closure' (*dúnad*). Where closure is absent, we may suspect that something is missing, but more importantly from the current perspective, we often find examples of multiple closures within a single verse text, in which case we may suspect that the poem has been continued and expanded by a later writer. Multiple closures should alert us to the possibility of the revision of a poem, although it has also been argued that they may merely indicate structural divisions within an integral piece (see Theuerkauf 2017: 63-4). The researcher, therefore, needs to make a judgement on whether a second closure is a structural marker or an indicator of later revision, but at the very least closure can direct the researcher to possible expansions in a poem.

Another possible factor to consider is the incorporation of older material into a poem by a known author. The poem 'Pure Ireland, island of the saints' (*Ériu óg inis na náem*) is attributed to the twelfth century poet Gilla Modutu úa Casaide. Its most recent editor accepts that Gilla Modutu penned the whole poem (Hemprich 2009), but Ní Mhaonaigh (2014: 287-8) has argued that he was responsible only for part of it and drew extensively on an earlier anonymous poem on the Christian kings of Ireland down to Máel Sechnaill mac Domnaill (d. 1022). Modutu himself wrote only the later eleventh- and twelfth-century material, adding just over twenty stanzas to a pre-existing poem of fifty-four. Thus, a poem, even if the attribution is thought to be genuine, may contain both older and more recent material.

1.3 Internal Evidence

A common method of providing a secure and precise date for a text involves the use of internal evidence, generally a reference within the text to a person or event of known date. At the most obvious level, a tale written about the

Battle of Clontarf, fought in 1014, cannot have been written before the year in which it occurred. This method almost invariably provides only a terminus post quem, but it can be used to date texts more closely. For example, references to dateable kings in the genealogies in the Book of Leinster suggest that that text was being compiled in the 1150s and early 1160s during the period of the writing of the manuscript (Duncan 2012a: 53), although we must bear in mind that this is just a continuation of a much longer process of compilation

Internal evidence is most useful in dating texts of a historical nature. 'The Phantom's Frenzy' (*Baile in Scáil*) can be dated on internal grounds, but again shows at least one period of revision. The text is framed as a prophecy of the kings of Tara, and for the first part, all the 'future' kings are named, the last in this series being Máel Sechnaill son of Máel Rúanaid who died in 862 (Murray 2004: 4). After this, kennings are used, and so the original composition is placed about the time of Máel Sechnaill. These kennings are then glossed with the names of historical kings, the latest identifiable one being Máel Sechnaill son of Domnall (d.1022) and so it is suggested that the text was redacted into its current form shortly after this. Similarly, Bhreathnach (2005: 61-2) concludes on the basis of the identification of kings listed in it that 'The Vision of Conn Hundred-battles' (*Baile Chuinn Chétchathaig*) was probably composed in two stints, one written during the reign of Fínsnechta Fledach, king of Tara 675-695, and a supplementary section dated to c.720. A poem on the Christian kings of Leinster (*Cóic ríg tríchat triallsat róe*) has been shown on the basis of internal evidence to comprise two separate poems (O'Brien 1955: 35). The first 38 stanzas were written while Fáelán mac Muiridaig (d.940) was still living, and the following two stanzas were added shortly afterwards. The second part of the poem (qq. 41-55) was added during the reign of Donnchad mac Dúnlaing (d.1036) who, again, is spoken of as being alive at the time of writing. Interestingly, despite this clear evidence for multiple strata, the editor finds 'little to differentiate the language of the two poets' (O'Brien 1955: 35-6), although there is a perceptible difference in the use of metre (Ó Cuív 1967-8: 281).

Some texts do not have a known author but are witnessed by dateable kings and clerics, in which case they can be dated relative to the signatories. 'The Law of Adomnán' (*Cáin Adomnáin*), also known as 'The Law of Innocents', was promulgated in 697 and the surviving text has the appearance of being contemporary with this promulgation. The guarantor list (§§28-32) can be dated on internal grounds to 697 (Ní Dhonnchadha 1982) and the core text (§§34-53) is generally accepted as original. However, the text as a whole is a compilation. The first section (§§1-27) is a later introduction belonging to the tenth or eleventh century. The last four paragraphs (§§49-53) are extant only in a single manuscript and Stifter (2013: 200-203) provides convincing linguistic and stylistic evidence to suggest that this was not part of the original. This is particularly significant because this is the section that treats primarily of women, and Stifter concludes that the original version 'was geared towards clerical interests; women played a subordinate role' (2013: 204).

Ireland has a large corpus of law tracts, the earliest of which date back to the seventh century. Occasionally, these can be dated by internal evidence, although it is more common to use linguistic evidence. The law tract on 'Bee Judgements' (*Bechbretha*) mentions the blinding of Congal Cáech (d.637), which provides a clear terminus post quem, although it does not of itself indicate how much longer after that date the tract might have been written (Charles-Edwards & Kelly 2008: 13). 'The Branched Purchase' (*Críth Gablach*) contains reference to two examples of promulgated law (*rechtge*) which Binchy links to dateable historical events, namely, a law for the expulsion of a foreign race, and the 'Law of Adomnán' which was promulgated in 697 (see above). The text gives an example of the first *rechtge* 'against the Saxons' which Binchy (1941: p. xiv) relates to a raid by the Northumbrian king, Egfrid, in 684. He concludes that these events must have been relatively recent and so places the date of composition in the early years of the eighth century.

Even fictional material set in the distant past may produce some internal dating criteria. Charles-Edwards (2015) adduces evidence from contemporary political geography to suggest an eighth-century date for the composition of Recension I of the Táin ('The Cattle-Raid of Cooley'). With regards to another tale, 'The Hostel of Da Coca' (*Bruiden Da Choca*), Ó Corráin (1994: 10-11) notes that it claims that St Columcille scattered the ashes of St Cíarán at a place called Mag nÚra. As this was granted in 1072 to the monastery of Clonmacnoise, which itself was founded by St Cíarán, it is likely that the incident concerning his ashes postdates this grant.

However, internal evidence of this type is often absent, vague or ambiguous for texts set in the prehistorical period, namely, the prehistoric sagas and synthetic history set in the ancient past, as they tend to lack internal references to securely dated events. In such cases there have been attempts to date these texts by their thematic content. Rodway (2013: 4-5) discusses efforts to date the Four Branches of the Mabinogi by internal evidence by 'fishing for possible hidden or coded contemporary allusions in the text' and notes a wide range of resulting dates: c.1018×1024 (Tolstoy), c.1050×1120 (Charles-Edwards), c.1060 (Williams), c.1093 (Goetinck), 1090s (Mac Cana), c.1120×1136 (Breeze), post 1140 (Huws), c.1164×1197 (Parker), c.1170×1190 (Lewis), first half or middle of the thirteenth century (Watkin), and c.1200×1275 (Daniel). These hidden codes differ from verifiable internal evidence insofar as they rely on the interpretation of the meaning of the text rather than recorded facts such as a king's reign. The current dominant theory of medieval Irish and Welsh literature holds that the tales are a product of the society in which they were produced, and it follows from this that we may be able to detect contemporary concerns in the writing. However, it is one thing to detect contemporary resonances in a text of known date, but quite another to use a perceived theme as a dating criteria. Rodway is less inclined to believe that medieval texts necessarily contain contemporary resonances, but more generally he argues that even where an author may have intended to reflect a contemporary situation, the problem remains that it 'cannot be proved satisfactorily' (2013: 8). The problem is twofold. Firstly, has the theme been correctly identified and secondly must it be of particular relevance at a certain time?

1.4 Manuscripts

An important dating criterion is the date of writing of the earliest manuscript in which a text is found. Manuscripts can frequently be dated on codicological or palaeographical grounds, and so a manuscript provides a terminus ante quem for any text contained within it. The Old Irish glosses are the primary source for knowledge of the grammar of Old Irish (c.700-c.900), but even here we are reliant on non-contemporary manuscripts for the main collections, as is evidenced by multiple layers and transcription errors. Ó Néill (2000) suggests 851 CE for the compilation of the St. Gall manuscript, but the glosses that it contains betray evidence of many years of additions and accretions (Stifter 2013: 166). The main body of the Würzburg glosses is dated to c.750, while those of the *prima manus* are dated to c.700. Notwithstanding complicating factors such as this, these texts are important for establishing a chronology of linguistic change during this early period.

Adomnán's *Life of St Columba* was penned by the abbot of Iona between 688 and 704 (Anderson & Anderson 1961: 96) and was transcribed probably before 713 by Dorrbéne and is preserved in Stadtbibliothek Schaffhausen, Switzerland, Generalia 1 (A). This gives us a near contemporary manuscript for the study of the text, although only some names are in the Irish language and there is some linguistic evidence to suggest that some of these might be from even older sources. The Latin lives of St Patrick by Muirchú (written 661×700) and Tírechán (c.690) are datable and also contain some Irish but they are found only in the Book of Armagh written over a century later c.807. The Cambrai homily provides us with an early text in Irish in continuous prose but it was transcribed with many errors by a continental scribe with no knowledge of the language in 763×780 (Ó Néill 1981).

Other Old Irish prose texts fair far worse. The Lambeth commentary is dated on internal evidence to c.725 but is preserved only in a tenth-century manuscript, Lambeth Palace Fragments 1229 (see Bieler and Carney 1972). 'The Dream of Óengus' (*Aislinge Óenguso*) is dated on linguistic grounds to the eighth century but survives only in a manuscript of c.1517 (see Appendix A). The Irish Life of St Brigit, thought to have been written in the ninth century, is not found in any manuscript before Oxford MS Rawlinson B.512 (fifteenth and early sixteenth centuries). This kind of gap between the putative date of composition and the extant recordings raises several problems of transmission, notably the possibility of corruption, modernisation and revision of the text to which we shall return below.

The earliest Gaelic manuscripts producing substantial continuous prose and verse texts belong to the late eleventh and twelfth centuries. Their relatively early date renders them key resources for this study and they will be described in more detail in Appendix A. Not only do they provide a shorter period of transmission for texts belonging to the Old Irish and early Middle Irish periods, but they also contain some contemporary or near contemporary texts which will prove particularly useful in this project. Moreover, they also present us with a potential terminus ante quem for texts contained within them. They are the Book of the Dun Cow (*Lebor na hUidre*), which is dated to c.1100, Oxford MS Rawlinson B 502, the older part of which was being worked on c.1130, and the Book of Leinster, which was begun in the 1150s. Other later manuscripts are also of significance, sometimes preserving better or older versions than these twelfth-century codices, and of course contain many texts of interest not found in the earlier manuscripts. In many cases they preserve good copies of early medieval originals that clearly indicate the date and content of the original text, and these will be used here as yardsticks for dating other texts. Most of the manuscripts of the fourteenth and fifteenth centuries contain much older texts, but some of the fifteenth century ones start to record contemporary or near contemporary texts, sometimes composed by the scribe, which are of interest here too as representative of that period.

1.5 Intertextuality

The largest, sustained dating exercise ever undertaken in Irish was Rudolf Thurneysen's 1921 study of Irish heroic and king tales, *Die irisches Helden- und Königsage*. This became the standard reference work for the best part of a century and dates proposed by him were only occasionally second guessed. Much of his dating was based on a linguistic evaluation of the texts. Although he usually gives few details, making arguing against the date rather difficult, his acknowledged pre-eminence in the language contributed greatly to the work's authority. However, another method favoured by Thurneysen was the establishment of intertextual relationships: if text A cited text B, then text B must be older than text A. Unfortunately, there is a fundamental flaw in this method which has meant that it has largely fallen into disfavour, although it is not without its usefulness, as it more or less assumes that all the copies of texts that survive are all that were written, whereas in fact we know that a great many manuscripts indeed the greater majority, have been lost. If one allows for the possibility of the erstwhile existence of other copies, then it becomes apparent that where texts A and B have the same fact or wording, then they might have been copied from a lost text, C. Therefore, it becomes extremely difficult to build a secure picture of the relationship between two texts. Nevertheless, the method has been applied successfully in certain areas. For example, L. Breatnach shows that *Uraicecht na Ríar* quotes from three other law tracts, *Cáin Fhuithirbe, Bretha Nemed Toísech* and *Bretha Nemed Dédenach*, and so he would place it chronologically after all three (1987: 78; 2005: 320-1; see also 2005: 354-55). Where the original text is named, this is a particularly strong argument for the relative chronology of texts.

One source of particular interest for dating frequently used by Thurneysen and others is the early Irish tale lists (Mac Cana 1980). These exist in two main versions, the introduction to one of which claims that the stories listed therein were to be recited by the poets to kings and lords (Mac Cana 1980: 41). The earliest copy is found in the Book of Leinster, but the original has been dated to the tenth century so that any title that appears in both versions can be assumed to have been in the archetype (see Toner 2000 on the earliest reconstructable form). It is now generally recognised, however, that any extant tale bearing a name or reflecting in its content a title found in the lists is not necessarily the same tale as referred to in the list. Indeed, the title *Togail Bruidne Da Choca* 'The Destruction of Da Coca's Hostel' appears to have been in the original list, but the corresponding surviving tale, *Bruiden Da Choca*, is a fresh composition of the twelfth century which bears an unknown relationship to the tale referred to in the lists (Toner 2007: 28-30). The original appears to have been lost and was unknown to the author of the extant version. The tale lists, therefore, prove nothing about the date of an extant tale, merely that a tale of that name did exist perhaps as early as the tenth century.

1.6 Metrics

Ó Cróinín (2013: 198) has recently argued that metrics is the feature most likely to provide a valid system of dating for the whole corpus of Irish historical literature. A distinct advantage of working with verse is that a sizeable number of poems have an ascription attached to them or can be dated from internal evidence, and so could provide the framework to which other unascribed poems could be attached. Ó Cuív (1967-68) shows an increase in metrical ornamentation, including rhyme and alliteration, over time between the eighth century and the Early Modern period (c.1200-c.1650 CE), drawing primarily from an analysis of the *deibide* metre. However, while Ó Cuív shows that these forms of ornamentation become more common and stricter (according to the rules of later Classical verse) over time, his statistics 'are not intended to do more than show the lines of development approximately' (Ó Cuív 1967-68: 275). For the Classical Early Modern Irish period, P. Breatnach (2017) has shown that the nature of the rhyme in opening couplets varies notably towards the end of the period and can be used effectively as a dating criterion.

An extensive survey has not yet been carried out that would allow metrics to be used with some degree of confidence in dating texts. The developments in Irish do not appear to be entirely linear. Although we see a general increase in the use of internal rhyme in the final couplet, Ó Cuív draws attention to the poem beginning *Maicne Echach ard a nglé*, attributed to the tenth-century poet, Flann mac Lonáin, in which there are no examples of the feature (Ó Cuív 1967-68: 280). Of three poems attributed to Gilla Cóemáin, *Ériu ard inis na ríg*, *Atá sund forba fessa*, and *Annálad anall uile* dealing with the history of Ireland, the latest chronologically (*Annálad anall uile*), which deals with events down to 1072, is also the least ornamented (Ó Cuív 1967-68: 283). Smith (2007: 91) concludes from his analysis of Gilla Cóemáin's verse that 'individual poets were capable of using different levels of ornamentation', and, importantly, that 'the trend toward the use of increased ornamentation can only be used as a rough guide in the process of textual dating'. One of the factors that would need to be considered, therefore, and may be fatal to the endeavour, is difference in genre and style. Rowland (2014: xxviii-xxix) suggests that metrical features can suggest a rough chronology for Welsh verse but warns that different practices may have obtained in official bardic praise poems and in mainly anonymous non-praise poetry genres.

Mac Mathúna also carries out a limited examination of the development of *deibide*, here with particular focus on early forms (1985: 299-319). He focusses on the distribution in *deibide* of rhymes between stressed words on the one hand and between stressed and unstressed rhymes (*rinn 7 airdrinn*), and on linking alliteration within and between stanzas (*fidrad freccomail*) on the other. He observes that linking alliteration between lines is generally absent from later poems but that internal rhyme in the second couplet becomes common in the tenth and increasingly in the eleventh century (Mac Mathúna 1985: 317). A mixture of stressed and unstressed (*rinn 7 airdrinn*) rhymes was common up until about 1100 (ibid. 301). Clearly, this is not a sufficiently refined tool in itself to enable accurate dating: Mac Mathúna (1985: 317) concludes from his metrical analysis only that the poems in 'The Voyage of Bran' (*Immram Brain*) were composed c.700-c.950.

The bulk of Irish verse is written in syllabic metres which were dominant from the seventh century until the seventeenth. An older form of verse, known as *roscad*, was stressed alliterative verse often with a fixed syllabic count in the final foot. This used to be taken as a guarantee of particular antiquity and even oral composition, but L. Breatnach (1984) has shown that several passages of *roscad* in *Bretha Nemed Toísech* are translations of material from the *Collectio Canonum Hibernensis* which can be dated to the eighth century. Clearly, poets continued to compose in *roscad* after the introduction of syllabic metres, and it is noteworthy, for example, that it remained the dominant verse form in legal tracts (Breatnach 2005: 370).

Composition of *roscad* continued into later centuries and was being actively cultivated in the twelfth century, but authors were reusing older texts as well as composing afresh. Liam Breatnach notes that the author of 'The Courtship of Luaine and the Death of Athairne' (*Tochmarc Luaine ocus Aided Athairne*) drew on a variety of sources when writing his *roscada*. The method is fairly crude and mechanical, for the author 'picks out phrases and verses from here and there, though mostly following the order in which they appear' in the source (Breatnach 1980: 4). The twelfth-century author of 'The Hostel of Da Coca' (*Bruiden Da Choca*) follows a similar technique, borrowing material from other earlier texts, some of which can still be identified. Where we know the source that he was using, it is clear that he is again following the order of the source text but does not slavishly do so (Toner 2007: 50). Rather, he picks out suitable lines from different parts of the exemplar and sometimes adapts them, including changing names, to fit the narrative of the text that he is writing. He writes some lines from scratch, and the appearance of certain phrases across a number of different poems suggests a degree of authorial cohesion.

Carney (1979) proposes a method for dating very early metrical texts, some of which he would place in the first half of the fifth century. The approach is based primarily on his interpretation of particular words as pre-syncope forms required by the metre. However, this is impossible to reconcile with known linguistic processes of syncope which entailed the loss of the second, fourth etc. syllables of words. Breatnach (1996: 75-6) and Stifter (2013: 185-6) reject the approach out of hand, saying that there is no need to assume that trisyllabic cadences were required. Corthals (1990) accepts that the pre-syncope forms are to be read as such, but for metrical purposes, in which case they do not support a very early date. Stifter (2013: 186) concludes that 'poems displaying Carney's aberrant feature need not go back to the pre-syncope period, but can contain a stylistic element of the poetic craft of, for example, the early 7th century, but this requires further study'. Carney (1979: 426-7) further proposes that some poems exhibit pre-anaptytic forms that would, for example, require *domun* 'world' to be read as a monosyllable. Stifter (2013: 187) notes that the only examples to have come to light so far are etymologically correct, but a fuller collection and analysis of examples would be required before it could be asserted that Carney's theory is valid. Qiu (2016: 206-7) has recently shown that the word *comaccomol* may vary in syllabic length according to metrical requirements, suggesting that anaptytic and pre-anaptytic forms could be freely used in verse.[1]

1.7 Linguistic Dating

Linguistic dating is key to the computational methods proposed elsewhere in this book as many of the same principles underpin both traditional and machine learning techniques. Linguistic dating may be defined as the dating of a document or text based on the chronological stage of the language within it. Languages change in various ways over time, including in their morphology, syntax, vocabulary and phonology, and any of these features can be used in dating. For example, Old Irish had three genders, masculine, feminine and neuter. The neuter died out about 1000 AD, so that we may conclude that texts that contain examples of this feature belong to the first millennium. In practice, these diagnostics are a little more complicated. For example, the neuter becomes petrified in placenames, as in Loch nEchach, modern Lough Neagh, where the n- indicates that *loch* is neuter. The neuter is also seen in chevilles – short line fillers used to make up the required length of line – in later poetry, and archaising tendencies sometimes caused scribes to artificially render originally masculine or feminine nouns into neuters. Also, certain fixed phrases

---

1 See also Carey 2002: 82-3.

preserved traces of the neuter for quite some time after its general demise,[2] and we must always be conscious of the virtual certainty that some dialects probably retained it longer than others (see 1.7.2 below). Nevertheless, with due allowance for these complications and others to be discussed below, the principle remains that changes in language may be used to date Irish texts. The level of precision that may be obtained is open to question however. We see occasional attempts by scholars in the field to date texts on linguistic grounds to within a quarter of a century. This is less than a generation and in principle it would seem impossible for linguistic dating to be that precise, except perhaps with a huge corpus of confidently dated texts from which to delineate linguistic developments. More generally, texts tend to be dated to the nearest half century or century, depending on the quality of comparable material and the state and size of the text being examined, and frequently the date range is much wider, particularly for short texts.

One of the problems facing the researcher in medieval Irish is the dearth of texts in contemporary manuscripts. Leaving aside the very large majority of texts that are preserved only in much later manuscripts, the vast bulk of the material that we rely on for our knowledge of Old and Middle Irish is not preserved in exactly contemporary manuscripts and in many cases shows signs of modernisation and misunderstanding (see above 1.4 and Appendix A). Secondly, these early manuscripts may themselves lack precise dates (see Appendix A) and in many cases they are dated based on the language of the texts within them, leading to a circularity in the argumentation. Add to this the tendency for scribes to use conservative or archaising orthography and grammar and we find that any level of absolute precision for linguistic change eludes us.

A further complicating factor is that one author could be significantly older than another one working at exactly the same time, and we might assume, therefore, that his writing could reflect an earlier stage of the language. For example, Adomnán was about 70 when he wrote his life of Columba, a factor that must be considered alongside his possible use of older sources (Stifter 2013: 170-1). According to Sharpe (1982: 13), Ferdomnach was already the master-scribe of Armagh when the codex was compiled between 807 and 808, nearly forty years before his death (AU 846.1). Linguistic dating can do little to cope

2 For example, *tech n-oíged* 'guest house' is found in an eleventh/twelfth-century poem (Stokes 1897: 62 § 29). See also from fourteenth- and fifteenth-century annals: 'Semmus O Flandagáin, .i. mac Persúin Indsi, neach … do bo maith teach n-aidedh, d'ég' (AU 1531.14); 'Brian, mac Feilim … nech ro bo mo aithne 7 einech 7 tech n-aidhedh do bí ina aimsir fein' (AU 1481.1). For the use of the nominative after the comparative in the latter example see Hoyne 2017: 169-73.

with these anomalies and it must be conceded that any date based solely on linguistic criteria could be up to 50 years in error simply due to the author's age.

Linguistic dating cannot directly provide an absolute date for a text, even within a broad framework, but all such dates are relative to a smaller set of texts with established or accepted absolute dates. Notwithstanding some problems of register and dialect discussed below, a particular text may, in theory, be placed between two texts of known date, thereby allowing us to propose an estimated absolute date. In practice, many of the key texts that might be used as anchor points have only approximate dates which are themselves based on linguistic analysis with the result that if the date of the anchor text is brought into doubt, then all dates based on that must also be revised.

1.7.1 *Linguistic Strata and Scribal Revision*

One of the fundamental problems which the textual historian must face in attempting to date a text is that documents may contain various textual strata or have suffered from periods of revision and modernisation. Binchy (1941: xi–ii) notes that the linguistic evidence from the law tracts, most of which date from the seventh and eighth centuries but are preserved only in late medieval manuscripts, must be used with great caution because of the existence of various strata within them. Thus, a tract may contain older layers, and both archaic and late Old Irish forms may exist side by side, but also modernised forms picked up during the long period of transmission.

Borrowing terminology from the field of palaeography, texts are sometimes described as palimpsests, that is, documents that have been (partially) erased and rewritten over the top. This is a useful analogy for thinking about the nature of the texts that we are dealing with, but it perhaps suggests a facile method for distinguishing old and new. Medieval Irish has produced a number of true palimpsests in which the work of later scribes is visible, most notoriously in the case of The Book of the Dun Cow (Appendix A) but the virtual palimpsests are much harder to detect and handle. To invoke another analogy already touched upon, textual history may be viewed as the uncovering of archaeological strata in the ground, each level indicating activity in a different period. However, while the archaeologist may peel away layer after layer, going back in time with depth, no such method is available to linguistic analysis. In a text, accretions may sometimes be obvious, but more often than not later scribes have combined originally separate texts together, added new sections, and modernised or corrupted older language. A better analogy is, therefore, to an archaeological site that has been dug over already by nineteenth-century antiquarians, leaving us with the artefacts but damaged stratigraphy. We might be able to date some of the artefacts, but the crucial strata that allow the archaeologist to associate one find with another and to build up a picture over time has been destroyed.

Breatnach (2015: 55) identifies four possible varieties of text in Middle Irish (c.900-c.1200) manuscripts that may be useful in linguistic dating:

1. a reasonably faithful copy of a text composed in the Old Irish period (c.700-c.900)
2. a copy of a text originally composed in Old Irish, but consciously modified or substantially revised in the Middle Irish period
3. a copy of a text composed earlier in the Middle Irish period
4. a copy of a text composed by a contemporary or a fair-copy of a text composed by the scribe himself.

While Breatnach is concerned here with those texts found in the great twelfth-century manuscripts, we may imagine similar situations for different periods. In Type 1, we might expect to find evidence of fairly undiluted Old Irish with just a few Middle Irishisms thrown in. We may assume the work of a conservative scribe who has attempted to copy the text faithfully but has only occasionally allowed more contemporary linguistic forms to intrude on the text. This may be because he was a faithful scribe whose primary interest was the preservation of the inherited text or simply that he had nothing to add to the text.

A complicating factor here is that the linguistic division between Old and Middle Irish is not always clear, and nor should we expect it to be. Old Irish is generally defined linguistically, as opposed to temporally, as the form of the language preserved in the Old Irish glosses and it is primarily from these collections that Thurneysen's canonical *Grammar of Old Irish* (1946) is constructed. However, McCone (1985) has shown that many of the developments that are associated with Middle Irish are already presented in the Old Irish glosses, and he proposes that these were emerging forms and structures in the spoken language that occasionally broke through into the written register.[3] This is potentially problematic for Type 1 because it could be argued that the proto-Middle Irish forms were used by the original author. Nevertheless, this is likely to be a minor issue and we may safely conclude in cases such as this that the text is substantially Old Irish.

By type 2, Breatnach is referring to Old Irish texts that were revised later in the Middle Irish period in a way that can be distinguished on a linguistic level from Type 1 by the extent of the interference with the original text. Such texts

3 Breatnach (2015: 53) argues that the term 'Middle Irish' should be applied only temporally (i.e. to texts of 900-1200) and so is inappropriate in this context.

are common in the Middle Irish period. In the Middle Irish version of 'The Courtship of Emer' (*Tochmarc Emire*), the redactor has taken an Old Irish text that exists independently, although unfortunately incomplete, and expanded on it almost line by line, adding new words and phrases as he goes (Toner 1998). He also adds completely new sections, much of which he has copied from other sources. Many texts as we have already seen are evidently compilatory, as for example two of the central tales of the early medieval period, 'The Destruction of Da Derga's Hostel' (*Togail Bruidne da Derga*) and 'The Cattle-Raid of Cooley' (*Tain Bó Cúailnge*). The former was formerly understood as an eleventh-century compilation from two ninth-century versions, but West (1999) has shown that it is in fact much more complicated than this and incorporated material from at least three versions.

Breatnach's Type 3 comprises texts composed early in Middle Irish but as no manuscripts containing extensive texts survive from before the end of the eleventh century they must necessarily be extant only in manuscripts of the later Middle Irish period. As a result, we should expect to find some degree of contamination of the original language. We could further subdivide this category into two subcategories corresponding to Types 1 and 2: namely a) reasonably unadulterated copies of early Middle Irish texts and b) more heavily reworked texts with all the features of Type 2 text discussed above.

Type 4 is of particular interest to the historical linguist as the texts in this category are contemporary or near-contemporary, and so can provide solid evidence of the chronology of linguistic changes. Such texts can be hard to identify in practice, of course, and frequently we can only safely conclude that the text is at least near-contemporary. We can attempt to link it to a particular scribe on the basis of the lateness of the language and, more particularly, on shared attributes with other texts copied by, but not authored by, the scribe. Mac Gearailt has made a special study of the late texts in the Book of Leinster and concludes, for example, that 'The Battle of Rosnaree' (*Cath Ruis na Ríg*) was composed by the scribe (see Appendix A). Thus, types 1 and 4 are considered to faithfully represent the original composition (to a lesser degree of course in type 1).

Types 2 and 3, which are in the majority, are more complex, both in theory and in practice. We must also consider the possibility of multiple layers of transcription and revision. 'The Expedition of Condlae' (*Echtrae Chondlai*), for example, is an Old Irish text existing in several manuscripts, the earliest of which, The Book of the Dun Cow, was copied c.1100. By a careful study of the stemma, McCone (2000: 45-7) has shown that the bulk of the extant manuscripts go back to a common node written in the tenth century. However, in many cases, earlier layers may become impossible to distinguish through textual study alone, particularly where a stemma cannot be constructed to demonstrate different stages of transmission.

While a linguistic analysis may be important in detecting different strata within a text, it should be noted that texts that are clearly composite do not necessarily reflect differences in language. We have seen in relation to the poem beginning *Cóic ríg tríchat triallsat róe* that despite clear evidence for more than one author, the language of the two major sections shows no palpable variation (see 1.3 above). Similarly, Murray (2017: 39) observes that there is little evidence for linguistic strata in texts of the Finn Cycle written before 1200 CE despite the fact that some texts are clearly composite. The differences may have been deliberately obscured or their constituent parts may themselves have dated from around the same time so that they would be linguistically indistinguishable. In any case, it should be clear that a linguistically homogenous text does not necessarily indicate a singular point of composition.

1.7.2 *Dialect*

There are other issues affecting the linguistic dating of text, particularly register and dialect. Bieler and Carney note (1972: 6) that dating linguistically assumes that scribal changes and changes in language happened evenly at literary centres all over Ireland, but this can hardly have been the case. It is generally agreed that early medieval Ireland, which was politically fragmented and covered a large area, must have had dialects but Old Irish shows a remarkable linguistic cohesiveness (e.g. Charles-Edwards 1995: 727; Russell 2005: 439). A major problem in the study of dialect in the Old Irish period is that few texts can be linked to any particular Gaelic-speaking area during this time. The features that characterise Modern Irish dialects emerge as late as the thirteenth and fourteenth centuries (Murray 2005) and there has been only limited success in tracing any earlier features. There is an intriguing reference in the tenth-century Glossary of Cormac to a word *naire* meaning 'indeed' which the writer claims to be 'old language' (*senbērla*) but, he says, was still then in use in west Munster (Corm. Y 82-3).[4] Variations in Old Irish in the prepositional relative construction (Ó hUiginn 2013) and the inflectional forms of the word for 'house' (*tech*, dat. *tig*/*taig*, gen. *tige*/*taige*) (Hughes 1994: 614) are advanced as further indications of dialect division. P. Kelly (1982) has shown that the law tracts of 'Judgements of the Privileged' (*Bretha Nemed*), which are associated with Munster, contain certain words for animals that are not used in 'The

4 Ó Muircheartaigh (2015: 121) suggests that it is also preserved in Scottish Gaelic *nàile* 'truly, indeed'.

Great Tradition' (*Senchas Már*) which was composed in the North, probably at Armagh (L. Breatnach 2011, 34-40).

The general absence of dialect forms in the early period would suggest that Old Irish is a written register or form of standardised, normative language. It is unlikely to represent directly any spoken form of Irish and it is generally accepted that it is a learned language of the elite (Charles-Edwards 1995: 727-8). Moreover, it does not appear to have been a purely written register, but the evidence, such as it is, 'points more to the rise in status of a single dialect.... Moreover, the orthographical variation suggests that it was not simply a *Schriftsprache* but rather an elite register spoken by the nobility as well as poets, churchmen, and judges' (Russell 2005: 443; cf. McCone 1985: 87; Charles-Edwards 1995: 728). Bisagni (2013-14: 15) describes it as 'a standard or at least supra-regional high-status language [which] was established, perhaps already in the seventh century, by the members of the Irish intellectual elite'. Ó Muircheartaigh (2015) argues cogently that the language of the glosses is based on a prestige dialect which he would connect with several monastic centres, notably Bangor, Co. Down, and the Scottish monastery of Iona, founded by the Irish saint, Columba, in 563, and which, most importantly, was adopted and cultivated at the monastery of Armagh in the second half of the seventh century.

Dialects are often sources of linguistic innovation, but they are just as likely to preserve conservative features that have been lost in others. Therefore, it is reasonable to suppose that more archaic forms and usages persisted in some dialects for longer than others, and one is reminded of the fact that the verbal morphology of modern Ulster Irish is more innovative that the southern dialects, particularly that of Munster, in exhibiting fewer inherited synthetic forms and greater use of independent subject pronouns. As a result, we cannot be certain that an older verbal form in one text beside an innovative form in another necessarily is indicative of age. It might be attributed to dialect, or indeed to scribal practice.

1.7.3 *Register*

The standard grammar of Old Irish, codified by Rudolf Thurneysen (1946) in his *Grammar of Old Irish*, is based almost entirely on the evidence of a number of collections of glosses on Latin texts, most especially on the three largest collections: the Würzburg glosses on the letters of St Paul, dated to the middle of the eighth century, the Milan glosses on a commentary in Latin to the Psalms, and the St Gall glosses on Priscian's grammar, both belonging to the ninth century (Thurneysen 1946: 4-6). The glosses sometimes contain older and younger forms side by side which McCone (1985) interprets as evidence for the use of a learned register: the older forms would represent the more conservative literary register while the younger forms that occasionally break through point to the scribe's own speech. McCone (1985: 85) warns that treating variation in the Old Irish glosses as the result of register 'may call for some rethinking of the dating and editorial methods appropriate to texts of presumed Old Irish provenance that survive only in later manuscripts'. Therefore, an editor should not seek to edit out apparently later forms from a perceived ninth-century text if those forms may already have existed, albeit only in a lower register, by that time. The implications for dating are probably even more severe, although the scholarly community has done little to engage with the issue. If it is true that Old Irish is a standardised register, then variation in linguistic features across different texts might have more to do with the author's level of adherence to the standard than the date of writing.

However, Russell (2005: 444-5) casts doubt on whether the glosses would be written in a high register:

> We would not expect glosses to be in a very high register of language, and even the non-deviant language of the glosses would not have been as high as registers of Old Irish could get… and indeed the whole context of the activity of glossing as producing a set of notes for private study, would suggest that the language of the glosses might well be more colloquial than it would be in a highly polished literary creation.

Bisagni (2013-14: 16) further implies that the glosses are an example of a purely 'functional' scholarly register which was relatively uninfluenced by literary models or aesthetic requirements. As we shall see, there are various registers available to an author writing in Old Irish, usually related to style, and some of the archaising features seen in them are absent from the glosses. However, all written language is conservative to some degree, and diverges to a greater or lesser extent from spoken language. The Old Irish glosses, therefore, would sit at the lower end of the elite register, and would lack the distinctive features of heightened language found in more formal texts.

An alternative view of the language of the Old Irish glosses is that variation within a single collection is the result of copying. Thurneysen (1946: 5) notes that 'slips of the pen' are frequent and it is well known that several of the collections that survive in manuscripts from that period are copies. The so-called St Gall glosses on Priscian, one of the major sources for the Grammar of Old Irish, are preserved in three manuscripts, the largest collection being that of Codex Sangallensis 904 preserved in the Stiftsbibliotek in Sankt Gallen. As Stokes and Strachan (1903: xxiii) observe, 'the collection of glosses is not homogenous, but comes from various sources and is of varying antiquity'. Errors common to the glosses in the three manuscripts of the commentary by Iunius Philargyrius on Virgil's *Eclogues* show that they go back to a common source (Stokes & Strachan 1903: xvii). The glosses in the prima manus in the Würzburg glosses were probably copied from another source as suggested by the omission of abbreviation marks and defective spellings, as well as some palaeographical evidence (Ó Néill 2002: 230-2). Moreover, it has been shown that the main glossator copied many if not all of his material from at least one other source as evidenced by some errors and the existence of the same glosses (in Latin) in another copy of the Pauline epistles (Bisagni (2013-14: 26-9) in Würzburg.[5]

1.7.4 *Archaism*

Written languages, particularly those in a higher register, tend to cultivate conservative features and this adds to their exclusivity and prestige. We may distinguish between conservative features and archaisms in principle, although it is much more difficult to determine which is occurring in practical examples. For the purposes of this discussion, we define a conservatism as a widely accepted preservation in writing of linguistic features that have disappeared from colloquial speech, whereas archaism is defined as the introduction of archaic linguistic features on stylistic or ideological grounds. It should be clear from the foregoing discussion that it can be difficult to determine whether a particular feature has disappeared from common speech as it may be obsolescent or, more probably, preserved in different dialects, so for practical reasons we must define conservatism as the continued use of older linguistic forms alongside innovative equivalents. Archaisms may be identified where conservative features are not or are no longer widely accepted, and so therefore stand out from contemporary writing. Conservatism must be learned, and so is deliberate, but it becomes with use mechanical and instinctual, whereas archaisms

5 Both the commentary and the glosses in the Milan codex are predominantly the work of a single scribe who calls himself Díarmait (Stokes & Strachan 1901: xv; Thurneysen 1946: 5), but he is otherwise unidentified. Dumville (1997: 29) notes various correspondences between the Milan and St Gall glosses and concludes that 'the two books appear to be contemporary, to share both scribes and sources, and in their intellectual background show connexions with Ulster'. If this were true, then the apparently more archaic language of Milan would have to be explained through some other means, such as McCone's register or by means of textual strata. As far as we know, it has not been shown that the Milan glosses were copied from an earlier source, although this is implied by Thurneysen. However, Díarmait has never been identified as a scribe of St Gall, nor does Dumville present any argument to that end.

are conscious departures from the norm on the part of the writer intended to imbue the text with a certain antique quality.

Conservatism is particularly evident in orthography, with redundant and archaic spellings becoming fossilised, as in the English *-gh-* in words like 'night' and *kn-* in 'knock' which then mask actual changes in the language. In Old Irish, the archaic voiceless dental fricative *-th* is replaced in final, unstressed position in Classical Old Irish by a voiced dental fricative, usually represented in spelling as *-d*. Stifter (2013: 173) notes that spelling with *-th* is very common in the Annals of Ulster up until the 730s, with instances of *-d* during that period representing interference from later copyists. Between 770 and 845, the proportion of older spellings drops to about a quarter, suggesting that we are now dealing with a conservative spelling that was, nevertheless, read as the voiced fricative. There may, of course, be other factors at play here, including dialect. There is a parallel shift about the same time from a voiceless guttural fricative to a voiced form under similar conditions and we witness a change from spellings in *-ch* to *-g*, and later *-gh*. However, the voiceless form is still found in unstressed final position in Scottish Gaelic and we must wonder, therefore, whether it persisted longer in certain parts of Ireland too. Therefore, it is clear that final unstressed *-th*/*-ch* cannot be taken as primary evidence for archaic origins. Indeed, C. Breatnach (2005: 96-7, 99) shows that *-th* re-emerges as a feature of thirteenth-century orthography. As Stifter (2013: 176) notes 'residual archaic spellings are no watertight proof that the old forms were still in use in the living language of a particular period, when evidence for progressive forms exists at the same time'.[6]

There are some remarkable cases of conservatism from later medieval sources. We may note, for example, that the perfective marker *ro* is replaced by *do* in late Middle Irish, but *ro* survives much longer in the manuscript tradition, including in Early Modern texts (Ó Catháin 1933: 11-16; Mac Gearailt 2012: 80), and one must conclude that this is probably a stylistic choice rather than a real linguistic survival. Similarly, Old Irish had a full set of object pronouns that were infixed into the verb or prefixed to it with an empty preverb. This was eventually replaced by a system of independent object pronouns, beginning already in the Middle Irish period. However, certain forms proved quite tenacious and continued in use into Early Modern Irish (c.1200-c.1650). They are particularly useful in verse in order to create the correct syllable count necessary for the metrics but the 3 sg. fem. (*-s-*) remains common in prose where

6 Stifter (2013: 176-7) also notes that *ō*, which later becomes *úa*, and is taken as an indication of archaic language is still found in the Annals of Ulster in the tenth century.

there is no external need for it. Thus, infixed pronouns continued to be used hundreds of years after they died out in ordinary speech (McManus 1994: 430).

Linguistic archaism and obscurity have a clear performative function in medieval Ireland. Carey (1996: 24) observes that convoluted syntax and the use of rare vocabulary in certain texts indicate that obscurity was deliberately cultivated, and Murray (2014: 298) observes that the use of obscure or archaic language was employed as a mechanism to make narratives look old. Elsewhere, Murray (2012a: 119) notes in the context of prophecies that 'Obscure and/or archaic language seems to be used [...] to give validity to narratives, to indicate to their audiences that learned, archaic and *inherently reliable* [author's italics] traditions lie behind the information being presented.'

The varieties of alliterative verse known as *roscad* (see 1.6) contain various linguistic elements such as tmesis and preposed genitives, which were once thought to belong to Archaic Old Irish but have now been shown to have been in use as late as the eighth century (L. Breatnach 1984). *Roscad* continued to be written into the tenth century, indicating that scribes were capable of using archaic structures long after they had ceased to be a part of the spoken language. Indeed, even in the twelfth century, earlier *roscad* was revived by certain scholars (see 1.6) and Murray (2014: 298) holds that its introduction could endow a text with particular authority. In terms of linguistic dating, deliberate archaisation such as this could be viewed as problematic, but the fact that the authors had to copy from authentic older texts, along with the decidedly more modern joining phrases, suggests that they had limited competence in the actual use of archaic language. They could read it, but they could not effectively write in it. We should also bear in mind that such passages are usually presented as part of a larger work which itself makes no pretence at archaisation. It seems quite possible that the reader was intended to believe that the verse passages contained the actual words as spoken in ancient times and that the archaic language was intended to imbue it with an air of authenticity. But the author still wrote the main body of the text in contemporary language in order to be understood by his audience.

Ó hUiginn (2013) shows that archaisation was being practiced in the sixteenth and seventeenth centuries, sometimes far in excess even of what was proposed in the Classical language of the later Middle Ages. 'The Life of Red Hugh' (*Beatha Aodha Ruaidh*) was composed in the first third of the seventeenth century, but while it employs many forms from Classical Irish, notably from the more archaic end of the permissible spectrum, it 'also makes liberal use of forms and constructions that were completely obsolete at the time the rules of that grammar were framed, and had no place in it' (Ó hUiginn 2013: 89). Indeed, the verbal forms would not have been 'out of place in a text composed five centuries before its time', although we do find examples of innovative use such as nasalisation after the negative particle *nach* (2013: 91). 'The Life of Red Hugh' lies at the extreme end of archaisation, but we see parallel efforts by many other authors of the period. Mac Gearailt (2012) discusses the many Middle Irishisms which exist alongside many neologisms in Tadhg Ó Cianáin's 'Journey of the Ulster earls from Ireland' (*Turas na dtaoiseach nUltach as Éirinn*), which was completed in 1616. The seventeenth-century Annals of the Four Masters show archaic features in those sections compiled from early medieval sources but also in those sections relating to more recent events (Ó hUiginn 2013: 92). It is significant that the Annals of the Four Masters is not as consistent in the pursuit of archaic forms as The Life of Red Hugh, and Ó hUiginn (2013: 93 n.40) observes that where the authors of the Annals include material from The Life, they sometimes substitute more modern forms for the Life's archaisms.

In a series of articles beginning in the final decades of the twentieth century, Tomás Ó Concheanainn challenged the traditional view of the relationship between later medieval copies of manuscripts and earlier manuscripts of the eleventh and twelfth centuries. It was his assertion that later medieval Irish scribes were well capable of correcting and even archaising texts that they were copying. In a number of papers, he argues, for example, that the Book of the Dun Cow contains the sole independent witnesses for certain texts. Copies in later manuscripts such as the Yellow Book of Lecan were previously taken as independent witnesses for these texts, but Ó Concheanainn argues that the later scribes had corrected errors, removed interpolated material, and archaised the texts. If this were indeed the case, it would render any attempt at stemmatics, and linguistic dating, void. However, Ó Concheanainn's methods have been shown to be flawed and his conclusions have now have been comprehensively rejected (see West 1990; Ó Cathasaigh 1990; Toner 1998; Herbert 2015).

Despite the cultivation of obscure style and the occasional effort at mimicking archaic linguistic features, authors and redactors seem not to engage in the forgery of texts. Certain texts are treated with fidelity in the copying, most notably the canonical sections of the law tracts (F. Kelly 2002: 234). However, many non-legal texts were modernised at different times in order to make them accessible to their readers and even the law tracts had to be heavily glossed with extensive commentary by later medieval scholars. A noteworthy feature is the near ubiquity of textual strata in texts from medieval Ireland, often accompanied by dateable differences in their language. Rather than deliberately archaising their language, therefore, authors were quite happy to mix clearly incompatible forms of language, even in a single sentence. Archaisation performed certain limited functions in writing, but the bulk of the surviving literature pays little heed to such efforts. Indeed, while a number of archaic linguistic features are preserved for largely stylistic reasons as we have seen, there appears to be very limited ability to write consistently in convincing archaic language.

Russell (2005: 446) concludes that the upshot of the last thirty years of research on register and archaisation is 'to bring into sharper focus ideas on register as opposed to attributing all variation of this type to different chronological layers of texts'. If correct, this has significant implications for linguistic dating. It is instructive, for example, that features that we know were obsolete or obsolescent in the Middle Irish period could still be in use in the later Early Modern period. Ó Catháin demonstrates (1933: 11), albeit on a very limited set of features, that the Irish 'Marco Polo' is indistinguishable from the language of the Annals of Ulster for the period 1156-1200 although it is based on the text of Francesco Pipino (1310×1314) and is likely to have been translated in the fourteenth or fifteenth centuries. Mac Gearailt (2012: 113) suggests that while scholars of the fifteenth to seventeenth centuries developed an interest in archaic language, there is no evidence that this was taught systematically:

> These differences suggest that while these authors, and probably most professional scholars from the twelfth to the seventeenth centuries, learned to read early Irish works and were conversant with their language, there was no common course of instruction on the use of the latter in new compositions and no commonly recognized corpus of early Irish forms for such purposes. Knowledge of the language of early Irish works with a view to using it in newly written works was probably not a widely recognised requirement in the schools of the late twelfth and thirteenth centuries, when there seems in any case to have been very little prose writing in Irish

The cultivation of high literary registers, archaic forms and pseudo-archaisms at different periods illustrates the pitfalls and challenges of linguistic dating. It might be expected that computational methods will encounter some of the same problems, if they are able to build a robust temporal model at all, but at the same time it might be hoped that they will provide independent corroboration of the linguistically-derived date.

1.7.5 *Lexical Dating*

Lexical dating may be defined as a method of establishing the chronology of a text through an examination of its vocabulary, and may be used on its own or in conjunction with other methods. For Ireland, its insular location has meant that its contacts with other cultures and languages is often thought to occur at discrete times in history, although in reality contact is more complex and prolonged than the great events view of history might suggest. The island was never conquered by the Romans so that the major contact with Latin came through the Christianisation of the country beginning in the fourth century CE. However, as the early texts in the Gaelic language hardly predate the seventh century, Latin loanwords alone are of little practical use in providing a chronology for the surviving texts. More useful information may be gleaned from later borrowings from Norse, Anglo-Norman French and English. Norse provides a number of loanwords in Irish, particularly in the realm of commerce and shipping.[7] As the first attack in Ireland is recorded in 795, this affords a neat terminus a quo for such borrowings, although Marstrander asserts that linguistic contact between Irish and Norse begins only c.820 (see Sommerfelt 1922, 176). According to Greene (1976), *erell* (= 'earl') is the earliest Norse loanword in Irish (cf. Ó Corráin 1987) but it is attested just once, in the record of the death of the jarl, Tomrair, in 848 (AU).[8] Most Norse loans are not attested until the Modern Irish period, although a number appear in the twelfth-century Book of Leinster (Breatnach 1994: 333).

The Anglo-Norman invasion of Ireland in 1169 provides another apparent linguistic horizon for loanwords in Irish. The leading nobles of the invasion were Anglo-Norman speakers, but the bulk of the settlers were English speaking. As in England, the use of Anglo-Norman was gradually displaced by English, and in Ireland also by Irish, from the thirteenth century (Risk 1968-69: 589). Most of the Romance borrowings in Irish are also found in Middle English, and so it can be difficult to determine the exact linguistic source, but in any case it is likely that they occurred after 1169 (Risk 1968-69: 591-4). Borrowings fall into several categories including architecture (*áirse* < *arche, castél* < *castel, gábla* < *gable, moirtél* < *morter, seómra* < *chaum(b)re*), war (*áirseoir* < *archer, batáille* < *bataille, caiptín* < *cap(i)taine*), law and administration (*báille* < *bailli, barún* < *barun, cúirt* < *curt/court, cunntáe* < *cuntee/countee, eighir* < *eir(e)*), food (*bagún* < *bacon, bitáille* < *vitaille, dínér* < *diner, festa* < *feste, galún* < *galun*), clothing (*aibít* < *habit, bróisde* < *broche, clóca* < *cloke, cóta* <

7 For example, in shipping and fishing we find *accaire* 'anchor' < *akkeri, bát* 'boat' < *bátr, trosc* 'cod' < *thorskr*, and *dorgha* 'fishing line' < *dorg*. Military: *ármann* 'officer', *suaittrech, suairtlech* 'mercenary' < *svartleggja* 'billeted soldier', *att* 'helmet' < *hattr*, Clothing and commerce: *cnapp* 'button' < *knappr, margad* 'market' < *markaðr* (Byrne 630-31).

8 Ó Cuív (1988: 81) notes that the earliest Viking name to be used of an Irishman was Gofraidh given to Gofraidh mac Fearghusa, the Gaelic king of Oirghialla (Annals of the Four Masters s.a. 835).

cote, *gúna* < *gune*) and the Church (*cailís* < *calis*, *grás*(*a*) < *grace*, *paróiste* < *paroche*, *pearsún* < *persun*) (McManus 1994: 441-2; Risk 1968-69: 586-8; Risk 1974-75: 72-91). Some borrowings appear soon after the arrival of the Anglo-Normans, for example, *rúta* and *sersénach* first appear in 1196, *caistél* in 1198 and *iustís* in 1203, while others, such as *garsún*, must have survived in the spoken language only (Risk 1968-69: 595). While it is likely that borrowings postdate the Anglo-Norman invasion, the potential for contact with the language must have been present since the Anglo-Norman invasion of England in 1066, although no examples have been advanced from the considerable body of material in the great twelfth-century manuscripts.

Borrowings from English may predate the Anglo-Norman invasion, with borrowings from Old English as well as Middle English. Frequently the form is an indicator of the period of borrowing in broad terms, for example (*h*)*alla* 'hall' < Middle English *halle* (cf. Old English *heall*) and *cing* < Middle English *cing* (Old English *cyning*) (see McManus 1994: 442-3). Irish *goistibe* 'godparent', although not attested before the twelfth century, is from Old English *godsibb* (eDIL), *sebac* 'hawk' < Old English *heafoc* and *ciste* 'chest, treasure' is probably from Old English *ciste* if not directly from Latin *cista* (Vendryes, Bachellery and Lambert 1987: 107). It can be difficult to disentangle Old English from Old Norse borrowings. Byrne (2005: 630) takes *pinginn* 'penny' as more probably from Old English *penning* rather than Old Norse *penningr* (Byrne 2005: 630) but F. Kelly (1998: 596) prefers an Old Norse origin, noting that the first Irish coins were minted during the reign of Sihtric III of Dublin in the late tenth century. It is noteworthy that the word does not appear in the canonical Old Irish law texts but only in later Middle Irish legal commentary. In this case, only extralinguistic considerations can guide us towards a probable period of borrowing.

However, caution must be exercised in establishing the significance of a loan for textual dating. Mac Eoin (1994) uses *ritire* 'rider, knight', a probable borrowing from Old English *rídere* 'knight', to date the work of the interpolator in the Book of the Dun Cow to the late twelfth century on the assumption that it cannot predate by much the first appearance of knights in Ireland during Anglo-Norman invasion of 1169. The earliest appearance of the term in a datable text is in the Annals of Tigernach. It is used in the phrase meaning 'knight of Christ' with reference to the Anglo-Saxon monk Ecgberht under the year 791, but this is clearly a later intrusion translating an original Latin *miles*.[9] Otherwise, *ritire* appears in these annals only in the years 1167-1177 to refer to the mounted soldiers of the Anglo-Norman lords. While they may not be exactly

9 Compare *miles Christi* (AU 729.1).

contemporary, they almost certainly were recorded shortly after the events described.[10] However, does that make 1167 the earliest attestation, let alone the date of introduction of the term? We must assume that the Irish knew of 'knights' before the arrival of the Anglo-Normans in Ireland, and certainly since soon after the invasion of England and Wales.[11]

Lexical dating is not commonly used in Ireland and where it is it tends to be particularly reliant on identifiable borrowings from other languages (e.g. Murray, 2012b: 42). It is more widely practiced elsewhere but its validity has been questioned (e.g. Rezetko 2003 and from a different angle by Holmstedt 2009). Young, Rezetko, and Ehrensvärd (2009) view lexical and morphological differences in biblical texts as relating to contemporary dialects rather than chronologically distinct periods. Rather than interpreting neologisms, including lexical borrowings, as indicative of a later period, they merely attribute them to different dialects so that Standard Biblical and Late Biblical Hebrew represent, in their view, diglossia rather than discrete periods of the language. The essence of the problem is that archaic features associated with Standard Biblical Hebrew are also found in Late Biblical Hebrew and neologisms found in the latter are also found in the former. Semantic developments within a language can be equally useful and may be easier to date precisely but it can be difficult to be assured of the precise meaning of a word in a particular context and a stable and robust lexical chronology presupposes the existence of a large series of securely dated texts in the first place.

1.7.6 *Methodology*

So far, we have examined the multiple issues involved in attempting to date medieval Irish texts, but now we must consider the impact of these on the nature of the methods that scholars may employ. Any methodology must take

10 For example, 'Robert Fitz Stephen came into Ireland with sixty mailcoats, and there was Earl Richard son of Gilbert, and they had two battalions, both knights (*ridire*) and archers', Stokes 1993: ii 279 = 1170 CE; '... one great and brave battalion of knights and officers and archers (*do ridirib 7 d'ármannaib 7 d'áirseóraib*)', ibid. 290 s.a. 1174. See also AU s.a. 1177, 1178.

11 The passage cited by Mac Eoin depicts three men as the *trí marcaig ind ríg* 'the three horse-riders of the king', which is glossed as *a thrí ritiri* 'his three knights' (Best & Bergin 1929: l.7622). There is nothing very distinctive in their appearance except that each carries a scourge (*sraigell*), and that their names all contain the word *ech* 'steed'. The curious thing is that *marcach* is a well-known word and would not have required glossing, except for the fact that it developed a secondary meaning 'messenger' at least as early as the twelfth century (O'Rahilly 1966). Presumably, it is this ambiguity that caused the scribe to add his explanatory gloss to indicate that these were not messengers but mounted warriors.

into account the survival of the vast majority of texts only in often much later manuscripts, with all the opportunities for modernisation and revision that this entails. To a large degree, we are not dating a text as such but its various stages. As noted above, these stages may not be neatly stratified, ready to be picked apart by a textual scholar, and so the method must be able to deal with texts in which the layers are not distinct. The absence of a clear chronology for language change is a further issue that must be addressed. If particular features cannot be dated precisely, then this has an impact on their usefulness in creating a textual chronology. This is further complicated by issues of dialect, register and archaism.

There have been some attempts to examine language change statistically, comparing, for example, the proportions of perfective *ro* to its later equivalent *do*. While those who have studied the annals have rightly looked at percentages, we may seriously doubt whether a simple proportional method can be applied to texts, either in principle or in the kind of complex textual tradition that pertains in Irish (see Mac Niocaill 1968). Linguistic changes would normally occur at a given time in the speech of an individual or community of speakers, although it may appear more gradual when considered at a regional, national or transnational level. While we might expect some degree of transition from one form or usage to another, we cannot expect that speakers at one point exclusively used *ro* and that there was a gradual decline over centuries, during which speakers employed a decreasing percentage of the form. As texts are produced by individuals or small groups of people, we might expect the language of the texts to reflect that of the individual writers, not of a whole language area. Where archaic features such as *ro* are preserved, it is almost certainly to do with archaisation as we have seen, and as a consequence they are generally recognised now as of limited value in linguistic dating.

In contrast to the underlying assumptions of the statistical method, we may conclude that the appearance of a single innovative form in a manuscript is evidence that that change had already occurred in the language of the writer. It doesn't matter whether there are ten equivalent conservative features – these may be due to the writer's source or his literary register. As McCone has usefully shown, even hypercorrect forms can indicate that a change had already occurred or was in the process of happening at the time of writing.[12]

12 We cannot readily distinguish between a change that had occurred at the time of writing and one that was in the process of developing. As noted above, an individual may use a mixture of early and late forms in their natural speech, in which case we must speak of the change being in development rather than having occurred, particularly as there is no inevitability of the completion and adoption of the change by the wider community.

Unfortunately, we are more frequently confronted with texts that do not occur in contemporary manuscripts, so that we must consider whether innovative forms arise from the process of transmission or alternatively point towards the 'original' text (presuming that that can be determined).

Dating by linguistic means is normally approached in two ways. One is to observe the profile of linguistic features of known or accepted date, such as the disappearance of the neuter c.1000 CE. Thus, any texts that contain evidence of the neuter may be placed in the first millennium, although we must of course bear in mind the possibility of archaisms (see 1.7). This directly provides an absolute date, although the certainty of the date may be somewhat illusory if the evidence on which it is based is itself founded on linguistic dating. The second approach is to sort texts chronologically through a comparison of their language overall. Thus, a text of unknown provenance can be dated relative to other texts of known, or more often accepted, dates (see, for example, L. Breatnach 2005, 354-55). In this way, an approximate absolute date can be computed but there is, of course, a danger here: if even one of the anchor texts is incorrectly dated, then any chronology that uses it will be flawed. Stifter (2013: 198) concludes that only relative dating is possible, but with the proviso that such dates are provisional and subject to change.

Given that few texts exist in pristine form, any dating method must attempt to distinguish the work of successive scribes and scholars. Textual studies or palaeographical concerns, along with a comparison of different copies, may enable the scholar to distinguish different contributions (see McCone, cited in 1.7.1 above, for example). In order to explore this further, we may consider a simple model of a Middle Irish text. Let's assume that it was written in the eleventh century and survives, with some scribal modernisation, in a single fifteenth-century manuscript. What we should expect to see, therefore, is a text that is predominantly Middle Irish, exhibiting only a few features of late Middle Irish or Early Modern Irish. The features considered must be truly diagnostic features. For example, it is not enough to notice the survival of a few cases of the infixed pronoun or isolated examples of deponent verbs if we know that those forms were still in use in the later language. On the other hand, the existence of a few late forms would not lead us to assume a late date for the composition of the text but rather we would assign these to a later scribe. There must be some consideration, therefore, of the proportions of certain features in order to determine whether or not they are original. Let us further assume that a text contains some quotations from an Old Irish text which does not otherwise survive. We can hardly expect these to survive in unadulterated form but we might expect them to exhibit some diagnostic Old Irish features, that is, forms that would no longer have been possible in the eleventh century. It is self-evident that a few quotations do not make the text as a whole Old Irish, so again we must consider both the percentage of early features and their distribution throughout the text. If they tend to be concentrated in a single passage, then they would point towards quotation, and this may be supported by textual analysis.

The model used here has been deliberately simplified for the purposes of illustration of the steps that need to be taken. In reality, texts tend to have a much more complicated history. A typical narrative may sew together two or more older versions of the story and incorporate other texts. Verse texts may be plundered to provide further information or to create the illusion of authenticity. Moreover, it is highly likely that multiple copies and revisions were made, most of which no longer survive, so where we might be able to uncover two or three strata within a text, in reality there could be traces of a dozen scribes and revisers. Clearly, linguistic dating is inadequate to deal with all these levels unless they survive independently in manuscripts. The reality of the situation is that the dating of a text is not based on a handful of isolated features but on a consideration of all its linguistic features. Moreover, we have seen that in some texts it is sometimes impossible to distinguish linguistically between two parts of a text that are known to have separate origins.

1.8 Conclusion

The complexity of linguistic dating is clear and remains controversial in many disciplines (for example, Kofoed 2006, Neidorf 2015). There may be disciplinary differences due to the nature of the surviving record. If a culture tends to record the time of writing or the names of dateable authors, then scholars may be less reliant on linguistic dating. Where a language is largely standardised, as in medieval Latin or classical Arabic, linguistic dating may be of limited value due to the lack of systematic change. This can be true of periods of a single language, as in Classical Modern Irish, where scholars have struggled to identify reliable diagnostic features.

Notwithstanding the problems of linguistic dating, it remains the primary method for establishing the chronology for many literatures, including Irish. The complications remain, however. In Irish, the bulk of the surviving material is extant in non-contemporary manuscripts and frequently contains layers of revision and expansion. Where a large number of texts survives in contemporary or autograph manuscripts, then linguistic dating will be more secure than in those cultures in which there is a long period of transmission and a practice of modification of texts. There are also issues of register and dialect to contend with. Authors may be under pressure to conform to a dominant register, but ultimately that is a choice depending on context and audience. Little is known about dialect variation in early Ireland and it must be conceded that linguistic dating methods are susceptible to dialect variation, as in biblical Hebrew.

In the next three chapters we set forth an alternative dating method using machine learning. Just as linguistic dating is complemented by other methods, we suggest that the machine learning method discussed here acts as a further tool in the textual scholar's toolbox.

CHAPTER 2

Computational Approaches to Text Dating

Although considerable advances in text dating have been made by domain experts using traditional models, computational and automatic approaches have been attracting more and more research interest in the last two decades. This chapter focuses on the computational problem of text dating, the solutions that have previously been attempted and some new methods that we are proposing. Firstly, we will provide a brief history and a formal description of text dating as a computational problem, then we will describe previous relevant techniques such as language modelling, regression, classification, and feature selection. Thirdly, we will propose some new solutions of multi-class classification with Flexible Time Intervals (FTI), Sliding Time Intervals (STI), Greedy Grouping (GG), and Temporal Landmark Selection (TLS). Finally, we will discuss the concept of datability to analyse the feasibility of text dating as a practical task.

2.1 A Brief History

The temporal dimension of texts can be essential for many Natural Language Processing tasks, such as event detection (Allan et al, 1998), document search (Lappas et al, 2009), text summarization (Wan, 2007), and information diffusion (Bakshy et al, 2012). These applications in turn output very useful information for traditional studies of discourse analysis, sense shifting, readability and narrative frameworks etc. in socio- and historical linguistics, and for emergent fields such as computational forensics, computational journalism, and clinical corpus analysis, etc. However, the timestamp of the text concerned may not be readily available. In this case, a likely time period can be estimated according to the information provided by the text. The task of estimating the time period when a text was composed is often called Text Dating (De Jong et al., 2005). It has also been described as document dating (Dalli and Wilks, 2006; Kanhabua and Norvag, 2009), temporal text classification (Ciobanu et al, 2013; Zampieri et al, 2015), or diachronic text evaluation (DTE) (Popescu and Strapparava, 2015).

 | DOI:10.1163/9789004410046_004

2.1.1 *Early Research*

Early research mostly focused on language modelling for temporal texts. Based on the language modelling approaches of Ponte and Croft (1998) and Li and Croft (2003), De Jong et al. (2005) employed prototype methods and unigram language models to classify Dutch texts with normalised log-likelihood ratio (NLLR) (Kraaij, 2004). They attempted to restore the diachronic relationship between terms which might be obscured by irregular patterns of language evolution and usage, while applying statistical language models. These models were supposed to be capable of supporting the automatic detection of semantic similarities between words and word ambiguities, and allow classification of a text according to the time span from which it originates. This approach involves building temporal profiles of words as longitudinal sections in a reference corpus and temporal language models as cross sections. To deal with continuous time, Wang et al. (2008) used Brownian motion for modelling topic change over time. Brownian motion refers to the Wiener process, a continuous-time stochastic process named in honour of Norbert Wiener. Their training process models the latent topics through a sequential collection of documents, where a "topic" is a pattern of word use that is expected to evolve over the course of the collection. This approach is simpler and faster but it cannot be directly applied to documents with different degrees of label uncertainty, such as interval labels. Employing a similar method as De Jong et al. (2005), Kanhabua and Norvag (2008; 2009) built temporal language models for dating texts by assigning a probability to a time partition according to word usage or word statistics over time. Kumar et al. (2011) also adopted language models and Kullback-Leibler distances in distribution space to classify temporal texts.

2.1.2 *Recent Research*

More recent research has employed machine learning techniques to build automatic text dating systems, which are often trained on a large corpus of texts annotated with timestamps. Classification is the most explored machine learning method employed for automatic text dating systems. Dalli and Wilks (2006) trained a classifier to date texts within a time span of nine years. The method uses lexical features and it is aided by words whose frequencies increase at some point in time, most notably named entities. Abe and Tsumoto (2010) propose similarity metrics to categorise texts based on keywords calculated by indexes such as tf-idf (that is, term frequency–inverse document frequency, a numerical statistic that is intended to reflect how important a word is to a document in a collection or corpus). Garcia-Fernandez et al. (2011) explore different NLP techniques on a digitised collection of French texts published between 1801 and 1944. Style-related markers and features, including readability features, have been shown to reveal temporal information in English as well as Portuguese (Stamou, 2005; Stajner and Zampieri, 2013). Ciobanu et al. (2013) proposed using supervised classification with unigram features with Chi-squared feature selection on a collection of historical Romanian texts, noting that the informative features are words that have changed form over time. The classification approach tackles text dating as a multi-class problem, with classes defined as time intervals such as months, years, decades or centuries. This approach has the drawback of having to arbitrarily delimit the intervals, and often leads to a model that is not informative for texts written within such a window. Niculae et al. (2014), therefore, resorted to another popular machine learning method: regression. They explored a solution to the drawback of classification by using a ranking approach, which comes from ordinal regression, where data points belong to inherently ordered classes.

2.1.3 *DTE Task*

In SemEval-2015 a novel task was introduced, namely the Diachronic Text Evaluation (DTE) task[1], which could be regarded as a landmark in the research of text dating (Popescu and Strapparava, 2015). The task was subdivided into three subtasks. Subtasks 1 and 2 require an automatic system to identify the time interval during which a piece of news was written. The intervals come in three grades: fine (6-year), medium (12-year) and coarse (20-year) according to their length. Subtask 3 aims to distinguish temporal phrases. The subtasks all concern specific types of information that might be available in news. Subtask 1 considers news items in which specific historical events, named entities etc. are clearly mentioned. Such information is excluded from subtask 2 where, however, enough surface information is provided to assign a time interval, at least for a human. DTE Subtask 2 is a typical text dating task in terms of its formulation and the size of training and test corpus. Zampieri et al. (2015) further improved the ranking method of Niculae et al. (2014) with a non-parametric memory-based distance function. They better dealt with the interval formulation of DTE Subtask 2, and won the second place for the DTE Subtask 2 competition. Szymanski and Lynch (2015), henceforth the UCD system, being unsatisfied with SVM regression and ordinal classification, chose standard multi-class SVM classification for DTE Subtask 2, and won first place.

2.1.4 *Features for Dating*

For both language modelling and machine learning methods, feature selection is essential because the training corpus for text dating often consists of highly

1 http://alt.qcri.org/semeval2015/task7/

complex time series data of multi-dimensional features which can be morphological, lexical, grammatical, stylistic, topical and even emotional. Most research mentioned above involved lexical features (Dalli and Wilks, 2006; Abe and Tsumoto, 2010; Kumar et al, 2011; Niculae et al, 2014; Zampieri et al, 2015; Szymanski and Lynch, 2015). Some also used topical features (Wang et al, 2008; Kotsakos et al, 2014), stylistic features (Zampieri et al, 2015), and external linguistic knowledge (Kanhabua and Norvag, 2009; Szymanski and Lynch, 2015). Morphological features or n-gram characters have been proven to be more effective than most other types (Szymanski and Lynch, 2015).

2.1.5 *Lazy Method*

In addition, the lazy machine learning method has also been employed for text dating. This approach involves a local part of a general temporal model for prediction. Kotsakos et al (2014) built a text dating system, BurstySimDater, which employed lexical similarity and term burstiness (Lappas et al, 2009). Term bursty intervals are computed beforehand from a reference corpus, then a set of similar texts is extracted for a query text in a manner similar to K-nearest Neighbor, and finally the largest overlap of bursty intervals of shared terms is returned as the estimated time for the query.

2.2 The Problem Stated

As for frequently used notation in this Chapter, we now denote x as a text, t as a timestamp, $y = P(t|x)$ as the probability of x being composed at t, n as the number of training texts, m as the number of classifying features, d as the number of time units or the length of the whole time period that the data covers, t' as the labelled date of a training text, $[t' - \delta, t' + \delta]$ as the required time interval, and δ as the dating tolerance, which is an integer that determines the size of a required granularity or the interval length $2\delta + 1$. We also denote $X \in R^{n \times m}$ as the matrix of training texts, and $Y \in [0, 1]^{n \times d}$ as the probability matrix of timestamps for the training texts. Moreover, the transpose of a vector or matrix is denoted by the superscript ^{T}, Y^+ denotes the Moore-Penrose pseudo-inverse of a matrix Y, $\|Y\|_2$ is the spectral norm, $\|Y\|_{\mathrm{F}}$ is the Frobenius norm, and $Y_{(i)}$ is the ith column of Y.

2.2.1 *Problem Formulation*

The problem of dating a text x can then be formulated as $f(x) \rightarrow [t - \delta, t + \delta]$. A supervised method can be used to train a model $f(X) \rightarrow Y$ on X labeled with Y. Figure 2.1(a) gives an example for the mapping between X and Y,

	1698	1699	1700	1701	1702	1703	1704	1705	...	2010
x_1	0	0	0	1	0	0	0	0	...	0
x_2	0	0	0	0	1	0	0	0	...	0
x_3	0	0	0	0	0	1	0	0	...	0
	...	...	...	...	...	...	...	...	...	...

(a) **Texts Labelled with Time Stamps Where $\delta = 0$**

	1698-1700	1701-1703	1704-1705	... ...	2008-2010
x_1	0	1	0	... ...	0
x_2	0	1	0	... ...	0
x_3	0	1	0	... ...	0
	...	...	...	... ...	...

(b) **Texts Labelled with Time Intervals Where $\delta = 1$**

<text id="378rn324911597">(x_1)

<textF yes="1698-1704" no="1705-1711" ...

<textM yes="1695-1707" no="1708-1720" ...

<textC yes="1691-1711" no="1712-1732" ...

(c) **DTE Format Time Intervals Where $\delta = 3$, 6 and 10**

	1698	1699	1700	1701	1702	1703	1704	1705	...	2010
x_1	1	1	1	1	1	1	1	0	...	0
x_2	0	1	1	1	1	1	1	1	...	0
x_3	0	0	0	1	1	1	1	1	...	0
	...	...	...	...	...	...	...	...	...	...

(d) **Binary Format for DTE Timestamps with $\delta = 3$**

FIGURE 2.1 Examples of data format and class labels in Y

where each text x_i is labelled with a time stamp corresponding to 1, and in this case $\delta = 0$. Although this is fine enough for text dating as regression if directly considered as a problem of classification, there will be as many class labels as the number of time units involved in the training and test corpus and it may not be suitable for practical classification due to data sparseness. A proper mapping of $\phi(Y) \rightarrow [t' - \delta, t' + \delta]$, where $\delta \geq 0$, therefore, often needs to be figured out for a more practical dating purpose, as illustrated in Figure 2.1(b), where texts are labelled with time intervals of a desired length, i.e. $2\delta + 1$. The DTE tasks centered the desired time interval symmetrically around the text's composing time (Popescu and Strapparava, 2015) as shown by Figure 2.1(c) in which the text was composed in 1701, with $\delta = 3$, 6 and 10. This is a straightforward mapping, where $y = P(t'|x)$ and δ doesn't reduce any variance of the time intervals. This mapping assigns two temporally close texts with incomparable class labels as shown in Figure 2.1(d) with $\delta = 3$, so is not suitable for practical classification because it leads to the same number of class labels as with $\delta = 0$ in Figure 2.1(a).

2.2.2 *Evaluation Methods*

Another important issue in text dating is the evaluation method because this is closely related to how a temporal language model should be built, how a machine learning model should be optimised, and what sorts of features should be included in these models. There have generally been two types of method for evaluation on a test set. One is based on distance or similarity, and the other is based on classification accuracy. All kinds of distance or similarity suitable for regression problems could be adopted for evaluating text dating results. Formally for a test set X labelled with Y, it is the distance or similarity between Y and Y^*, the predicted probability matrix by a text dating system. Some common measures include least squares, norms such as $\|Y - Y^*\|_1$, $\|Y - Y^*\|_2$, and log likelihood. However, these straightforward measures are intensely sensitive to scales, so an outlier may easily bias the evaluation if relevant values are not normalised. Therefore, some normalisation or limitation for controlling the scale tends to be introduced in practice. For example, Popescu and Strapparava (2015) employed 10 rules as loss function to punish any predicted dates with 0 to 9 or more time intervals off the standard labels (Table 2.1). Outliers of predicted dates with 9 or more intervals off would thus compose no bias and be punished by the same degree.

When text dating is modelled as classification, accuracy could be used directly as an evaluating measure, but the classification accuracy can be too sensitive to how the time intervals are segmented as class labels. It means that any prediction would be considered as incorrect if it were just one time-unit off the segmented time interval. For example, if the text in Figure 2.1(c) is dated as 1699-1705, it will be evaluated as wrong because it doesn't match the three given standards 1698-1704, 1695-1707, and 1691-1711. The DTE task evaluates dating performance by the ratio of how many times a text dating system can find exactly the DTE defined time intervals. Since the DTE time intervals are overlapping (see Figure 2.1(d)), Szymanski and Lynch (2015) created their

TABLE 2.1 Loss function on off intervals (Popescu and Strapparava, 2015)

Intervals off	Loss
0	0
1	0.1
2	0.15
3	0.2
4	0.4
5	0.5
6	0.6
7	0.8
8	0.9
≥9	0.99

own non-overlapping classes by segmenting the whole period into adjacent intervals of respective DTE granularities, i.e. 6, 12 and 20 years, and assigned a query text with any given year range of the DTE format that has the greatest overlap with the predicted time interval. In other words, the dating prediction of a text was considered correct if over half of the dated period fell in the standard time interval of relevant granularity. For example, for adjacent intervals of "1691-1697, 1698-1704, 1705-1711" in DTE format, if a predict is "1696-1701" and its overlaps with the DTE intervals are respectively "2, 3, 0", the middle DTE interval of "1698-1704" will be assigned as the final dating result.

In our experiments, we introduce the concept of dating tolerance δ, which means a dating error of $\pm\delta$ can be tolerated for some practical purposes. Our evaluation employs **dating accuracy** which is the ratio of those texts that are correctly dated with regard to a given tolerance δ, such as 3, 6, and 10-year tolerance corresponding to the DTE granularities of 6, 12 and 20 years. Thereafter, a predicted date t^* is considered correct if $t' - \delta \leq t^* \leq t' + \delta$. Because the temporal order ensures that there are at most only two adjacent intervals for any time interval, our evaluation method technically works for the DTE task in the same way as that of Szymanski and Lynch (2015).

2.3 Previous Solutions

Previous solutions for automatic text dating could be roughly grouped into three approaches, namely language modelling, regression/ordinal ranking, and classification. This section will describe the general process of each approach and the basic techniques involved.

2.3.1 *Language Modelling*

This approach was inspired directly by the traditional linguistic dating methods of manual analysis. It consists of a pipeline process of three stages. First, a temporal language model is established explicitly either by human experts or automatically via some machine learning methods. This language model may include different types of elements, such as words, topics, and events. Second, a mapping function is defined to compute a text by the established model, or to simply represent a text with elements from the language model. Third, a dating function is learned from a training corpus of texts labelled with timestamps, or simply defined by linguists or domain experts.

Many early efforts (Ponte and Croft, 1998; Li and Croft, 2003; De Jong et al, 2005) in text-dating research focused on language modelling, mainly due to the shortage of a large enough training corpus and the purpose of academic research in which the linguistic analysis and qualitative explanations are considered indispensable. The temporal language model might lead to both qualitative and quantitative explanations about why a given text is dated to a certain time, which is the most compelling aspect of the language modelling approach. However, the language model can be very expensive to build and its scalability, compatibility and consistency are difficult issues to solve.

The text dating system of BurstySimDater (Kotsakos et al, 2014) could also be grouped as a language modelling approach. Though involving a lazy learning method, the system employs term burstiness, which serves in a way like a general language model, and lexical similarity for dating a query text by K-nearest Neighbor.

2.3.2 *Ordinal Regression/Ranking*

During recent decades, many Natural Language Processing tasks, such as event detection, document search, text summarisation, and information diffusion, have essentially been deploying temporal information of relevant texts. Moreover, there are more and more time-stamped texts available for training text dating systems. Machine learning approaches based on a large training corpus, therefore, have become a major stream for text dating research. Since timestamps can be regarded as numeric values, the training of a text dating function $f(X) \rightarrow Y$ on X labeled with Y may be modelled as a regression problem. Regression analysis may help us understand how some components of a text are varied while other components are held fixed when the time changes, and thus it may lead to a qualitative explanation about how a text could have been dated. However, due to the sparseness of data points, a regression problem may not be solved directly, especially for text dating tasks where a long time period is covered. Instead, a formalisation of ordinal regression has been employed by some text-dating research.

Ordinal regression is a ranking approach, which amounts to ordering a set of inputs with respect to some measure. Niculae et al. (2014) and Zampieri et al. (2015) modelled the training of text dating as an ordinal ranking task. This ranking model is supposed to learn a direction along which the temporal order of training texts is preserved as much as possible. First, the training corpus X is converted into a pairwise dataset with each element formed as $(x_i, x_j | y_i < y_j)$; then, a linear function $f(x) = w \cdot x$ is learned such that $f(x_i) < f(x_j)$ for each element in the pairwise dataset; finally, for dating a query text x', $w \cdot x'$ can be compared to $w \cdot x^T$ of some typical texts for each required time interval, or to $w \cdot x^K$ of K-nearest neighbours of x' in the training corpus. More recently, Belinkov, Magidow, Romanov, Shmidman, and Koppel (2016) used the ranking method in SRILM toolkit (Stolcke, 2002; Stolcke et al., 2011) and a 5-gram language model for dating Arabic texts of unspecified genres.

The regression approach doesn't have to segment the concerned time period, and, moreover, remains suitable for the evaluation measure of classification accuracy with any given dating tolerance δ (See Section 2.2.2). Besides, because the construction of the pairwise dataset is based on the partial ordering of the timestamps, where texts labelled with the same timestamp are not ordered, a regression approach can be very flexible for the format of timestamp labelling. This means that this approach may take in as the training corpus texts labelled with incompatible time intervals.

2.3.3 *Classification*

The classification approach also seems a straightforward choice for text dating, since timestamps labelled on training texts could simply serve as multi-class labels, and there are lots of machine learning methods to choose from. Actually, both language modelling and ordinal regression, mentioned in the above sections, involve some classification techniques either for prediction or for training. After building a temporal language model, a classifier using elements of the model as features could be either defined manually or trained automatically on labelled texts, and employed for dating query texts. Ordinal regression often takes advantage of the simplicity of binary classification training on a pairwise dataset converted from time-stamped texts. However, due to the long time period that the corpus may cover and the potential data sparseness in the training corpus, classifiers may not be trained directly on the time-stamped texts in the original format. Fortunately, for practical dating purposes, a query text is usually not required to be dated to an exact time unit. An error of $\pm\delta$ ($\delta \geq 0$) can be tolerated in accordance with some domain specific requirements. The originally labelled timestamps could thus be converted into non-overlapping time intervals of 2δ or $2\delta + 1$ time units, and a classifier then trained on the converted corpus. For dating a query text, the predicted time interval could be a cheap and efficient answer, or be mapped to some required format such as that of DTE task solved by Szymanski and Lynch (2015).

Though it has been proved to work well in many dating applications, the segmentation of time intervals is problematic in quite a few aspects. First, the regular intervals of equal length run contrary to the intuition that a language may well have been changing irregularly along its history; second, because the boundaries of each interval depend a lot on the arbitrary starting point of the covered time period, it can be very difficult to train any model that is expected to be informative for texts written within such windows; third, in a classification model, the time intervals as class labels are assumed temporally independent from each other, and thus no ordinal information could be modelled.

2.3.4 *Feature Selection Methods*

Features used for text dating can be morphological, lexical, grammatical, stylistic, topical, emotional, and even meta-linguistic, such as the length of a text, or extra-linguistic, such as the handwriting style or font types used for printing. The number of a set of candidate dating features can be too large to choose from manually. For automatic text dating, almost all research selects features automatically. Some research, especially for the dating approaches of language modelling and ordinal regression (de Jong et al., 2005; Dalli and Wilks, 2006; Niculae et al, 2014; Zampieri et al, 2015), often employed a separate statistical method for selecting and building up the feature set, and then used a different statistical or machine learning method to learn a dating model and predict for new texts. Other research, especially for the classification approach (Szymanski and Lynch, 2015), only involved one machine learning method for both feature selection and text dating. Normally, features were selected by optimising the dating performance of the chosen machine learning method on a separate corpus called the development set, and then the selected features were used to train the final dating model on the whole training corpus and to make predicts for new texts.

2.3.5 *Regression vs Classification*

The approaches of regression and classification are the two most popular ones in recent text dating research. Unlike the language modelling approach, which explicitly builds a language model, both regression and classification build

TABLE 2.2 State-of-the-art dating performances on DTE Subtask 2 (Popescu and Strapparava, 2015)

Systems	Approaches	Features involved	Dating accuracy		
			Fine	Medium	Coarse
UCD	SVM classification	Character and word 1-3grams, POS, syntactic rules, and Google n-gram database	46.3%	47.2%	54.2%
AMBRA	Ordinal regression	Document length, stylistics, POS, and word n-grams	14.3%	14.3%	29.2%

implicit language models via their respective machine learning algorithms. The difference is that the implicit language model built via regression aims to detect rigid temporal patterns from the training corpus while that of classification simply ignores any temporal patterns. A regression method tries to preserve the temporal order of training texts as much as possible by learning a linear function $f(x) = w \cdot x$ on the converted pairwise dataset, so the linear function keeps most of the partial order of the timestamps labelled on training texts. Class labels for classification are assumed independent from each other, so nothing of the temporal order among the timestamps can be captured by this approach. This leads to the fact that regression and classification are at opposite extremes in terms of exploring the temporal information provided in the training corpus.

Previous research (Szymanski and Lynch, 2015; Popescu and Strapparava, 2015), as well as our preliminary study, proved that modelling text dating as a multi-class classification task could outperform other approaches that define text dating as regression or ranking problems. Table 2.2 gives the state-of-the-art evaluation results of typical regression and classification approaches on DTE Subtask 2. It shows that the multi-class classification approach greatly outperformed that of regression. Therefore, it seems that the temporal distribution is not worth exploring. Besides, if the predefined window of the time intervals is too large, the output is not useful for most systems; if the window is too small, learning is impractical because of the large number of classes. Particularly for the problem of historical datasets, learning a year-level classifier would not work, because some class might be represented by a single document, and for many time units, such as years, there would be no documents available. The temporal independence assumption obviously conflicts with what we understand of the evolution of lexicons and languages (Cucera and Stulka, 2010; Altschuler et al, 2013), and breaks the historical relation between things "before and after" (Lévi-Strauss, 1966).

Some important issues, therefore, are: what the real temporal distribution underlying the training corpus looks like; whether this distribution could be modelled; and, if so, how much of it could be modelled. All these issues can be very challenging because training corpora often consist of highly complex time series data of multi-dimensional aspects. Furthermore, factors influencing the evolution of a language can be varied, including geography, economy, politics, genetics, the population size, language contacts, migration movements, etc. These factors may leave either explicit or implicit traces in the form of a language and its representation, so it can be too difficult to fully model the temporal distribution of a training corpus, especially when the corpus is large.

2.4 New Solutions

From this analysis of previous research on text dating we can conclude that: a) the approach of multi-class classification outperforms other approaches such as regression or ranking; b) due to the temporal independence assumption, the classification approach neglects the temporal distribution within a training corpus; and c) the temporal distribution within a training corpus could be difficult to model directly. On the basis of multi-class classification, we proposed five solutions to improve dating performance by exploring the temporal distribution within the training corpus: a) Flexible time intervals (FTI), b) Sliding time interval (STI), c) Greedy grouping (GG), d) Temporal landmark selection (TLS), and e) a compound solution of FTI&TLS. FTI and STI exploit the temporal distribution implicitly, while GG and TLS exploit the distribution explicitly.

2.4.1 *Flexible Time Interval* (FTI)

The approach of multi-class classification to dating texts (Dalli and Wilks, 2006; Szymanski and Lynch, 2015) normally employs time intervals that are fixed by a required dating tolerance δ, segmented equally and deployed linearly along the time span, as illustrated in Figure 2.2(a) which gives a segmentation example of $\delta = 2$. To better visualise the mechanism, we represent the similarity between each pair of adjacent texts by the graphical distance. Thus, the fixed class labels in Figure 2.2(a) might be formatted as 't_{0-4}', 't_{5-9}', etc. Since classifiers tend to group a text into the class with more similar texts to it, text *x*' in Figure 2.2(a) might very possibly be wrongly predicted by the multi-class classifier as class 't_{0-4}' instead of 't_{5-9}'. If the time intervals could be set

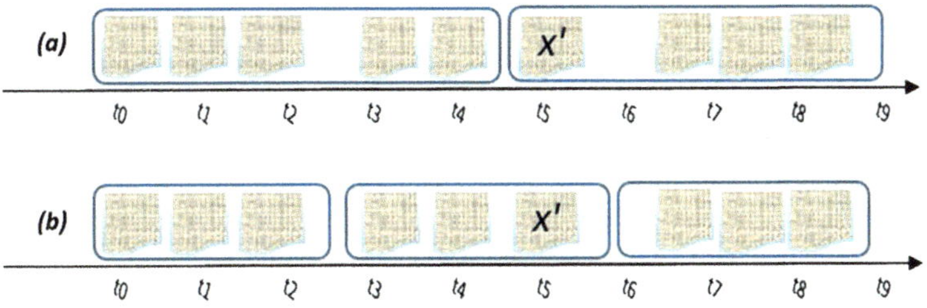

FIGURE 2.2 Fixed (a) and flexible (b) time intervals for multi-class classification

flexibly as illustrated in Figure 2.2(b) with tunable tolerance of $\delta' = 1$, all texts would be classified correctly into classes of 't_{0-2}', 't_{3-5}' and 't_{6-8}' etc., and thus the advantage of multi-class classification for text dating could be kept and its disadvantage of temporal independence be overcome to some degree. Therefore, we can tune δ' on the training corpus to find the optimal segmentation of time intervals, satisfying the condition that the overall text dating accuracy will be optimised.

Our FTI method aims to improve the multi-class classification approach for dating texts by tuning δ' to find the best segmentation of time intervals, instead of simply segmenting with the given dating tolerance δ. This method exploits the temporal distribution of the training corpus implicitly and partially since the whole distribution hasn't been estimated and the regular segmentation via δ' reveals only some temporal characteristics of the training texts. Algorithm 2.1 gives the steps for tuning δ' on a training corpus for using any multi-class text classifier. After tuning δ', dating new texts is then as straightforward as employing the classifier trained with flexible time intervals of the tuned δ' as class labels. This can be suitable for any given multi-class classification models.

2.4.2 *Sliding Time Interval* (STI)

Figure 2.3 illustrates our motivation and the basic mechanism of STI. Here, we also represent the similarity between each pair of adjacent texts by the graphical distance, and the class labels in Figure 2.3(a) might be formatted as 't_{0-3}', 't_{3-6}', etc. A multi-class classifier tends to group text x_2 in Figure 2.3(a) into the class of 't_{3-6}'. If we slide the time intervals one unit forward as in Figure 2.3(b), text x_2 would be correctly predicted but at the cost of text x_1. Further sliding in Figure 2.3(c) secures both x_1 and x_2 but may cause other errors (such as x_3 and x_4). Nevertheless, this sliding mechanism implicitly captures to some extent the temporal characteristics shared by those adjacent classes of texts.

Our preliminary study proved the above hypothesis. Three NBM classifiers were trained on the DTE Subtask 2 training corpus with class labels of time

ALGORITHM 2.1 Dating texts by classification with flexible time intervals

---

Input: δ, the given dating tolerance; T, a corpus of texts labeled with writing/publishing timestamps t; b, the beginning of the overall time span; and D, a hyper-parameter of the largest possible width of time intervals for a language in concern.

Output: δ', that determines the optimal segmentation of time intervals.

Steps:

1. From T, randomly extract T_d as developing set, and use $T_t = T - T_d$ as training set;
2. **for** $\delta' = 0$ to D:
3. Label each text in T_t with the time interval of $[b + i * \delta', b + (i + 2) * \delta']$, where i is an integer such that for the timestamp of the text t, we have $b + i * \delta' \leq t \leq b + (i + 2) * \delta'$;
4. Train a multi-class classifier on T_t;
5. Classify each text in T_d with the trained classifier;
6. For a text predicted of class label $[x, y]$, return $x + (y - x)/2$ as the estimated date;
7. A text is considered correctly dated if $t - \delta \leq x + (y - x)/2 \leq t + \delta$;
8. **end for**;
9. Retrieve δ' that led to most correctly dated texts in T_d for dating new texts.

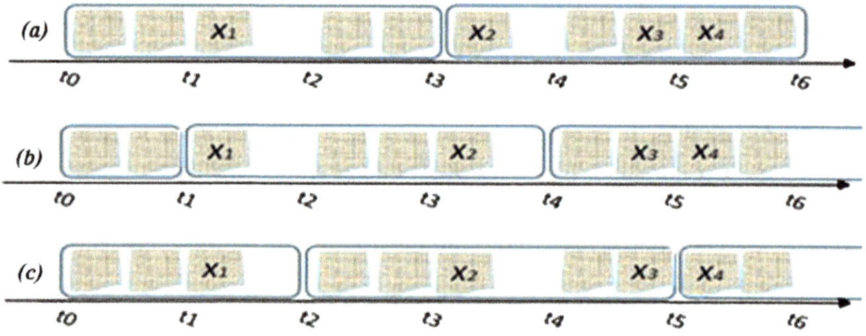

FIGURE 2.3 Fixed and sliding time intervals for multi-class classification

intervals from three different segmentations. 4,500 character n-gram ($n = 1$, 2 and 3) features were used to transform the texts into string vectors: all letters were converted to lowercase, no stop word removal or stemmer was performed, and other parameters were kept default. Histograms in Figure 2.4 gives the 10-cross validation per-class dating precisions of the classifiers on labelling the texts published from 1700 to 1760. Values of precision for yearly class classification, i.e. with the dating tolerance $\delta = 0$, were given to contrast the predicting performances for overlapping time spans. Obviously, the three classifiers behaved very differently, and the upper line links maximum values for each year which shows the room for improvement.

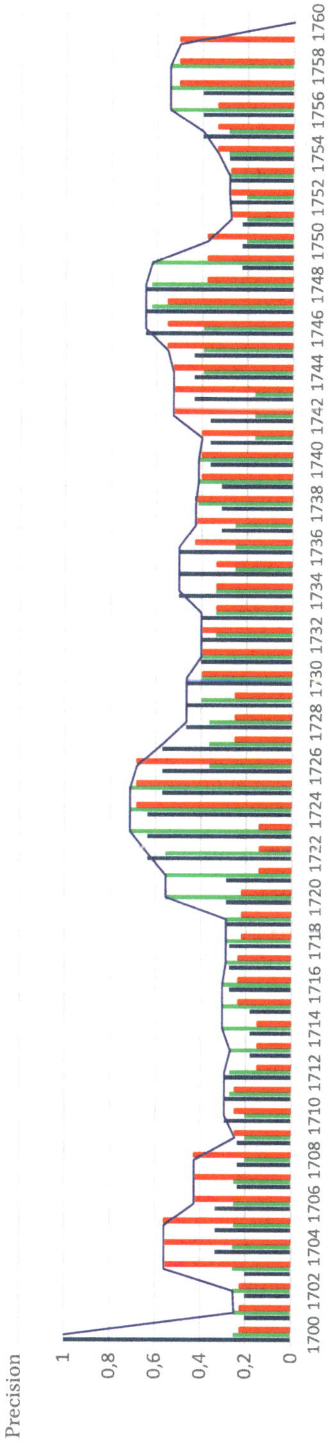

FIGURE 2.4 Per-class dating precisions of three NBM classifiers trained on texts labeled with time intervals from three different segmentations

Our STI method is aimed at exploring the room for potential improvement by ranking the prediction results of trained classifiers. We defined three STI parameters to be tuned on a held-out development corpus. Interval width **w** is the largest time span for all STI classes, which remains the same except at the beginning and end of the overall time span where smaller values might be caused due to sliding. Sliding step **s** is the number of time units skipped over at each step, and $\mathbf{s} \leq \mathbf{w}$ so that there won't be duplicated segmentations. Performance coordinator λ is used to integrate the training precision and predicting confidence, for which we adopted the log-linear interpolation. There are also two other parameters, namely, the dating tolerance δ and the sliding freedom $n = ceiling(w/s)$, which is the integer that is just larger than w/s. δ is required for practical dating and evaluating purposes to allow the predicting result of 2δ time unit deviation, i.e. a span of $[t - \delta, t + \delta]$ where t is the real writing or publishing time (Refer to Section 2.2). n determines the number of standard multi-class classifiers to be involved and avoids duplicated sliding intervals. Detailed steps for tuning w, s and λ are listed in Algorithm 2.2. This is also suitable for any given multi-class classification models.

2.4.3 *Greedy Grouping* (*GG*)

One problem with the classification approach to text dating is the class labels of regular and fixed time intervals, such as those in Figure 2.2. This leads to the disregarding of temporal characteristics which can be very irregular and non-linear (Popescu and Strapparava, 2013; 2014; 2015). To achieve some irregular temporal segmentation, we also proposed the approach of classification with greedy grouping (GG). The motivation is quite straight forward, as illustrated in Figure 2.5. There would be no potential classification errors as shown in Figure 2.3 with texts x_{1-4} if temporally adjacent texts were grouped in order according to the similarities among them.

We proposed two greedy grouping versions: the basic GG and GG_{MI} (Greedy Grouping via Mutual Information), which exploit some temporal characteristics in the training corpus by making the time segmentation irregular. They both adopt a bottom-up grouping method, which starts from the smallest granularities and gradually groups texts of bad classifying performances into their neighbor classes. For GG the grouping will be accepted if the overall classifying performance is thereby improved. For GG_{MI} the grouping will be accepted if the mutual information between two neighbor classes is higher than a trained threshold and the overall classifying performance could be thus improved. Algorithm 2.3 gives the pseudo codes for GG, and Algorithm 2.4 lists steps for that of GG_{MI}.

ALGORITHM 2.2 Dating texts by classification with sliding time intervals

---

Input: δ, a corpus of texts dated with writing/publishing time D, the beginning of the overall time span b, and the ending e;

Output: n classifiers and the optimum λ;

Steps:

1. Randomly extract D_d as developing set from D, and use $D_t = D - D_d$ as training set;
2. Label each text in D_d with time interval $T_{[t-\delta,t+\delta]}$;
3. **for** $w = 1$ to 2δ:
4.   **for** $s = 0$ to w:
5.   Label each text in D_t with $STI_{[b+s+i*w,b+s+i*w+w]}$, where $i \geq 0$ and ensures the interval cover the writing or publishing time; if $b + s + i * w + w > e$, the ending point of the STI interval is set as e;
6.   Train a multi-class classifier on the new D_t;
7.   **end for**;
8.   **for** $\lambda = (0, 0.1, 0.2, 0.3, \ldots, 0.9, 1)$:
10.   Predict for texts in D_d with trained classifiers;
11.   Rank for each text the predicting results by $\lambda \log \mathit{Precesion} + (1 - \lambda) \log \mathit{Confidence}$;
12.   Label the text with the top-one STI L;
13.   Calculate the precision by counting the text as correctly dated if $|L \cap T_{[t-\delta,t+\delta]}| > w/2$;
14.   Store the best precision, classifiers and λ till now for comparison and retrieving;
15.   **end for**;
16. **end for**;
17. Retrieve the classifiers and λ for dating new texts.

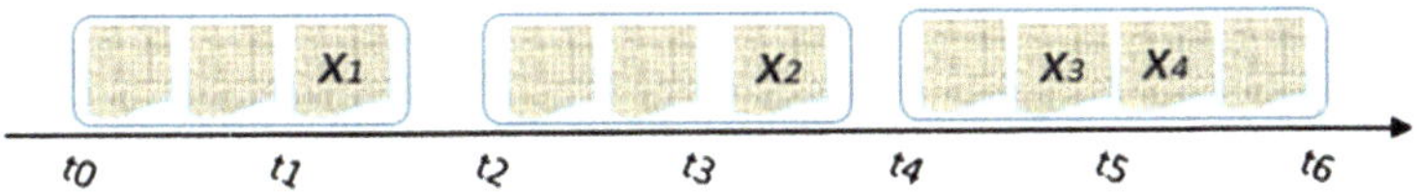

FIGURE 2.5 Greedy grouping according to the similarities among temporally adjacent texts

In Algorithm 2.4, we use K-means clustering to calculate the mutual information between two adjacent classes (Step 4 and 5). K-means clustering is a method of vector quantification originally from signal processing, that is popular for cluster analysis in data mining. It aims to partition a given number of data points into a given number of clusters in which each data point belongs to the cluster with the nearest mean, serving as a prototype of the cluster (Lloyd, 1982).

2.4.4 *Temporal Landmark Selection* (TLS)

The classification approach to text dating formats time intervals as classes equally and linearly along the time span, as illustrated in Figure 2.6(a). Fig-

ALGORITHM 2.3 Dating texts by classification with greedy grouping

---

Input: D, a corpus of texts dated with writing/publishing time T; δ, the given dating tolerance.

Output: T^*, the list of time intervals of optimal epoch segmentation; f^*, a classifier for dating new texts.

Steps:

1. Randomly extract D_d as developing set from D, and use $D_t = D - D_d$ as training set;
2. Train classifier f on D_t with 10-fold cross-validation, and ascending sort the per-class performances P;
3. **for** $i = 1$ to $2\delta + 1$, and for the texts in each class of performance P:
4. Group them into their neighbor class and set $f = f'$, if a trained new classifier f' on D_t outperforms f;
5. Evaluate f' on the task of dating D_d with i, and set $f = f'$ if the dating performance is improved;
6. **end for**;
7. Set $f^* = f'$, and T^* as the list of grouped time intervals on D_t, and use them for dating new texts.

ALGORITHM 2.4 Dating texts by classification with greedy grouping via mutual information

---

Input: D, a corpus of texts dated with writing/publishing time T; δ, the given dating tolerance.

Output: T^*, the list of time intervals of optimal epoch segmentation; f^*, a classifier for dating new texts.

Steps:

1. Randomly extract D_d as developing set from D, and use $D_t = D - D_d$ as training set;
2. Train classifier f on D_t with 10-fold cross-validation, and date texts in D_d;
3. **for** $c = 2$ to $2\delta + 1$,
4. Perform K-means clustering with c clusters on texts in D_t without considering T;
5. Calculate the mutual information MI between pairs of adjacent classes according to the clustering results, $MI(X,Y) = \sum_{x\in X}\sum_{y\in Y} p(x,y)\log\frac{p(x,y)}{p(x)p(y)}$, where X and Y are adjacent classes, x and y are cluster labels for their texts;
6. **for** $mi = 0.2$ to 1 and for $i = 1$ to $2\delta + 1$,
7. Merge X and Y if $MI(X,Y) > mi$ and the time interval width is smaller than i, i.e. $w(X) + w(Y) < i$;
8. Modify T accordingly to be T';
9. Train classifier f' on $D_{t'}$ with 10-fold cross-validation, and date texts in D_d;
10. **end for**;
11. If the dating result of f' outperforms that of f, set $f = f'$, $T = T'$ and $D_t = D_{t'}$; else stop;
12. **end for**;
13. Set $f^* = f$, and $T^* = T$ as the list of grouped time intervals on D_t, and use them for dating new texts.

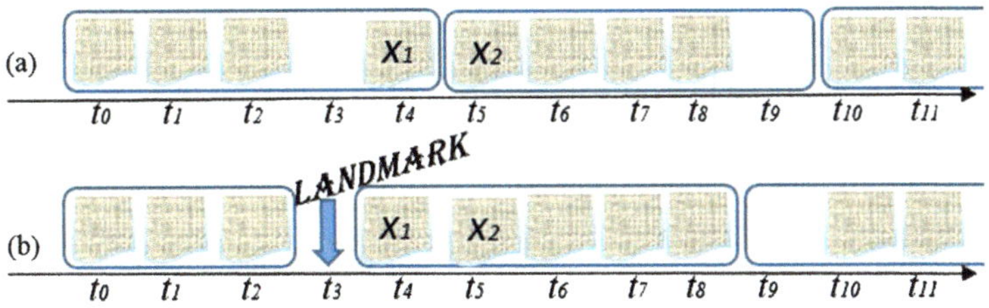

FIGURE 2.6 Reformat the time intervals by selecting a landmark

	1698	1699	1700	1701	1702	1703	1704	1705	...	2010
x_1	1	1	1	1	1	1	1	0	...	0
x_2	0	1	1	1	1	1	1	1	...	0
x_3	0	0	0	1	1	1	1	1	...	0
	...	...	...	Y ...	...	...	...	...	...	...

FIGURE 2.7 Example of binary format for timestamps with $\delta = 3$

ure 2.6 gives a segmentation example of $\delta = 2$. Again, classifiers tend to group a text into the class with more similar texts to it, so text x_1 in Figure 2.6(a) might well be wrongly predicted as class 't_{5-9}' instead of 't_{0-4}'. If t_3 could be treated as a landmark that separates t_2 and t_4, the segmentation would then consist of 't_{0-2}', 't_{3-3}' and 't_{4-8}' etc. as shown in Figure 2.6(b), and thus the advantage of the classification approach could be kept and its disadvantage of temporal independence be overcome to some degree. Therefore, we define a landmark for text dating as a special timestamp that can separate its neighbouring timestamps, and the overall text classifying accuracy will be increased if it is treated as a unique segment.

After analysing some corpus material, we found three interesting points about a landmark: a) At a landmark timestamp there can be either many fewer or more texts than at its neighbouring timestamps; b) Texts at the landmark timestamp distinguish themselves significantly from those at its neighbouring timestamps; and c) Texts at the time interval preceding a landmark are very much different from those at its following time interval. In other words, there are some more natural temporal break points in the corpus rather than simply chopping the timeline into equally sized chunks, and our method of landmark selection can make the temporal chunks match those natural breakpoints instead.

We trialled the selection of temporal landmarks in the class label matrix Y of timestamps. Timestamps in the labelled training data such as DTE can be organised in a binary format as illustrated in Figure 2.7 (see also Figure 1).

Cutting off those irrelevant timestamps beyond the DTE range of 1700-2010 produces the matrix Y of the least possible size (in the dashed rectangle). Y is of the same format as a label matrix for multi-label classification, and thus is suitable for any landmark selection algorithms. However, the true timestamp of a training text x is t', and only at t' could the composing probability of x be estimated as 1. This means that a binary matrix Y is not suitable for representing the probabilities of texts being composed during the time interval of $[t' - \delta, t' + \delta]$. Alternatively, we employed four smoothing methods to estimate the probability distribution of x's composing time and to formulate Y. They are the uniform distribution, normal distribution, trained distribution, and trained normal distribution. For timestamps beyond $[t' - \delta, t' + \delta]$, x's composing probabilities remain as 0 as in the binary format. For timestamps within $[t' - \delta, t' + \delta]$, in the uniform distribution matrix Y (UM) it is assumed that

$$y = 1/(2\delta + 1), \tag{1}$$

and in the normal distribution matrix Y (NM) it is assumed that

$$y = e^{-\frac{1}{2}|t'-t|^2}/\sqrt{2\pi}. \tag{2}$$

UM and NM are formulated in an unsupervised way, where X is not considered. For the other two methods, a classifier $\varphi(x)$, capable of predicting a complete distribution, is trained on X with binary Y and $\delta = 0$. These two methods are thus supervised. For timestamps within $[t' - \delta, t' + \delta]$, the trained distribution matrix Y (TM) assumes that

$$y = \varphi(x), \tag{3}$$

and the trained normal distribution matrix Y (TNM) assumes that

$$y = \varphi(x)e^{-\frac{1}{2}|t'-t|^2}/\sqrt{2\pi}. \tag{4}$$

We adopted Column Subset Selection (CSS) (Boutsidis et al., 2009) for temporal landmark selection. Given a matrix Y and a positive integer k, CSS seeks to find exactly k columns of Y so as to span Y as much as possible. In other words, CSS needs to select an index set C with cardinality k such that the residual $\|Y - Y_c Y_C^+ Y\|_F$ is minimised (Bi and Kwok, 2013). Here, Y_c denotes the sub-matrix consisting of the k columns in Y, and $Y_C Y_C^+$ is the projection matrix onto the k-dimensional space spanned by the columns of Y_C. Therefore, C indexes the landmarks along Y's second dimension, i.e. the columns, which are

ALGORITHM 2.5.1 Temporal landmark selection via Column Subset Selection

---

Input: Y, the class label matrix of timestamps; k, a given number for landmarks to be selected.

Output: C, the index set of temporal landmarks.

Steps:
1. Compute V_k, the top k right singular vectors of Y.
2. Compute the sampling probability p_i for each column in Y using (5).
3. $C \leftarrow \Phi$.
4. **while** $|C| < k$ **do**
5.   Select an integer from $\{1, 2, 3, \ldots, d\}$ where the probability of selecting i is equal to p_i.
6.   **if** $i \notin C$ **then**
7. $C \leftarrow C \cup \{i\}$.
8.   **end if**
9. **end while**
10. Return C as the index set of temporal landmarks.

---

thus the temporal landmarks along the temporal axis of the training corpus. The CSS method for selecting landmarks is shown in Algorithm 2.5.1.

The computational peg is Singular Value Decomposition (SVD), a popular method for identifying and ordering the features along which data points exhibit the most variation. Once the most variant features have been identified, it is possible to find the best approximation of the original data points using fewer dimensions. For a given matrix Y, SVD can be written as $Y = USV^T$, where S is a diagonal matrix containing the square roots of eigenvalues from U or V in descending order, $U^TU = I$, and $V^TV = I$. As in previous research (Drineas et al., 2006; Boutsidis et al., 2009; Bi and Kwok, 2013), we first perform partial SVD on Y and pick the top k right singular vectors $V_k \in \Re^{n \times k}$. The columns in Y are sampled with replacement, with the probability for selecting the ith column being

$$p_i = \frac{1}{k}\|(V_k^T)_{(i)}\|_2^2. \tag{5}$$

As in Bi and Kwok (2013), we continue sampling until k different columns are selected (steps 4-9). This ensures that within $O(k \log k)$ sampling trials the residual $\|Y - Y_C Y_C^+ Y\|_F$ will be minimised with a probability of at least 0.9.

After selecting appropriate temporal landmarks, text dating could be simply treated as a multi-label classification problem, and the adjacent predicted labels could be joined as an estimated time interval for a query text. In this way, a classifier $f(\cdot)$ should be first trained from $\{X, Y_C\}$, then for a new text

ALGORITHM 2.5.2 Merging timestamps into class labels

Input: C, the index set of temporal landmarks.

Output: L, the set of merged class labels.

Steps:

1. $L \leftarrow \Phi$.
2. **for** each index C_i in C
3. $\quad L \leftarrow L \cup \{t_{C_i}\}$, where t_{Ci} is the timestamp at C_i.
4. **end for**
5. **for** each pair (C_i, C_j) where $C_i < C_j$ in C
6. $\quad s \leftarrow C_i + 1$, and $e \leftarrow s + 2\delta + 1$.
7. $\quad$ **while** $e < C_j$ **do**
8. $\quad\quad L \leftarrow L \cup \{t_{[s,e]}\}$, where $t_{[s,e]}$ is the time interval at $[s, e]$.
9. $\quad$ **end while**
10. $\quad L \leftarrow L \cup \{t_{[s,C_j-1]}\}$.
11. **end for**
12. Return L as the set of merged class labels.

---

x a binary vector y' could be obtained by rounding $f(x)^T Y_c^+ Y$, and finally the time interval corresponding to the longest sequence of truth values in y' could be deemed as the composing time t for x. However, in spite of a reduced number of timestamps as labels, this multi-label classification problem is still very time consuming, because k classifiers are usually involved. Besides, the mapping $\phi(x) \rightarrow t$ also remains a non-trivial problem to be solved. To avoid the expensive computing complexity and to exploit the advantage of the UCD time intervals, we used Algorithm 2.5.2 to merge timestamps into class labels for using a single multi-class classifier. All temporal landmarks indexed by C are regarded as new class labels (steps 2-4). Timestamps between any adjacent pair of landmarks are merged into UCD time intervals and regarded as new class labels (steps 5-11). It is obvious that labels in L are temporally non-overlapping and thus suitable for classification.

The procedure for classification and prediction is given in Algorithm 2.5.3. Training texts are re-annotated with corresponding labels in L (steps 1-7). A classifier $f(\cdot)$ of any multi-class classification method could be trained on the newly labelled training texts (step 8). For dating a new text x, we first apply to it the learned classifier $f(x)$, and then return the midpoint timestamp t^* of the classified time interval as the predicted date (step 9-10).

For landmark selection on a training set, the only parameter that needs to be tuned is k, the number of temporal landmarks to be selected. This could be done via a held-out development set or cross-validation. Since the upper

ALGORITHM 2.5.3 Classification and prediction with merged class labels

---

Input: X, the training set of texts annotated with timestamps.

Output: f, a classifier trained on X labelled with the merged classes.

Steps:

1. **for** each training text x in X
2.   **if** x's annotated timestamp $t' = t_{C_i}$ $(t_{C_i} \in L)$
3.   Label x with t_{Ci}.
4.   **else if** $t_s \leq t' \leq t_e$ $(t_{[s,e]} \in L)$
5.   Label x with $t_{[s,e]}$.
6.   **end if**
7. **end for**
8. Train a classifier $f(\cdot)$ on the newly labelled X.
9. Given a new text x, $t^* \leftarrow t_{C_i}$ if $f(x) = t_{C_i}$ $(t_{C_i} \in L)$; $t^* \leftarrow t_{(s+e)/2}$ if $f(x) = t_{[s,e]}$ $(t_{[s,e]} \in L)$.
10. Return t^* as the predicted date for x.

---

bound complexity of Algorithm 2.5.1 is $O(ndk) + O(k \log k)$ (Bi and Kwok, 2013), that of Algorithm 2.5.2 is $O(d)$, that of Algorithm 2.5.3 is $O(f(\cdot))$, and $0 \leq k \leq d$, tuning k will thus cost $d(O(ndk) + O(k \log k) + O(f(\cdot)) + O(d)) = O(nd^2k) + O(dk \log k) + O(df(\cdot)) + O(d^2)$, which can be very expensive for large X and/or d. Instead of tuning k directly, we can adopt a two-stage approximation. First, we can tune $K = \mathbf{round}(100k/d)$,[2] in which $0 \leq K \leq 100$ and $k \approx Kd/100$; secondly, we can tune k within $[\mathbf{round}(Kd/100) - 5, \mathbf{round}(Kd/100) + 5]$. This method will return an approximately optimised k, and costs only $(101 + 10)(O(ndk) + O(k \log k) + O(f(\cdot)) + O(d)) = O(111ndk) + O(111k \log k) + O(111f(\cdot)) + O(111d) = O(ndk) + O(k \log k) + O(f(\cdot)) + O(d)$. When $k = 0$, there will be no temporal landmarks selected and our approach retreats to the traditional multi-class classification method. When $k = d$, all timestamps will be considered as unique landmarks, and δ will have no influence on the training process.

2.4.5 *Compound Solution of* FTI&TLS

Instead of simply segmenting the whole time period with a given dating tolerance δ, our FTI method exploits the temporal distribution on the training corpus implicitly and partially by tuning δ' to find the best segmentation of time intervals, which optimises the dating performance on a development set or in terms of 10-fold cross-validation. Our TLS method exploits the temporal distribution of the training corpus explicitly by selecting temporal landmarks,

---

2 Here **round**$(\cdot)$ is a mathematic function that returns the integer part of a float variant.

ALGORITHM 2.6 Dating texts by classification with FTI&TLS

Input: δ, the given dating tolerance; T_t, a corpus of texts labeled with timestamp matrix Y; T_d a corpus of texts labeled with timestamps as developing set; D, a hyper-parameter of the largest possible width of time intervals for a language in concern.

Output: C, the index set of temporal landmarks; δ', that determines the optimal segmentation of time intervals; L, the set of merged class labels; and f, a classifier for dating new texts.

Steps:

On T_t execute Algorithm 2.5.1 and return C, the index set of temporal landmarks.
$L \leftarrow \Phi$.
for each index C_i in C
    $L \leftarrow L \cup \{t_{C_i}\}$, where t_{Ci} is the timestamp at C_i.
end for
for $\delta' = 0$ to D
    for each pair (C_i, C_j) where $C_i < C_j$ in C
        $s \leftarrow C_i + 1$, and $e \leftarrow s + 2\delta' + 1$.
        while $e < C_j$ **do**
            $L \leftarrow L \cup \{t_{[s,e]}\}$, where $t_{[s,e]}$ is the time interval at $[s, e]$.
        end while
        $L \leftarrow L \cup \{t_{[s,C_j-1]}\}$.
    end for
    Re-label each text in T_t with a corresponding label in L.
    Train a multi-class classifier on T_t, and classify each text in T_d with the trained classifier.
    For a text predicted of class label $[x,y]$, return $x + (y - x)/2$ as the estimated date.
    A text is considered correctly dated if $t - \delta \leq x + (y - x)/2 \leq t + \delta$.
end for
Retrieve C, δ', L and f that led to most correctly dated texts in T_d for dating new texts.

---

which could be regarded as more natural break points in the temporal distribution of the training texts. For re-labelling the training texts, these selected landmarks are then used as segmenting points, while the given dating tolerance δ is still in use for segmenting any time interval between two landmarks with a size larger than $2\delta + 1$. Therefore, it is straightforward to combine FTI and TLS to further exploit the temporal distribution by replacing δ in TLS with δ' in FTI. Algorithm 2.6 lists the training process of FTI&TLS.

2.5 Datability

How practically a task of text dating can be solved depends in the first place on how regular the evolution process of a language is. The text dating task can be more feasible if the language evolution has experienced more traceable patterns. Here we introduce the term Datability $\mathcal{D}_\rho$ to quantify how feasible or practical a text dating task could be. Given a dating approach, $\mathcal{D}_\rho$ is then dependent on the time unit, language and corpus. It can be very difficult to measure $\mathcal{D}_\rho$ for a language since the evolution process of most languages tends to be extremely complicated and is compounded by stylistic choices on the part of authors as we have seen in Chapter 1. By employing the following expectation (6), we try to estimate $\mathcal{D}_\rho$ by the normalised dating accuracy of a given dating approach on a training corpus. In probability theory, the expectation or expected value of a random variable, intuitively, is the long-run average value of repetitions of the experiment it represents. For example, the expected value in rolling a six-sided die is 3.5, because the average of all the numbers that come up in an extremely large number of rolls is close to 3.5.

$$\begin{aligned} \mathcal{D}_\rho &\cong \text{Expectation}(P|C, H, \delta) \\ &\cong \text{Expectation}\left(P/(1 + e^{C-H/(2\delta+1)})\right) \\ &\cong \text{Expectation}(P)|\delta \to 0. \end{aligned} \qquad (6)$$

Here Expectation(x) returns the expected value of the variable x, H is the history period or the number of time units covered by the training corpus, δ is the required dating tolerance, P is the estimated dating accuracy, and $C - 1$ is a guess of the smallest number of natural break points in H. Normally, we can set $C = 2$, i.e. the training corpus should at least be separable at one point along the temporal distribution of the texts involved. The logistic regression of $1/2 \leq 1/(1 + e^{C-H/(2\delta+1)}) < 1$ is used to smoothly punish P when δ is getting larger. When δ gets large enough to be close to $(H - 2)/4$ and $C = 2$, $\mathcal{D}_\rho$ could be estimated as Expectation$(P)/2$. When δ gets small enough and H is large enough, $\mathcal{D}_\rho$ could be roughly estimated as Expectation(P).

2.6 Conclusion

In this chapter, we briefly reviewed the existing research of automatic text dating, including relevant techniques such as language modelling, regression, classification, and feature selection. According to existing research and our preliminary study, the dating approach of multi-class classification by far outperforms the approaches of regression or ordinal ranking. However, when text dating is modelled as classification and classification accuracy could be used directly for evaluating dating performance, the classification accuracy can be too sensitive to how the time intervals are segmented as class labels. Furthermore, the assumption of temporal independence of multi-class classification does not comply with what we understand of the evolution of lexicons and languages, and breaks the historical relation between things "before and after". On the other side, the failure of regression and ranking approaches has revealed the great difficulty in exploring the temporal distribution among training texts. We, therefore, decided to base our research on multi-class classification and exploit, as far as possible, the temporal characteristics in a training corpus. We have examined solutions of Flexible Time Intervals (FTI), Sliding Time Intervals (STI), Greedy Grouping (GG), Temporal Landmark Selection (TLS), and a compound solution of FTI&TLS. Among these solutions, FTI and STI exploit the temporal distribution implicitly by selecting one or several segmentations of time intervals as class labels, while GG and TLS exploit the distribution explicitly by determining irregular segmenting points for time intervals. In the next chapter, we will turn to the application of these methods to a range of texts from different genres in both English and Irish.

CHAPTER 3

Trials in English and Medieval Irish Texts

This chapter presents the results of testing of the methods proposed in Chapter 2 with the aim of establishing the most efficient and effective methods for dating texts. Using Weka 3.7 (Witten et al, 2011) Java Library,[1] we ran extensive experiments on multi-class classification with Flexible Time Intervals (FTI), Sliding Time Intervals (STI), Greedy Grouping (GG), Temporal Landmark Selection (TLS), and a compound of TLS&FTI. In order to compare our results with existing research, we used tolerance $\delta = 3, 6, 10$ and/or 25, as was required in DTE task and adopted by the UCD system (Szymanski and Lynch, 2015).

In order to test the methods across linguistic and historical boundaries, we used several corpora of modern English and medieval Irish texts. The English corpora include the historical newspaper items used in DTE Subtask 2 and a group of public posts collected from the Freecycle Network UK.[2] For medieval Irish, we employed three sets of annals – narrative accounts that purport to record contemporary events annually from the fifth century until the sixteenth century.[3] Both the DTE texts and the Irish annals present untagged language in non-standard orthography, allowing us to investigate the applicability of the methods to raw texts. The Irish texts are particularly interesting because the language is highly inflected and the orthography is widely heterogeneous, so that they provide a challenging testbed for the methods. A complex transmission of the Gaelic material also increases the complexity of the texts which makes them interesting for testing.

3.1 Dating English Texts

For both manual and automatic text dating, English was certainly the language focused on in most existing research. We, therefore, first tested our solutions with English texts and compared the results with previous dating approaches.

1 http://www.cs.waikato.ac.nz/ml/weka/downloading.html
2 https://www.freecycle.org/browse/UK
3 http://www.ucc.ie/celt/published/

 DOI:10.1163/9789004410046_005

TABLE 3.1 English corpora and relevant information

Corpus		Temporal range	Number of texts	Average length	Character n-grams (types)	Word n-grams (types)
DTE2	train	1700-2010	4,116	69.7 words	2500 for SVM	500 for SVM
	test	1700-2010	1,036	65.5 words	4500 for NBM	1000 for NBM
Freecycle	train	1/10/2014-25/7/2015	2,127	20.5 words	2500 for NBM	1500 for NBM
	test	1/10/2014-22/7/2015	300	22.2 words	2500 for NBM	1500 for NBM

3.1.1 *Data and Features*

Our two English corpora with some relevant information are listed in Table 3.1. The DTE2 corpus is adopted from DTE Subtask 2. The DTE resource was obtained by the task organisers from large newspaper archives such as NPA,[4] SPR,[5] and BDY[6] (Popescu and Strapparava, 2015). It consists of 6,477 news snippets, of which 5,436 make up the training data and 1,041 the test data. However, after removing errors (repeated items, items containing no text, items with invalid dates) we only got 4,116 texts for the training set and 1,036 texts for testing. The DTE2 corpus covers a period of 310 years between 1700 and 2010. We also harvested Freecycle texts from the Freecycle Network UK. These are public posts made by people who are giving or getting goods for free within their own towns in the UK. The contents of these texts can be seasonal because people may want or offer different items at different times of the year. The covered temporal range for this corpus is altogether 180 days.

For feature selection in our present research, we simply chose the most effective and informative text dating features (Szymanski and Lynch, 2015) of character and word n-grams, with $n = 1, 2,$ and 3. These features are readily available in any language, while other features such as part of speech tags and syntactic rules need pre-processors that themselves might well be sensitive to temporal language changes. To make the comparison between different methods straightforward and easy, we determined the set of feature types by optimising the classifying efficiency of the Support Vector Machine (SVM) or Naïve Bayes Multinomial (NBM) classifier with $\delta = 3$, which corresponds to

4 http://newspaper.archive.com
5 http://archive.spectator.co.uk
6 http://www.bodley.ox.ac.uk/ilej/

our baseline of the fixed time intervals of a UCD system based on SVM or NBM for the fine granularity of DTE tasks. The last two columns of Table 3.1 list the numbers of types we empirically set for each corpus. The same feature set was then used for all relevant classifiers trained on them.

3.1.2 *Choosing Basic Classifiers*

Since our solutions are all intended to explore the temporal distribution by setting better time intervals for class labels, the hyper parameters for time segmentation need to be tuned by optimising the dating performance of a basic classification model. Therefore, an efficient classification model will determine the final computational cost. Using the DTE2 training corpus with $\delta = 3$, we checked the efficiency of several models for text classification on a Dell laptop with 2.3GHz CPU and 8GB RAM. For the top four most efficient models, Table 3.2 compares the computing time in seconds, and Figure 3.1 compares the classifying accuracies.

The features include character and word n-grams ($n = 1, 2,$ and 3), and in each feature set there are one half of character n-grams and one half of word n-grams. The SMO model is the Weka implementation of the Sequential Minimal Optimization algorithm (Platt, 1998) for training an SVM classifier. The J48 model is the Weka version of C4.5 for decision trees (Ross Quinlan, 1993). NB and NBM are respectively Weka's Naïve Bayes and multinomial Naïve Bayes classifiers (Witten et al, 2011). All algorithmic parameters of each model were kept as default. Results in Table 3.2 and Figure 3.1 show clearly that NBM is by far the most efficient and most accurate classification model for our task.

TABLE 3.2 Computing time (in seconds) comparison of different classification models on DTE2

Features	SMO	J48	NB	NBM
100	182	38	9	1
200	306	96	17	1
300	376	187	25	1
400	425	272	35	1
500	479	390	45	1
600	497	583	54	1
700	556	697	56	1
800	632	876	74	1
900	658	1035	95	2
1000	687	1278	95	2

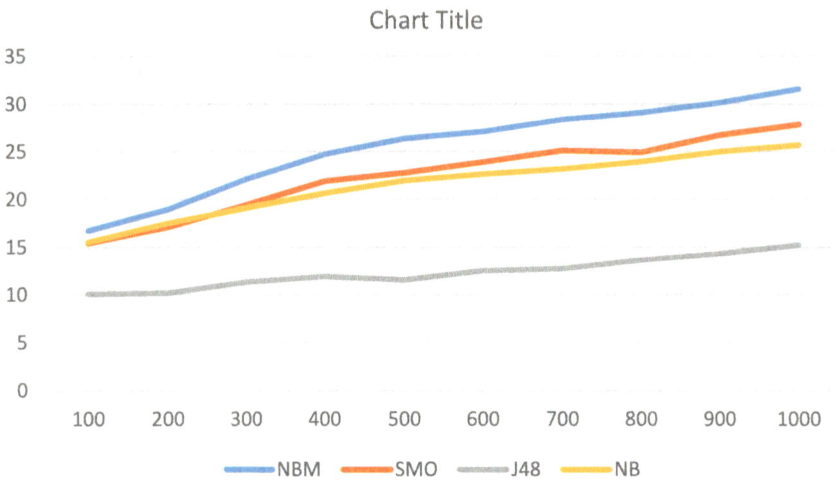

FIGURE 3.1 Classifying accuracy comparison of different classification models on DTE2

TABLE 3.3 FTI tuning results of ẟ′ values on the training set of DTE2

Fine (ẟ = 3)		Medium (ẟ = 6)		Coarse (ẟ = 10)	
ẟ′	Accuracy %	ẟ′	Accuracy %	ẟ′	Accuracy %
		Part of sorted tuning results for NBM			
1	46.93*	3	47.65*	5	51.65*
2	45.74	1	46.98	2	50.62
4	45.35	2	45.78	6	49.58
3	44.96	5	45.30	1	48.63
		Final tuned results for SVM			
2	46.66*	4	47.32*	4	50.76*

3.1.3 *Experiments and Results*

We tested our FTI and STI solutions with SVM and NBM on texts in the corpus of DTE2, our GG, GG_{MI}, TLS and TLS&FTI solutions with NBM on DTE2, and all the solutions with NBM on the corpus of Freecycle.

3.1.3.1 FTI and STI with SVM and NBM on DTE2

Table 3.3 lists the 10-fold cross-validation tuning results of ẟ′ for FTI on the training set of DTE2. Parts of the sorted results for NBM are listed in the upper part of the table, while the tuned values of ẟ′ for SVM are given at the lower part. To make predictions for a text in the test set, we assigned it whichever given year range of the DTE format that has the greatest overlap with our dated flexible time interval. Evaluation performances are measured by dating accu-

TABLE 3.4 Dating accuracies (%) of FTI and UCD SVM on the test set of DTE2

	Fine	Medium	Coarse
FTI SVM	46.62	47.43	54.28
FTI NBM	46.71*	48.76*	55.44*
UCD SVM	46.30	47.20	54.20

TABLE 3.5 Tuning results of STI parameters on the training set of DTE2

Fine (δ = 3)				Medium (δ = 6)				Coarse (δ = 10)			
w	***s***	**λ**	Precision	***w***	***s***	**λ**	Precision	***w***	***s***	**λ**	Precision
Part of sorted tuning results for NBM with STI											
3	1	0.1	42.81*	7	3	0.4	47.33*	9	5	0.8	49.88*
3	2	0.6	42.57	7	3	0.9	45.17	3	2	0.1	49.64
3	2	0.7	42.47	11	8	0.9	44.69	2	1	0.5	49.62
6	4	0	42.18	11	8	0.8	39.29	9	5	0.9	49.60
3	2	0.8	41.99	9	8	0	39.00	3	2	0.2	49.39
4	3	0.9	41.99	8	5	0.9	38.32	2	1	0.6	48.66
Final tuned results for SVM with STI											
3	2	0.2	37.50*	7	4	0.2	41.22*	8	4	0.4	47.56*

racy (see Section 2.2.2 and Section 2.4.1 Algorithm 2.1: Steps 6 and 7), which is the ratio of how many times the method found exactly the DTE defined time intervals. Evaluation results on the test set of DTE2 and those of the state-of-the-art UCD system are listed in Table 3.4. It shows that both our SVM and NBM with tuned flexible time intervals significantly outperformed the state-of-the-art with t-test p-value of 0.048 and 0.045.

Table 3.5 lists the 10-fold cross-validation tuning results of STI parameters on the training set of DTE2. Parts of the sorted results for NBM are listed in the upper part of the table, while the optimal values for SVM are given in the lower part. On the whole training corpus, we then trained the basic SVM and NBM classifiers also by 10-fold cross-validation. The number of basic STI classifiers for each time granularity is the upper bound integer of w/s. Dating accuracies of basic classifiers involved are listed in Table 3.6. Prediction and evaluation are implemented in the same way as for FTI. Evaluation results on the test set of DTE2 and those of the state-of-the-art UCD system are listed in Table 3.7. It shows that our STI NBM significantly outperformed UCD with one-tailed t-test p-value of 0.048, while

TABLE 3.6 Dating accuracies (%) of basic STI classifiers on the training set of DTE2

Basic STI classifiers		f_1	f_2	f_3
NBM	Fine (δ = 3)	34.94	34.94	35.93
	Medium (δ = 6)	39.65	39.77	40.74
	Coarse (δ = 10)	40.55	42.10	
SVM	Fine (δ = 3)	30.66	33.05	
	Medium (δ = 6)	34.95	37.20	
	Coarse (δ = 10)	36.44	39.34	

TABLE 3.7 Dating accuracies (%) of STI and UCD SVM on the test set of DTE2

	Fine (δ = 3)	Medium (δ = 6)	Coarse (δ = 10)
STI SVM	42.81	46.97	55.17
STI NBM	47.01*	49.90*	55.92*
UCD SVM	46.30	47.20	54.20

our STI SVM performed comparably to UCD with two-tailed t-test p-value of 0.563.

The UCD system employed four SVM classifiers with fixed time intervals of 6, 12, 20 and 50 years, involving many more feature types of character n-grams, word n-grams, POS-tags, syntactic rules, and Google syntactic database (Szymanski et al., 2015). From Table 3.4 and 3.7, we can see that our methods of FTI and STI performed much better though with only feature types of character and word n-grams. Furthermore, NBM was proved to be more efficient than SVM, so in the following experiments for both English and medieval Irish corpora we only employed NBM for classification.

3.1.3.2 GG, GGMI, TLS and TLS&FTI with NBM on DTE2

We tested both GG and GG_{MI} with NBM multi-class classification on DTE2. For the developing set, we randomly extracted 440 texts from the training corpus. The remaining 3,690 texts served as the training set. Our output T^* for GG consists of time intervals with irregular granularities of 1 to 3 years, while that for GG_{MI} varies along the dating tolerance δ, as shown with parameter i in Table 3.8 as well as the dating performances on the DTE2 test set for both GG and GG_{MI}. Compared to the state-of-the-art dating performance of UCD (46.3%, 47.2%, 54.2% respectively for δ = 3, 6 and 10 years) on the DTE2 test set, both greedy grouping methods have achieved better test-

TABLE 3.8 GG and GGMI training results and dating performances (%) on DTE2

δ	*GG parameters*	GG_{MI} parameters	GG training	GG_{MI} training	GG test	GG_{MI} test
3-year	$i = 3$	$c = 4, mi = 0.6, i = 3$	37.43	38.57	46.51	46.72
6-year	$i = 3$	$c = 5, mi = 0.5, i = 5$	40.8	45.56	47.23	47.28
10-year	$i = 5$	$c = 5, mi = 0.5, i = 6$	44.89	48.14	54.33	54.27

ing results, but the improvement was much less significant than that of FTI or STI.

The TLS experiment with NBM included tuning the landmark parameter k and training a corresponding classification model using 10-fold cross-validation to tune the TLS parameters. The first part of Table 3.9 lists the results of landmark selection by TLS with four different timestamp matrices of uniform distribution matrix (UM), normal distribution (NM), trained distribution (TM) and trained normal distribution (TNM). We give here the percentages K and numbers k of temporal landmarks, where k is tuned within $[\mathbf{round}(Kd/100) - 5, \mathbf{round}(Kd/100) + 5]$ (see Section 2.4.4). The second part of Table 3.9 gives the estimated dating performances of TLS and a UCD system with NBM for classification, including average dating accuracies and corresponding standard deviations. These were estimated via 10-fold cross-validation on the training set. The best and comparable results (according to the pairwise t-test with 95% confidence) are highlighted in bold. It shows that our TLS approach as a whole significantly outperformed the corresponding UCD method with NBM. We also evaluated all the trained TLS dating systems on the DTE2 test set. The last part of Table 3.9 gives the comparison of dating accuracies by different systems. It shows that as δ gets larger, the TLS approach dates the test texts in a much steadier way than the UCD method. Furthermore, the TNM dating system significantly outperformed the best state-of-the-art results of 46.3%, 47.2% and 54.2% given by the UCD system with SVM and many more classification feature types (Popescu and Strapparava, 2015).

Table 3.10 gives the TLS&FTI training results of 10-fold cross-validation and dating performance on the test set of DTE2. The first part of the table lists the results of landmark selection by TLS&FTI with four different timestamp matrices, which actually duplicates the landmark selection results of the TLS method since we selected the landmarks at first and then tuned the FTI parameter δ′. The second and third parts of Table 3.10 list respectively the estimated and testing dating performances of TLS&FTI and a UCD system with NBM for classification. Compared to TLS, TLS&FTI produced more stable improvement

TABLE 3.9 TLS training results of 10-fold cross-validation and dating performance (%) on the test set of DTE2

1. Percentage *K* and number *k* of temporal landmarks selected

δ	UCD_{NBM}		UM		NM		TM		TNM	
	***K*%**	***k***	***K*%**	***k***	***K*%**	***k***	***K*%**	***k***	***K*%**	***k***
3-year	N/A	N/A	0%	0	0%	0	1%	3	1%	3
6-year	N/A	N/A	1%	3	3%	9	1%	3	2%	6
10-year	N/A	N/A	1%	3	3%	9	0%	0	1%	3

2. Training performance estimated by 10-fold cross-validation

δ	UCD_{NBM}	UM	NM	TM	TNM
3-year	$43.03_{\pm 2.7}$	$44._{\pm 2.7}$	$43.03_{\pm 2.7}$	$45.45_{\pm 2.8}$	$\mathbf{44.55}_{\pm 2.8}$
6-year	$46.72_{\pm 2.5}$	$\mathbf{48.79}_{\pm 1.9}$	$\mathbf{49.25}_{\pm 2.9}$	$47.76_{\pm 1.9}$	$46.65_{\pm 1.8}$
10-year	$55.18_{\pm 3.0}$	$\mathbf{55.27}_{\pm 2.8}$	$55.18_{\pm 3.0}$	$55.18_{\pm 3.0}$	$\mathbf{55.57}_{\pm 2.8}$

3. Dating performance on the test set

δ	UCD_{NBM}	UM	NM	TM	TNM
3-year	44.69	45.75	45.75	45.87	**46.61**
6-year	45.56	49.42	**49.61**	48.34	48.73
10-year	52.51	53.38	53.65	53.65	**54.82**

over the UCD method with fixed time intervals for all the four different timestamp matrices, and standard deviations of the estimated performances are generally smaller.

3.1.3.3 All Solutions with NBM on Freecycle

Table 3.11 gives the training results of 10-fold cross-validation on Freecycle for all our solutions with NBM and the UCD_{NBM} method of fixed time intervals, and Table 3.12 lists the corresponding dating accuracies by evaluation on the test set. Both the estimated and evaluation dating accuracies of our solutions unanimously outperformed the UCD_{NBM} method significantly. GG, GG_{MI}, TLS&FTI with UM and NM labeling matrices achieved the top performance. Besides, the tuned values for parameters of FTI (δ'), STI (w, s, λ), GG (i) and

TABLE 3.10 TLS&FTI training results of 10-fold cross-validation and dating performance (%) on the test set of DTE2

1. Percentage K and number k of temporal landmarks selected

δ	δ'	UCD$_{NBM}$		UM		NM		TM		TNM	
		K%	***k***	***K%***	***k***	***K%***	***k***	***K%***	***k***	***K%***	***k***
3-year	1	N/A	N/A	0%	0	0%	0	1%	3	1%	3
6-year	3	N/A	N/A	1%	3	3%	9	1%	3	2%	6
10-year	5	N/A	N/A	1%	3	3%	9	0%	0	1%	3

2. Training performance estimated by 10-fold cross-validation

δ	δ'	UCD$_{NBM}$	UM	NM	TM	TNM
3-year	1	$43.03_{\pm2.7}$	$46.95_{\pm1.4}$	$47.01_{\pm2.3}$	**47.51**$_{\pm2.9}$	**47.56**$_{\pm2.4}$
6-year	3	$47.78_{\pm1.5}$	**48.89**$_{\pm1.6}$	**49.58**$_{\pm2.2}$	$47.79_{\pm1.3}$	$48.66_{\pm1.7}$
10-year	5	$55.18_{\pm3.0}$	**56.62**$_{\pm2.1}$	$56.18_{\pm2.0}$	$56.18_{\pm2.0}$	**56.54**$_{\pm2.1}$

3. Dating performance on the test set

δ	δ'	UCD$_{NBM}$	UM	NM	TM	TNM
3-year	1	44.69	46.35	46.35	**46.86**	**46.86**
6-year	3	45.56	49.44	**49.61**	49.54	**49.73**
10-year	5	52.51	**55.75**	55.44	55.44	**55.93**

$GG_{MI}(k, i)$ are generally smaller than those tuning results of corresponding solutions on DTE2; and the numbers of landmarks selected for TLS and TLS&FTI are much larger than those numbers selected for DTE2. This means that there are more changes in Freecycle than in DTE2 during the period that the corpus covers.

3.2 Dating Medieval Irish Texts

For medieval Ireland, we have an extensive and continuous set of annals that contain supposedly contemporary notices of the deaths of important individuals, battles, plagues, extreme weather events and unusual celestial

TABLE 3.11 Training results of 10-fold cross-validation for all solutions on Freecycle

		δ = 3 days		δ = 6 days		δ = 10 days	
		Accuracy (%)	Parameters	Accuracy (%)	Parameters	Accuracy (%)	Parameters
UCD_{NBM}		$20.17_{\pm 3.0}$	N/A	$26.18_{\pm 3.4}$	N/A	$34.80_{\pm 2.5}$	N/A
FTI		$22.85_{\pm 1.2}$	$\delta' = 1$	$31.93_{\pm 2.0}$	$\delta' = 2$	$38.32_{\pm 1.6}$	$\delta' = 4$
STI		$23.36_{\pm 1.4}$	$w = 3, s = 1, \lambda = 0.2$	$32.25_{\pm 1.6}$	$w = 4, s = 2, \lambda = 0.3$	$39.34_{\pm 1.6}$	$w = 6, s = 3, \lambda = 0.3$
GG		**$23.61_{\pm 1.6}$**	$i = 3$	**$33.32_{\pm 1.4}$**	$i = 3$	**$39.68_{\pm 1.4}$**	$i = 4$
GG_{MI}		**$23.86_{\pm 1.6}$**	$c = 3, mi = 0.5, i = 3$	**$33.50_{\pm 1.8}$**	$c = 4, mi = 0.6, i = 5$	**$40.44_{\pm 1.8}$**	$c = 4, mi = 0.6, i = 5$
TLS	UM	$21.47_{\pm 1.5}$	$K = 30\%, k = 54$	$29.94_{\pm 2.3}$	$K = 30\%, k = 54$	$38.87_{\pm 2.4}$	$K = 35\%, k = 63$
TLS	NM	$21.53_{\pm 1.6}$	$K = 20\%, k = 36$	$29.99_{\pm 2.4}$	$K = 20\%, k = 36$	$38.92_{\pm 2.5}$	$K = 30\%, k = 54$
TLS	TM	$21.06_{\pm 1.6}$	$K = 20\%, k = 36$	$28.39_{\pm 2.3}$	$K = 30\%, k = 54$	$38.79_{\pm 2.4}$	$K = 35\%, k = 63$
TLS	TNM	$20.27_{\pm 1.5}$	$K = 20\%, k = 36$	$29.49_{\pm 2.2}$	$K = 20\%, k = 36$	$38.57_{\pm 1.9}$	$K = 30\%, k = 54$
TLS&FTI	UM	**$23.55_{\pm 1.6}$**	$K = 30\%, k = 54, \delta' = 2$	**$33.48_{\pm 1.8}$**	$K = 30\%, k = 54, \delta' = 2$	**$39.98_{\pm 1.4}$**	$K = 35\%, k = 63, \delta' = 4$
TLS&FTI	NM	**$23.63_{\pm 1.4}$**	$K = 20\%, k = 36, \delta' = 2$	**$33.59_{\pm 2.1}$**	$K = 20\%, k = 36, \delta' = 3$	**$40.52_{\pm 2.1}$**	$K = 30\%, k = 54, \delta' = 5$
TLS&FTI	TM	$23.12_{\pm 1.4}$	$K = 20\%, k = 36, \delta' = 2$	$31.13_{\pm 2.2}$	$K = 30\%, k = 54, \delta' = 2$	**$39.76_{\pm 1.4}$**	$K = 35\%, k = 63, \delta' = 4$
TLS&FTI	TNM	$23.18_{\pm 1.4}$	$K = 20\%, k = 36, \delta' = 2$	$32.35_{\pm 2.4}$	$K = 20\%, k = 36, \delta' = 4$	**$39.87_{\pm 1.3}$**	$K = 30\%, k = 54, \delta' = 4$

phenomena such as eclipses and comets. These annual notices are arranged chronologically and have been supplied with Anno Domini (AD) dates, and as such are ideal for testing the applicability of our methods to pre-Modern language.

The data is complicated by the fact that no copies have survived in contemporary manuscripts from the early medieval period. Later annalists not only maintained records of events in their own time but also revised existing entries, expanding on them by adding new information, or retrospectively adding entirely bogus new entries. Therefore, in addition to the fundamental issue of dating, the method, if it is to be successful, needs to distinguish between those annals that are written in contemporary language and those that have been contaminated or inserted by later copyists.

TABLE 3.12 Dating accuracy (%) for all solutions on freecycle test set

		δ = 3 days	**δ = 6 days**	**δ = 10 days**
UCD$_{NBM}$		19.25	28.64	31.92
FTI		22.85	31.93	38.32
STI		23.36	32.25	39.34
GG		**24.26**	**31.25**	**42.37**
GG$_{MI}$		**24.33**	**31.58**	**41.94**
TLS	UM	23.47	28.64	40.38
TLS	NM	23.94	29.11	40.38
TLS	TM	22.56	28.62	38.74
TLS	TNM	23.96	29.11	39.29
TLS&FTI	UM	23.95	**31.08**	**42.66**
TLS&FTI	NM	**24.36**	**31.25**	**42.56**
TLS&FTI	TM	22.76	30.76	**42.54**
TLS&FTI	TNM	23.61	30.50	**42.57**

3.2.1 *The Corpus: the Irish Annals*

It is widely agreed that Irish annals were maintained contemporaneously from as early as the mid-sixth century (Dumville 1982: 322; Charles-Edwards 2006: 8). Charles-Edwards (2006: 57-8) argues that some retrospective entries were added at this time, but going back no further than c.500 CE, and that material for the fifth century was added later, possibly in the mid-eighth century.[7] This early set of annals was compiled on the Scottish island of Iona in the monastery of St Columcille, which was part of the greater Gaelic-speaking area, and moved c.740 CE to the Irish midlands (Charles-Edwards 2006: 13-14). Known as the Chronicle of Ireland, no single text survives but copies of it as far as the year 911 are embedded in the extant major collections of annals (Grabowski & Dumville 1984: 93; Evans 2010: 2-3; 225; cf. McCarthy 2008). The two main branches of the annals, exemplified by the Annals of Ulster and the Clonmacnoise group, are relatively independent thereafter but a smaller number of shared entries between 912 and 1100 suggest a continued relationship at a later stage (Evans 2010: 91-114). We have used three sets of annals in our experiments: the Annals of Inisfallen, the Annals of Ulster and the Annals of Loch Cé.

7 McCarthy provides a radically different view of the history of the annals. His views remain controversial and are not further considered here. Good summaries are available in Charles-Edwards 2009-10 and Evans 2010: 3-6).

3.2.1.1 Annals of Inisfallen

The Annals of Inisfallen is found in the manuscript Rawlinson B.503 which is held in the Bodleian Library, Oxford, and is the earliest manuscript copy of any Irish annals. Approximately half of the manuscript, down to the middle of the year 1092, is the product of a single scribe, after which the work was continued by a series of thirty-eight or thirty-nine annalists whose entries are more or less contemporary with the time of writing (Mac Airt 1951: xiii, xxviii). Of these, Mac Airt (1951: xxx-xxxi) believes that 1092-1214 and 1258-85 are contemporary or near contemporary. The scribe identified as Hand 30 is responsible for a large group of annals covering the years 1216-52, 1299, and 1301-1311, and there is some evidence to suggest that he worked in or shortly after 1311.

The loss of leaves from the manuscript has resulted in some gaps in the surviving record, notably for the (partial) years 1130-1159, 1181-89 and 1286-1294 (Mac Airt 1951: xxviii), and not all years have entries. From the middle of 1311 until 1319 the entries are written in Latin, and so are not relevant here, and after this date there is only a small number of sporadic entries written chiefly in Irish which are not used in this study. The period of chief concern to us, therefore, is 1092-1311. Although Hand 30's entries for the first half of the twelfth century are hardly exactly contemporary, they are included here as having been copied within a century of their date of composition. It should be noted that a great deal of the relevant material is written in Anglo-Norman or Anglo-Irish scripts rather than Irish script, and that the orthography is often unusual (e.g. *Gallybh* for *Gallaibh* and *oyth* for *uadh* s.a. 1271).

3.2.1.2 Annals of Ulster

The Annals of Ulster is central to this project as it covers the greatest historical span of all the usable annals and is widely regarded as the most reliable of the Irish annals for the early medieval period. Charles-Edwards (2006: 19-20) concludes that most of the entries in the Annals of Ulster up until 911 were in the Chronicle of Ireland, while the other major sets of annals suffered greater levels of intrusion. Ó Máille (1910: 6) observes that the language of consecutive entries becomes contemporary only in the last few years of the seventh century, while there is some evidence of contemporary language as early as the sixth century. More recent research has called some of Ó Máille's assertions into doubt but tends to confirm the early date of some sixth-century forms (Stifter 2013). For the later medieval period, it is likely that the vast majority of records are contemporary or near contemporary (Simms 2009: 22).

However, the Annals of Ulster are preserved only in much later copies of the fifteenth and sixteenth centuries, so that they are prone to some degree of linguistic modernisation. The oldest copy is that in Trinity College Dublin

H.1.18 (catalogue no. 1282) which was written by Ruaidhrí Ó Luinín (d.1528) as far as the year 1489 (Mac Airt & Mac Niocaill 1983, ix),[8] and continued by two other scribes down to 1504. The basic text of this copy has received numerous interpolations and glosses by four scribes identified as H1, H2, H3, and H4 (see Mac Airt & Mac Niocaill 1983, viii), as well as several other late scribes. They used various sources, probably including a representative of the Clonmacnoise group (Evans 2010: 8). Another copy of the Annals of Ulster is found in Rawlinson B. 489 in the Bodleian Library, Oxford, which also contains a number of additional entries extending its range down to 1588 (Mac Airt & Mac Niocaill 1983, ix). It was generally accepted that Rawl. B. 489 is a copy of H.1.8 but C. Breatnach (2015) has recently argued that both manuscripts are copies of another now lost exemplar. Neither manuscript is complete but gaps in one can be made good, to some extent, by reference to the other. A notable lacuna occurs in the Trinity manuscript for 1115 (part) to 1162 (part), only part of which can be made good by the Rawlinson manuscript, leaving a gap in the record for the critical period 1131 (part) to 1155 (part).

We are reliant for this present study on two separate editions of the Annals of Ulster: the nineteenth-century edition by Hennessy & Mac Carthy (1887-1901), which covers the entire span of the Annals, and the incomplete edition by Mac Airt & Mac Niocaill (1983) which covers the period only as far the lacuna in 1131. Hennessy & Mac Carthy do not consistently distinguish between the different hands, with the result that the interpolations cannot be identified in all cases. However, Mac Airt & Mac Niocaill print the interpolations in a different font and indicate the hand. For this analysis, we draw on both editions as digitised by the CELT project. The electronic edition is based on Mac Airt & Mac Niocaill as far as 1131 and on Mac Carthy's edition in volumes 2 and 3 of the nineteenth-century publication.

3.2.1.3 Annals of Loch Cé

The Annals of Loch Cé is extant in two late sixteenth-century manuscripts, Trinity College Dublin H.1.19 (1293) and British Library Add. 4792. They cover events, mainly in Connacht and its neighbouring regions, from 1014 to 1590, but like both the Annals of Ulster and of Inisfallen, there is a lacuna in the middle years of the twelfth century (1139-1169). There is another large gap from 1315 to 1378 which Hennessy (1871), in the standard edition, fills with material from the Annals of Connacht, and this in included in CELT's digital edition used here.

8 McCarthy 2008: 317-8 argues that H1 and H2 used the same source as the main scribe and that their work should be treated as a single piece.

From its beginning in 1014 down to 1223, the Annals of Loch Cé shares a common core with the Annals of Ulster and throughout the eleventh century contains very little unique material apart from its expanded account of the battle of Clontarf in 1014 (Evans 2010: 10). From 1180, it starts to draw on a separate source (Mac Niocaill 1959: 18) and is, for the most part, independent of Ulster during this period. It does not draw directly on the extant versions of the Annals of Ulster, and we can regard the Annals of Loch Cé from its commencement until c.1180 as an independent copy of the same text as the Annals of Ulster (see C. Breatnach 2015: 227-8). From 1224 until 1590, the Annals of Loch Cé are independent of the other Annals. As the record in the Annals of Ulster becomes scarce after c.1225 until the late fourteenth century (Ó Corráin 2017: 932), Loch Cé can be used to supplement the record for that period.

3.3 Implementation

To save computing time and involve more features for further statistical analysis, our experiments of dating medieval Irish texts only employed NBM classifiers, which in fact proved better than SVM in our experiments on DTE2 (See Section 3.1.2). Since the medieval Irish texts treated here are composed much earlier than the English corpus, we adopted four labelling granularities of $\delta = 3, 6, 10$ and 25 years in order to reveal more temporal characteristics.

3.3.1 *Data Pre-Processing and Features for Classification*

Our medieval Irish annals were harvested from the CELT website which contains digital copies of the most authoritative scholarly editions.[9] As the Annals of Inisfallen exist in their contemporary form and are therefore potentially the most accurate record of the language of the time, we began testing with annals written around the 11th to 14th century. As the aim ultimately is to build a model of a specific language, during pre-processing we removed any Latin words or sentences. We also removed Roman numbers that may have encoded the date, and subsequently we eliminated any annals of less than five words. Table 3.13 lists some important statistics for our three medieval Irish documents and a corpus of their combination after the pre-processing.

For dating the Irish texts, we only used character n-grams ($n = 1, 2$ and 3) as classification features because: a) character n-grams was proved to be the most effective and informative text dating feature (Szymanski and Lynch, 2015);

9 http://www.ucc.ie/celt/published/

TABLE 3.13 Our medieval Irish corpora

Corpus	Temporal range	Training set	Test set	Average length
Inisfallen	1092-1309	760	106	22.4 words
Ulster	1092-1378	2,020	250	20.1 words
Loch Cé	1014-1348	2,000	490	28.2 words
Combination	1014-1378	4,780	846	23.6 words

TABLE 3.14 Numbers of feature types for our text dating experiments on medieval Irish corpora

	Inisfallen	Ulster	Loch Cé	Combination
Character n-grams	3500	4500	4500	4500

b) our preliminary study showed that the addition of other features, such as words, had little impact on multi-class text classification for medieval Irish,[10] and c) there is no extensive parsed corpus of texts for medieval Irish. As with our feature selection for dating English texts, we determined the set of feature types by optimising the classifying efficiency of the NBM classifier with $\delta = 3$, which corresponds to the UCD system based on NBM for the fine granularity of DTE tasks. Table 3.14 lists the numbers of types we empirically set for each corpus. The same feature set was then used for all relevant NBM classifiers trained on them.

3.3.2 *Experiments and Results*

We tested the UCD_{NBM} dating method of NBM classification with fixed time intervals, and our solutions of FTI, STI, GG, GG_{MI}, TLS and TLS&FTI with NBM on the four corpora listed in Table 3.13. To compare the performances of different dating methods, we report the training and testing results for each corpus separately. Tables 3.15, 3.17, 3.19 and 3.21 give the respective training results of 10-fold cross-validation on each corpus for our solutions and UCD_{NBM}, and Tables 3.16, 3.18, 3.20 and 3.22 list respectively the dating accuracies by evaluation

10 The major reason is that the spellings of many medieval Irish words vary along the history and among different scribes. This also leads to the fact that character n-grams actually play a more important role for dating medieval Irish than for dating English texts.

TABLE 3.15 Training results of 10-fold cross-validation for all solutions on Inisfallen

	δ = 3 years		δ = 6 years		δ = 10 years		δ = 25 years	
	Accuracy (%)	Parameters	Accuracy (%)	Parameters	Accuracy (%)	Parameters	Accuracy (%)	Parameters
UCD_{NBM}	$32.24_{\pm3.2}$	N/A	$46.84_{\pm3.6}$	N/A	$53.29_{\pm3.5}$	N/A	$66.97_{\pm3.2}$	N/A
FTI	$36.62_{\pm2.9}$	$\delta' = 4$	$48.31_{\pm2.6}$	$\delta' = 7$	$58.56_{\pm2.6}$	$\delta' = 8$	$69.47_{\pm2.6}$	$\delta' = 12$
STI	**38.16**$_{\pm3.2}$	$w = 9$, $s = 1$, $\lambda = 0.4$	**52.10**$_{\pm3.6}$	$w = 17$, $s = 5$, $\lambda = 0.4$	**62.63**$_{\pm2.9}$	$w = 16$, $s = 1$, $\lambda = 0.7$	**74.74**$_{\pm3.4}$	$w = 22$, $s = 11$, $\lambda = 0.0$
GG	$32.60_{\pm3.6}$	$i = 6$	$43.52_{\pm2.8}$	$i = 6$	$49.88_{\pm1.2}$	$i = 6$	$64.71_{\pm2.6}$	$i = 11$
GG_{MI}	$32.86_{\pm4.5}$	$c = 4$, $mi = 0.5$, $i = 6$	$45.56_{\pm2.8}$	$c = 8$, $mi = 0.5$, $i = 6$	$50.64_{\pm1.8}$	$c = 9$, $mi = 0.5$, $i = 6$	$64.93_{\pm2.2}$	$c = 9$, $mi = 0.6$, $i = 11$
TLS UM	$32.24_{\pm3.2}$	$K = 0\%$, $k = 0$	$46.97_{\pm3.5}$	$K = 1\%$, $k = 1$	$53.82_{\pm2.4}$	$K = 3\%$, $k = 7$	$70.32_{\pm3.0}$	$K = 2\%$, $k = 3$
TLS NM	$32.79_{\pm3.7}$	$K = 1\%$, $k = 2$	$46.93_{\pm2.8}$	$K = 1\%$, $k = 1$	$54.23_{\pm2.9}$	$K = 1\%$, $k = 2$	$69.76_{\pm2.2}$	$K = 3\%$, $k = 7$
TLS TM	$32.24_{\pm3.2}$	$K = 0\%$, $k = 0$	$46.84_{\pm3.6}$	$K = 0\%$, $k = 0$	$53.96_{\pm2.2}$	$K = 2\%$, $k = 3$	$68.86_{\pm2.6}$	$K = 3\%$, $k = 7$
TLS TNM	$32.87_{\pm3.7}$	$K = 1\%$, $k = 1$	$46.84_{\pm3.6}$	$K = 0\%$, $k = 0$	$53.31_{\pm3.1}$	$K = 1\%$, $k = 2$	$71.65_{\pm3.1}$	$K = 3\%$, $k = 7$
TLS& FTI UM	**37.55**$_{\pm1.3}$	$K = 0\%$, $k = 0$, $\delta' = 5$	**51.81**$_{\pm1.9}$	$K = 1\%$, $k = 1$, $\delta' = 7$	$60.98_{\pm1.5}$	$K = 3\%$, $k = 7$, $\delta' = 8$	**74.85**$_{\pm3.8}$	$K = 2\%$, $k = 3$, $\delta' = 13$
TLS& FTI NM	**38.03**$_{\pm3.4}$	$K = 1\%$, $k = 2$, $\delta' = 5$	$51.59_{\pm2.3}$	$K = 1\%$, $k = 1$, $\delta' = 7$	$61.55_{\pm2.1}$	$K = 1\%$, $k = 2$, $\delta' = 9$	$73.61_{\pm3.1}$	$K = 3\%$, $k = 7$, $\delta' = 12$
TLS& FTI TM	$36.22_{\pm1.2}$	$K = 0\%$, $k = 0$, $\delta' = 6$	$48.35_{\pm2.6}$	$K = 0\%$, $k = 0$, $\delta' = 6$	$59.78_{\pm1.9}$	$K = 2\%$, $k = 3$, $\delta' = 8$	$72.78_{\pm3.1}$	$K = 3\%$, $k = 7$, $\delta' = 15$
TLS& FTI TNM	**38.15**$_{\pm2.4}$	$K = 1\%$, $k = 1$, $\delta' = 6$	$51.65_{\pm2.8}$	$K = 0\%$, $k = 0$, $\delta' = 7$	**62.87**$_{\pm1.4}$	$K = 1\%$, $k = 2$, $\delta' = 8$	**74.75**$_{\pm3.4}$	$K = 3\%$, $k = 7$, $\delta' = 13$

on the corresponding test set. Numbers for dating accuracy in bold fonts represent top comparable performances among the dating methods with a given dating tolerance, i.e. along a column of accuracy in each table.

As with the experiment on English texts, the 10-fold cross-validation process was employed to tune temporal parameters, namely, the training texts were randomly divided into ten sections of equal sizes, nine of which were used for training, and one for tuning parameters. The optimum values of the temporal parameters were retrieved by sorting the averaged dating accuracies.

TABLE 3.16 Dating accuracy (%) for all solutions on Inisfallen test set

		δ = 3 years	δ = 6 years	δ = 10 years	δ = 25 years
UCD$_{NBM}$		42.03	52.34	58.88	69.16
FTI		**43.35**	54.77	62.54	71.81
STI		42.06	**56.07**	**65.42**	**73.83**
GG		42.12	51.36	57.66	64.25
GG$_{MI}$		42.23	52.25	58.10	66.34
TLS	UM	42.03	53.44	60.39	70.32
TLS	NM	**43.34**	53.01	61.81	71.55
TLS	TM	42.03	52.34	60.04	71.25
TLS	TNM	**43.28**	52.34	61.29	71.64
TLS&FTI	UM	**43.40**	**55.95**	**65.60**	72.55
TLS&FTI	NM	**43.28**	55.12	63.88	72.64
TLS&FTI	TM	42.18	53.90	62.07	71.98
TLS&FTI	TNM	**43.37**	**56.11**	64.56	72.76

The predicting and evaluation is the same as that for dating English texts. To make predictions for a new Irish text, we assigned it whichever given year range of the DTE format has the greatest overlap with our dated time intervals. In other words, the dating prediction of a text was considered correct if over a half of the dated period fell in the standard time interval of a relevant granularity. Tables 3.15-22 show that, with the exception of GG and GG$_{MI}$, our solutions significantly outperformed the baseline of UCD$_{NBM}$ method on both training and test corpora. Although our solutions of GG and GG$_{MI}$ were beaten by the baseline on Inisfallen, Ulster and Loch Cé, on the combination corpus they both significantly outperformed UCD$_{NBM}$. Analysis of the results shows the reason: sparse medieval Irish data made the greedy algorithms converge quickly at some locally optimal points, while the combination enriched the dataset. Among our solutions, STI ranks the top one and TLS&FTI with UM and NM have performed comparably.

3.4 Temporal Parameters

The five solutions we proposed all aim to improve the dating performance of multi-class classification by exploring the temporal distribution within the training corpus. Our analysis of the text dating task and existing research (Chapter 2) shows that the temporal distribution within the training corpus could be difficult to model directly. We, therefore, indirectly and partially mod-

TABLE 3.17 Training results of 10-fold cross-validation for all solutions on Ulster

		δ = 3 years		δ = 6 years		δ = 10 years		δ = 25 years	
		Accuracy (%)	Parameters	Accuracy (%)	Parameters	Accuracy (%)	Parameters	Accuracy (%)	Parameters
UCD$_{NBM}$		18.91$_{\pm 2.6}$	N/A	28.56$_{\pm 2.4}$	N/A	38.47$_{\pm 2.3}$	N/A	62.87$_{\pm 2.7}$	N/A
FTI		20.10$_{\pm 1.8}$	$\delta' = 4$	30.96$_{\pm 2.2}$	$\delta' = 6$	43.44$_{\pm 1.7}$	$\delta' = 9$	65.23$_{\pm 1.9}$	$\delta' = 10$
STI		**20.79**$_{\pm 1.8}$	$w = 9$, $s = 5$, $\lambda = 0.2$	**34.36**$_{\pm 1.8}$	$w = 11$, $s = 2$, $\lambda = 0.1$	**46.14**$_{\pm 1.9}$	$w = 17$, $s = 2$, $\lambda = 0.1$	**68.12**$_{\pm 2.3}$	$w = 21$, $s = 2$, $\lambda = 0.0$
GG		20.04$_{\pm 2.9}$	$i = 6$	26.33$_{\pm 2.4}$	$i = 7$	36.28$_{\pm 1.9}$	$i = 7$	58.36$_{\pm 1.3}$	$i = 13$
GG$_{MI}$		20.16$_{\pm 3.6}$	$c = 6$, $mi = 0.4$, $i = 6$	27.09$_{\pm 1.8}$	$c = 11$, $mi = 0.4$, $i = 7$	36.24$_{\pm 1.1}$	$c = 11$, $mi = 0.5$, $i = 7$	59.55$_{\pm 1.5}$	$c = 11$, $mi = 0.5$, $i = 12$
TLS	UM	19.47$_{\pm 1.6}$	$K = 1\%$, $k = 3$	29.99$_{\pm 2.1}$	$K = 1\%$, $k = 3$	41.87$_{\pm 2.1}$	$K = 2\%$, $k = 6$	65.34$_{\pm 1.8}$	$K = 3\%$, $k = 7$
TLS	NM	20.36$_{\pm 1.7}$	$K = 1\%$, $k = 3$	29.99$_{\pm 2.1}$	$K = 1\%$, $k = 3$	40.92$_{\pm 2.1}$	$K = 2\%$, $k = 5$	64.66$_{\pm 1.9}$	$K = 3\%$, $k = 8$
TLS	TM	19.06$_{\pm 1.8}$	$K = 1\%$, $k = 2$	28.32$_{\pm 2.2}$	$K = 1\%$, $k = 3$	38.72$_{\pm 2.6}$	$K = 3\%$, $k = 8$	63.14$_{\pm 2.1}$	$K = 3\%$, $k = 8$
TLS	TNM	20.71$_{\pm 1.4}$	$K = 1\%$, $k = 3$	29.84$_{\pm 2.2}$	$K = 1\%$, $k = 3$	39.75$_{\pm 1.8}$	$K = 3\%$, $k = 8$	65.87$_{\pm 1.6}$	$K = 3\%$, $k = 8$
TLS& FTI	UM	**20.55**$_{\pm 1.5}$	$K = 1\%$, $k = 3$, $\delta' = 2$	**33.95**$_{\pm 1.1}$	$K = 1\%$, $k = 3$, $\delta' = 4$	42.54$_{\pm 1.9}$	$K = 2\%$, $k = 6$, $\delta' = 9$	66.55$_{\pm 2.1}$	$K = 3\%$, $k = 7$, $\delta' = 15$
TLS& FTI	NM	**20.62**$_{\pm 1.6}$	$K = 1\%$, $k = 3$, $\delta' = 3$	33.22$_{\pm 2.1}$	$K = 1\%$, $k = 3$, $\delta' = 5$	42.65$_{\pm 2.1}$	$K = 2\%$, $k = 5$, $\delta' = 8$	67.14$_{\pm 3.7}$	$K = 3\%$, $k = 8$, $\delta' = 17$
TLS& FTI	TM	19.14$_{\pm 1.4}$	$K = 1\%$, $k = 2$, $\delta' = 3$	30.36$_{\pm 2.4}$	$K = 1\%$, $k = 3$, $\delta' = 5$	39.77$_{\pm 1.4}$	$K = 3\%$, $k = 8$, $\delta' = 9$	64.10$_{\pm 2.5}$	$K = 3\%$, $k = 8$, $\delta' = 11$
TLS& FTI	TNM	**20.39**$_{\pm 1.1}$	$K = 1\%$, $k = 3$, $\delta' = 3$	32.50$_{\pm 2.2}$	$K = 1\%$, $k = 3$, $\delta' = 6$	42.17$_{\pm 1.2}$	$K = 3\%$, $k = 8$, $\delta' = 9$	**67.92**$_{\pm 2.1}$	$K = 3\%$, $k = 8$, $\delta' = 17$

el the temporal distribution by tuning the time intervals used as class labels. In all our solutions, the tuning is implemented by optimising the dating performance and estimating the best values for respective temporal parameters. As a summary, temporal parameters for each solution are listed and briefly described in Table 3.23.

According to Popescu and Strapparava (2013, 2014 and 2015), epochs for temporal texts tend to change much faster in later or modern times than in earlier ones. Our tuned parameters seem to have also proved this assumption,

TABLE 3.18 Dating accuracy (%) for all solutions on Ulster test set

		δ = 3 years	δ = 6 years	δ = 10 years	δ = 25 years
UCD_{NBM}		17.53	27.09	36.25	62.95
FTI		17.96	29.78	40.32	64.85
STI		**18.12**	**30.68**	**44.22**	**66.53**
GG		16.83	28.78	36.21	61.55
GG_{MI}		17.31	28.90	36.21	61.76
TLS	UM	17.85	28.45	40.22	65.02
TLS	NM	17.62	27.95	41.36	64.55
TLS	TM	17.56	27.34	38.18	63.29
TLS	TNM	17.62	29.08	41.25	65.11
TLS&FTI	UM	**18.23**	**30.56**	43.25	**66.60**
TLS&FTI	NM	**18.23**	**30.52**	**44.35**	65.42
TLS&FTI	TM	17.95	29.21	41.11	65.03
TLS&FTI	TNM	**18.27**	**30.66**	**44.35**	**66.48**

i.e. the texts in Freecycle have been changing faster than the newspaper items in DTE2, which in turn have been changing faster than the medieval Irish texts. We may take the case where $\delta = 10$ to illustrate how our dating experiments have revealed the shifting speed of change in the language used.

Figure 3.2 compares the tuning results of δ' for FTI and four TLS&FTI dating models on the training texts of our six corpora. Our FTI solution of Algorithm 2.1 in Section 2.4.1 and Algorithm 2.6 in Section 2.4.5 groups any texts with a timestamp t between $b + i * \delta'$ and $b + (i + 2) * \delta'$, where b is the beginning of the overall time span on the training corpus and $i \geq 0$ is an integer such that $b + i * \delta' \leq t \leq b + (i + 2) * \delta'$. A bigger δ' groups more temporally adjacent texts, which means more adjacent texts are similar to each other, while a smaller δ' groups fewer temporally adjacent texts, which means more adjacent texts are different from each other. Therefore, bigger δ' was caused by slow language change while smaller δ' came from fast language change. Figure 3.2 shows that δ' values for Freecycle are generally smaller than δ' value for DTE2, which are in turn smaller than those of the four medieval Irish corpora.

Figure 3.3 compares the tuning results of w and s for our STI dating model on the training texts of our six corpora. Our STI solution of Algorithm 2.2 in Section 2.4.2 groups any texts with a timestamp t between $b+s+i*w$ and $b+s+i*w+w$, where b is the beginning of the overall time span on the training corpus and $i \geq 0$, ensures that the interval covers t. In a similar manner as δ', a bigger w revealed slow language change, while a smaller w came from fast language change. Figure 3.3 shows that the w value for Freecycle is smaller than that for

TABLE 3.19 Training results of 10-fold cross-validation for all solutions on Loch Cé

		δ = 3 years		**δ = 6 years**		**δ = 10 years**		**δ = 25 years**	
		Accuracy (%)	**Parameters**	**Accuracy (%)**	**Parameters**	**Accuracy (%)**	**Parameters**	**Accuracy (%)**	**Parameters**
UCD_{NBM}		18.70$_{\pm2.1}$	N/A	30.81$_{\pm2.6}$	N/A	37.60$_{\pm2.1}$	N/A	55.55$_{\pm1.8}$	N/A
FTI		20.42$_{\pm1.5}$	$\delta' = 4$	32.56$_{\pm1.8}$	$\delta' = 7$	42.88$_{\pm1.8}$	$\delta' = 9$	60.05$_{\pm1.6}$	$\delta' = 11$
STI		**23.40**$_{\pm1.8}$	$w = 9$, $s = 2$, $\lambda = 0.3$	**34.80**$_{\pm2.1}$	$w = 13$, $s = 4$, $\lambda = 0.1$	**45.50**$_{\pm2.1}$	$w = 17$, $s = 6$, $\lambda = 0.0$	**63.45**$_{\pm1.7}$	$w = 21$, $s = 8$, $\lambda = 0.1$
GG		18.61$_{\pm2.6}$	$i = 6$	30.32$_{\pm2.4}$	$i = 6$	36.98$_{\pm2.4}$	$i = 7$	54.33$_{\pm1.6}$	$i = 11$
GG_{MI}		18.80$_{\pm3.2}$	$c = 5$, $mi = 0.5$, $i = 6$	30.51$_{\pm1.8}$	$c = 6$, $mi = 0.6$, $i = 7$	37.84$_{\pm2.8}$	$c = 11$, $mi = 0.6$, $i = 7$	55.64$_{\pm1.9}$	$c = 9$, $mi = 0.6$, $i = 11$
TLS	UM	22.65$_{\pm1.6}$	$K = 1\%$, $k = 2$	32.73$_{\pm1.1}$	$K = 1\%$, $k = 1$	41.53$_{\pm1.0}$	$K = 1\%$, $k = 1$	60.14$_{\pm1.6}$	$K = 2\%$, $k = 5$
TLS	NM	22.17$_{\pm1.9}$	$K = 1\%$, $k = 4$	33.01$_{\pm1.8}$	$K = 2\%$, $k = 5$	42.57$_{\pm2.4}$	$K = 2\%$, $k = 7$	60.42$_{\pm1.9}$	$K = 1\%$, $k = 4$
TLS	TM	22.22$_{\pm1.7}$	$K = 2\%$, $k = 5$	31.83$_{\pm1.1}$	$K = 1\%$, $k = 2$	41.06$_{\pm1.0}$	$K = 1\%$, $k = 1$	58.06$_{\pm1.3}$	$K = 1\%$, $k = 4$
TLS	TNM	22.35$_{\pm1.6}$	$K = 1\%$, $k = 4$	32.54$_{\pm1.8}$	$K = 1\%$, $k = 2$	42.63$_{\pm3.5}$	$K = 1\%$, $k = 1$	59.48$_{\pm1.1}$	$K = 1\%$, $k = 4$
TLS& FTI	UM	**23.35**$_{\pm1.6}$	$K = 1\%$, $k = 2$, $\delta' = 4$	33.54$_{\pm1.8}$	$K = 1\%$, $k = 1$, $\delta' = 5$	**45.68**$_{\pm2.3}$	$K = 1\%$, $k = 1$, $\delta' = 9$	**64.05**$_{\pm2.3}$	$K = 2\%$, $k = 5$, $\delta' = 11$
TLS& FTI	NM	**23.42**$_{\pm1.4}$	$K = 1\%$, $k = 4$, $\delta' = 4$	**34.69**$_{\pm1.9}$	$K = 2\%$, $k = 5$, $\delta' = 7$	44.62$_{\pm2.1}$	$K = 2\%$, $k = 7$, $\delta' = 9$	**63.64**$_{\pm1.9}$	$K = 1\%$, $k = 4$, $\delta' = 11$
TLS& FTI	TM	20.12$_{\pm1.4}$	$K = 2\%$, $k = 5$, $\delta' = 3$	31.37$_{\pm2.2}$	$K = 1\%$, $k = 2$, $\delta' = 7$	40.09$_{\pm1.8}$	$K = 1\%$, $k = 1$, $\delta' = 7$	60.88$_{\pm1.6}$	$K = 1\%$, $k = 4$, $\delta' = 11$
TLS& FTI	TNM	**23.28**$_{\pm1.4}$	$K = 1\%$, $k = 4$, $\delta' = 4$	**34.35**$_{\pm1.2}$	$K = 1\%$, $k = 2$, $\delta' = 5$	**45.80**$_{\pm2.2}$	$K = 1\%$, $k = 1$, $\delta' = 7$	62.74$_{\pm1.8}$	$K = 1\%$, $k = 4$, $\delta' = 11$

DTE2, which is in turn smaller than those of the four medieval Irish corpora. For a given w value, s determines how many basic classifiers are involved. The number of basic classifiers $n = ceiling(w/s)$, and larger values of n reflects greater complexity of changing pattern or irregularity in the language of the corpus. Figure 3.3 shows that medieval Irish, as evidenced in our corpus, might have changed much more irregularly than modern and contemporary English.

Figure 3.4 compares the tuning results of i for our GG dating model, and Figure 3.5 compares the tuning results of i and c for our GG_{MI} dating mod-

TABLE 3.20 Dating accuracy (%) for all solutions on Loch Cé test set

		δ = 3 years	δ = 6 years	δ = 10 years	δ = 25 years
UCD_{NBM}		22.24	33.47	42.04	58.16
FTI		23.36	35.50	**44.60**	61.55
STI		**24.49**	**36.53**	**44.49**	**62.65**
GG		21.55	32.78	43.43	57.97
GG_{MI}		22.36	33.54	43.26	57.86
TLS	UM	23.60	35.46	43.56	59.35
TLS	NM	23.24	35.66	44.28	60.37
TLS	TM	22.55	34.31	42.33	59.21
TLS	TNM	22.86	35.35	43.97	60.78
TLS&FTI	UM	**24.51**	**36.75**	**44.45**	61.62
TLS&FTI	NM	23.69	**36.56**	**44.45**	61.71
TLS&FTI	TM	23.15	34.88	43.63	60.85
TLS&FTI	TNM	24.78	35.85	**44.45**	**62.70**

el. Our GG solution of Algorithm 2.3 and GG_{MI} solution of Algorithm 2.4 in Section 2.4.3 groups any pair of texts (T_1, T_2) with timestamps t_1 and t_2, and $|t_1 - t_2| \leq 2i$ if the overall dating performance can be improved and the similarity between T_1 and T_2 is large enough in the case of GG_{MI}. In a similar manner as δ', a bigger value of i reveals slow language change, while a smaller i results from fast language change. Figures 3.4 and 3.5 show that i values for Freecycle are smaller than those for DTE2, which are generally smaller than those of the four medieval Irish corpora. In GG_{MI}, c is the number of clusters used for calculating the similarity of mutual information. Larger values of c comply with greater complexity of changing pattern or irregularity in the language of the corpus. Figure 3.5 also shows that medieval Irish might have changed much more irregularly than English.

Figure 3.6 compares the tuning results of K and k for our eight dating models of TLS and TLS&FTI. Algorithm 2.5.1 in Section 2.4.4 ensures that the selected temporal landmarks represent the timestamps at which texts are of the greatest variance. Therefore, more landmarks selected roughly corresponds to a greater number of changes during the temporal range concerned. The Freecycle corpus is the most recent, and our approach selected many more landmarks for dating it than for all the other five corpora. Furthermore, the selected landmarks also reflect the temporal characteristics of texts in the training corpus. By selecting an appropriate number of timestamps as landmarks, our dating approach captures to some extent the temporal distribution of the training texts. Since we employ UCD or FTI time intervals between each

TABLE 3.21 Training results of 10-fold cross-validation for all solutions on combination

	$\delta = 3$ years		$\delta = 6$ years		$\delta = 10$ years		$\delta = 25$ years	
	Accuracy (%)	Parameters	Accuracy (%)	Parameters	Accuracy (%)	Parameters	Accuracy (%)	Parameters
UCD_{NBM}	$23.06_{\pm 1.9}$	N/A	$30.72_{\pm 2.4}$	N/A	$38.92_{\pm 1.8}$	N/A	$54.28_{\pm 1.7}$	N/A
FTI	$25.33_{\pm 1.3}$	$\delta' = 4$	$32.84_{\pm 1.6}$	$\delta' = 7$	$41.55_{\pm 1.6}$	$\delta' = 9$	$60.63_{\pm 1.8}$	$\delta' = 10$
STI	**26.53**$_{\pm 1.4}$	$w = 5$, $s = 4$, $\lambda = 0.1$	**35.84**$_{\pm 1.8}$	$w = 13$, $s = 5$, $\lambda = 0.1$	**44.31**$_{\pm 1.9}$	$w = 20$, $s = 5$, $\lambda = 0.0$	**63.20**$_{\pm 1.9}$	$w = 23$, $s = 13$, $\lambda = 0.8$
GG	$23.79_{\pm 1.6}$	$i = 5$	$32.36_{\pm 1.8}$	$i = 6$	$40.65_{\pm 1.7}$	$i = 6$	$58.43_{\pm 1.8}$	$i = 9$
GG_{MI}	$23.86_{\pm 1.7}$	$c = 9$, $mi = 0.6$, $i = 5$	$32.58_{\pm 1.6}$	$c = 11$, $mi = 0.6$, $i = 6$	$41.45_{\pm 1.8}$	$c = 11$, $mi = 0.5$, $i = 7$	$59.24_{\pm 1.8}$	$c = 11$, $mi = 0.5$, $i = 9$
TLS UM	$25.48_{\pm 1.5}$	$K = 1\%$, $k = 4$	$34.29_{\pm 2.1}$	$K = 2\%$, $k = 5$	$42.53_{\pm 2.4}$	$K = 1\%$, $k = 3$	$58.64_{\pm 1.6}$	$K = 1\%$, $k = 3$
TLS NM	$25.53_{\pm 1.6}$	$K = 1\%$, $k = 4$	$33.91_{\pm 2.1}$	$K = 2\%$, $k = 6$	$42.66_{\pm 2.5}$	$K = 2\%$, $k = 5$	$59.45_{\pm 1.7}$	$K = 2\%$, $k = 5$
TLS TM	$24.26_{\pm 1.5}$	$K = 1\%$, $k = 3$	$31.90_{\pm 2.3}$	$K = 2\%$, $k = 5$	$39.79_{\pm 2.1}$	$K = 2\%$, $k = 6$	$57.60_{\pm 1.5}$	$K = 2\%$, $k = 7$
TLS TNM	$25.67_{\pm 1.6}$	$K = 2\%$, $k = 5$	$34.49_{\pm 2.1}$	$K = 1\%$, $k = 4$	$42.57_{\pm 1.8}$	$K = 2\%$, $k = 5$	$61.05_{\pm 1.8}$	$K = 2\%$, $k = 5$
TLS& FTI UM	**26.55**$_{\pm 1.4}$	$K = 1\%$, $k = 4$, $\delta' = 4$	**35.78**$_{\pm 1.8}$	$K = 2\%$, $k = 5$, $\delta' = 6$	$43.68_{\pm 1.4}$	$K = 1\%$, $k = 3$, $\delta' = 7$	**64.15**$_{\pm 2.7}$	$K = 1\%$, $k = 3$, $\delta' = 9$
TLS& FTI NM	**27.23**$_{\pm 1.9}$	$K = 1\%$, $k = 4$, $\delta' = 4$	**36.59**$_{\pm 2.6}$	$K = 2\%$, $k = 6$, $\delta' = 6$	$43.52_{\pm 2.1}$	$K = 2\%$, $k = 5$, $\delta' = 7$	**64.09**$_{\pm 2.5}$	$K = 2\%$, $k = 5$, $\delta' = 7$
TLS& FTI TM	$26.02_{\pm 1.8}$	$K = 1\%$, $k = 3$, $\delta' = 4$	$34.93_{\pm 2.2}$	$K = 2\%$, $k = 5$, $\delta' = 7$	$42.87_{\pm 1.3}$	$K = 2\%$, $k = 6$, $\delta' = 9$	$62.33_{\pm 1.7}$	$K = 2\%$, $k = 7$, $\delta' = 11$
TLS& FTI TNM	**27.18**$_{\pm 1.9}$	$K = 2\%$, $k = 5$, $\delta' = 4$	**36.35**$_{\pm 2.4}$	$K = 1\%$, $k = 4$, $\delta' = 6$	**44.83**$_{\pm 1.3}$	$K = 2\%$, $k = 5$, $\delta' = 7$	**64.24**$_{\pm 2.9}$	$K = 2\%$, $k = 5$, $\delta' = 9$

pair of adjacent landmarks, more selected landmarks indicate that our algorithms have learned more about the temporal distribution than the UCD or FTI method. In particular, when $k > d/(2\delta + 1)$ the boundaries of our time intervals are mostly determined by the selected landmarks, and the corresponding UCD or FTI method may have recovered very little temporal information. This happened with the Freecycle corpus for many values of δ or δ'. As to the opposite extreme point, if no landmarks were selected, our approach retreats to the UCD or FTI method. It means that the segmentation of the UCD or FTI time

TABLE 3.22 Dating accuracy (%) for all solutions on combination test set

		δ = 3 years	δ = 6 years	δ = 10 years	δ = 25 years
UCD_{NBM}		23.40	30.94	37.11	49.43
FTI		25.73	32.98	**39.60**	56.57
STI		**27.17**	**33.84**	**39.62**	**58.87**
GG		24.54	32.08	**39.45**	55.63
GG_{MI}		24.75	33.11	**39.45**	55.75
TLS	UM	25.02	32.35	37.96	55.85
TLS	NM	25.55	32.67	38.45	56.77
TLS	TM	24.80	31.18	37.55	55.23
TLS	TNM	26.35	33.20	38.92	57.21
TLS&FTI	UM	26.63	**33.75**	**39.71**	**59.02**
TLS&FTI	NM	**27.31**	**33.94**	**39.68**	**58.75**
TLS&FTI	TM	25.85	32.38	**39.55**	57.35
TLS&FTI	TNM	**27.26**	**33.94**	**39.73**	**58.85**

TABLE 3.23 Temporal parameters for each of our solutions

	Parameters	Description
FTI	δ'	The span of optimal time intervals.
STI	w	The largest span for all time intervals.
	s	The number of time units skipped over at each step, and $s \leq w$.
GG	i	The largest possible span for time intervals.
GG_{MI}	c	The number of clusters.
	i	The largest possible span for time intervals.
TLS	K	The percentage of timestamps that could be selected as landmarks.
	k	The number of timestamps that could be selected as landmarks.
TLS&FTI	K	The percentage of timestamps that could be selected as landmarks.
	k	The number of timestamps that could be selected as landmarks.
	δ'	The span of optimal time intervals.

intervals already captured all possible temporal characteristics on the training corpus. This situation often occurs when the data is sufficiently large and intensive, and especially with large tolerance δ, because enough data points have already ensured the classification performance.

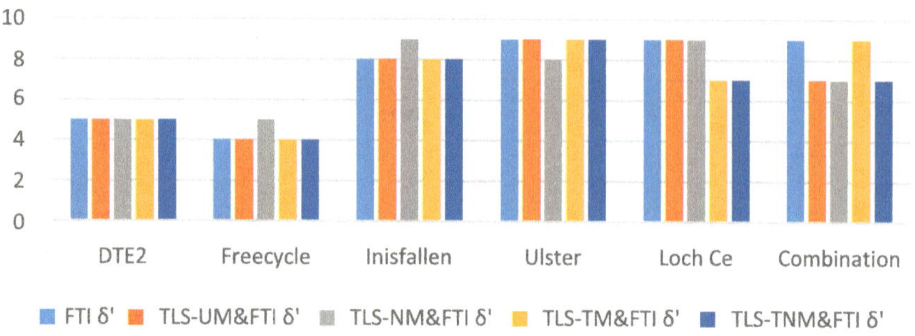

FIGURE 3.2 Tuning results of FTI δ'

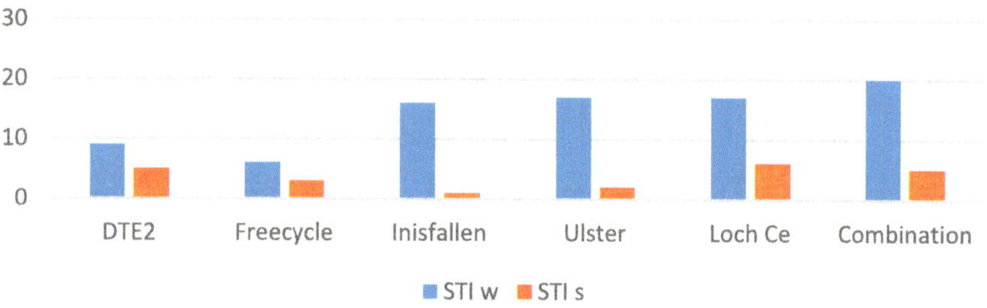

FIGURE 3.3 Tuning results of STI w and s

3.5 Datability

In Section 2.5 we introduced the term Datability $\mathcal{D}_\rho$ to measure how feasible a text dating task can be. Though it is very difficult to calculate $\mathcal{D}_\rho$ directly for a language, we can estimate it by the normalised dating accuracy of a given dating approach on a training corpus, as Equation (6) in Section 2.5. To compare the datability of languages in our six corpora, we estimated $\mathcal{D}_\rho$ for $\delta = 10$ by

$$
\begin{aligned}
\mathcal{D}_\rho &\cong \text{Expectation}\left(P/(1+e^{C-H/(2\delta+1)})\right) \\
&= \text{Expectation}(P)\left(1/(1+e^{C-H/(2\delta+1)})\right),
\end{aligned}
$$

where Expectation(P) was approximated with the averaged dating accuracy on the training corpus of our twelve dating models, i.e. FTI, STI, GG, GG_{MI}, TLS-UM, TLS-NM, TLS-TM, TLS-TNM, TLS-UM&FTI, TLS-NM&FTI, TLS-TM&FTI and TLS-TNM&FTI, and C was set as 2. Table 3.24 lists the values of H, i.e. the historical period or the number of time units covered by the training corpus. Figure 3.7 gives the estimated datability of the text dating tasks on our six corpora.

Freecycle contains modern English posts and only covers 180 days, so is the least datable given $\delta = 10$. The annals of Inisfallen were maintained more or

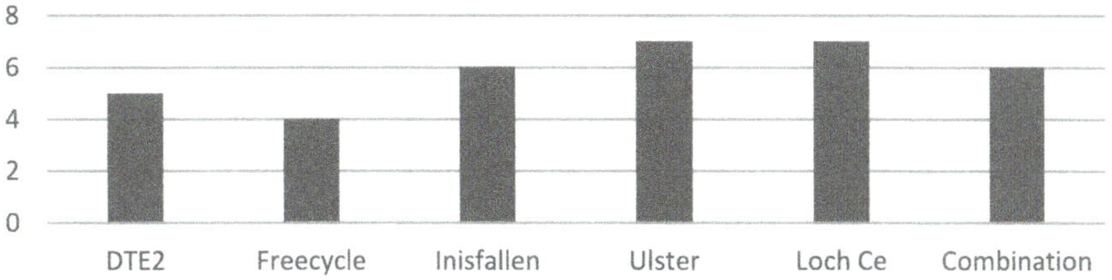

FIGURE 3.4 Tuning results of GG *i*

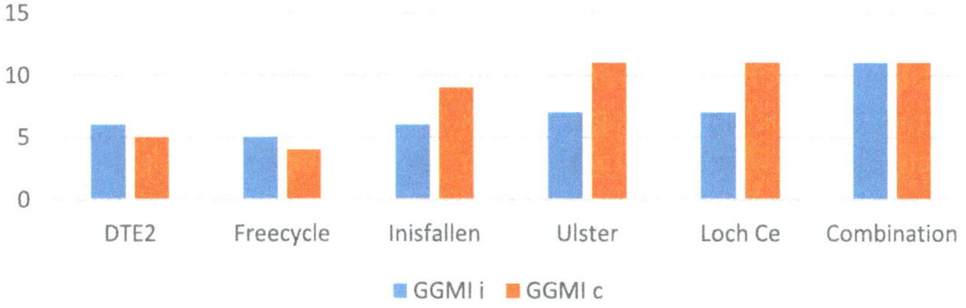

FIGURE 3.5 Tuning results of GG_{MI} *i* and *c*

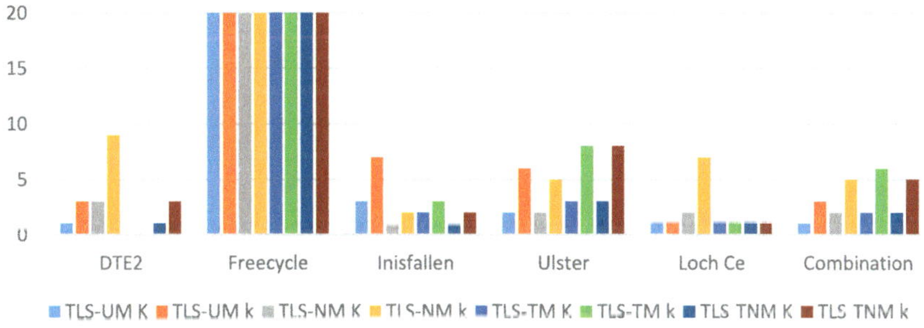

FIGURE 3.6 Tuning results of *K* and *k* in TLS and TLS&FTI

TABLE 3.24 *H*, the history period covered by the training corpus

DTE2	Freecycle	Inisfallen	Ulster	Loch Cé	Combination
310 (years)	180 (days)	218 (years)	286 (years)	335 (years)	365 (years)

less annually from 1092 and the original writers can be distinguished in the surviving manuscript. It is not surprising, therefore, that Figure 3.7 shows that the Inisfallen annals are more datable than the other sets of annals which survive only in later copies with their propensity towards modernisation and levelling. The Annals of Ulster and Loch Cé are similarly datable, with Loch

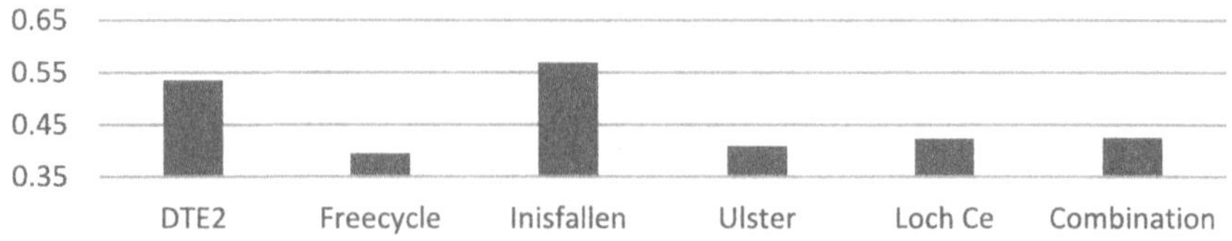

FIGURE 3.7 Estimated datability for dating our six corpora with δ = 10

Cé producing slightly better results suggesting that it may be more conservative than the Ulster annals for this period. The newspaper corpus from DTE2 produces good datability but not quite as good as the annals of Inisfallen. Like Inisfallen, the journalistic items are contemporary records and so do not suffer from the problems of long transmission that we see in the other sets of annals. There may be several reasons why the newspapers are not as datable as Inisfallen, but chief among these must be that the annals are the product of less than 40 individual scribes writing on a limited set of historical events whereas the newspapers are drawn from a wide range of international titles penned by a huge number of journalists writing about a much broader range of topics. Linguistic change, therefore, is not the only factor in determining the datability of a corpus.

3.6 Conclusion

This chapter describes our extensive experiments on dating modern English and medieval Irish texts. We compared the dating performance of a baseline method of UCD_{NBM} and our twelve dating models as outlined in Chapter 2. With the exception of GG and GG_{MI}, our dating models significantly outperformed the baseline on all six corpora, and STI and TLS-UM&FTI proved to be the best. The STI and FTI methods proved more efficient and more accurate than existing methods involving multiple feature types including character n-grams, word n-grams, POS-tags, syntactic rules, and Google syntactic database, despite the fact that we used only character and word n-grams for dating English, and only character n-grams for dating Irish. This is significant because it also enables us to use these methods on unparsed and untagged corpora, thereby saving considerable effort and expense and raising the possibility of applying the methods to material in other languages.

In tackling the medieval Irish material, we had to deal with problems that are not present in modern corpora, primarily, the dearth of genuinely contemporary material and the often long periods of transmission of earlier material with the resulting potential for the modernisation and corruption of texts. We are able to achieve accuracy results of 73.83% at ±25 years for the more-or-less contemporary records in the Annals of Inisfallen, but the cost of longer periods of transmission is seen in decreased accuracy for Ulster and Loch Cé. Nevertheless, it is clear that the methods described here are capable of revealing underlying pattern changes even in non-contemporary training texts with accuracy rates in excess of 66% at ±25 years. In the next chapter, we will seek to extend the chronological range of texts used in the training and then to use the trained corpus in the dating of other non-annalistic texts.

CHAPTER 4

Dating Long Documents

4.0 Introduction

In the previous chapter we examined methods for dating short annalistic texts of known or supposed dates, and we have seen that it is possible to build a generally reliable predictive model. The question arises, then, whether it is possible to apply this model to otherwise undated or insecurely dated texts beyond the annalistic collections. This is what we will explore in this chapter. In Chapter 1, we examined the traditional methods available to scholars in the field including the use of internal and linguistic evidence. It is generally recognised that almost all datings are provisional and contingent on the dating of other texts, yet a great deal of effort is required to examine the textual history of a text and its possible evidence for dating. A computer-assisted method could provide a powerful tool to scholars working in ancient and medieval literatures. A complicating factor is that medieval Irish texts rarely survive in contemporary or near-contemporary manuscripts and that many texts have undergone sometimes radical revision subsequent to their first composition. This raises the possibility, indeed near certainty, of encountering multiple strata in any text under consideration, an environment in which traditional methods struggle to achieve clarity, and ideally a computer-based method would be able to deal with texts for which a single, simple date for a text cannot be realised.

This chapter proposes a general approach to dating long documents. First, by exploiting temporal characteristics learned by dating models we described in Chapter 2, we can build up a large training corpus by incrementally selecting temporally typical texts from Irish annals and then construct a dating model trained on this large annals corpus. We will then use this model to attempt to date longer texts. We will first use a range of long texts for which there is general agreement about their dating. This will enable us to determine the accuracy of our model and any weaknesses within it. We will refine the method to allow for the possibility of multiple strata and to control for particularly dominant strata or biases within our model. We will then apply the method to other texts, some of which have a more complex transmission history. The aim of this chapter, therefore, is to test the robustness of our method against texts of known or agreed dates, and to work towards the foundation of a tool for dating texts of unknown or uncertain dates.

 | DOI:10.1163/9789004410046_006

4.1 Building a Datable Medieval Irish Corpus

As we have seen, the Annals of Inisfallen were kept contemporaneously for the period c.1092-1309, while the other sets of annals on which we are relying were copied only in later centuries with the result that they have undergone various degrees of modernisation, revision and augmentation. As a result, the Inisfallen subset that we have examined is thought to be the best representative of contemporary language for this period and this has been borne out by our dating experiments in Section 3.2. However, the size of our Inisfallen corpus is very small – there are only 866 texts left after pre-processing – and it only covers a limited period of 1092-1309 when we actually want to date long documents for the whole of the Irish medieval period c.700-c.1600. Therefore, we tried to extend the dating methods proposed in Section 2.4 in order to build a larger and more datable medieval Irish training corpus.

The problem of non-contemporaneity decreases in significance in the later annalistic entries as we get closer to the date of transcription, but it becomes increasingly substantial the further we go back in time. The most direct method would have been simply to add more records from the annals to those already examined for 1092-1309, but this would introduce much material that is not contemporary and therefore may distort the resulting model. Therefore, our aim was to extend the temporal patterns learned from Inisfallen corpus with more Ulster and Loch Cé annals and incrementally improve the final dating performance on short medieval Irish texts. Our hypothesis is that the learned temporal parameters of our dating methods could have revealed some of the temporal characteristics/patterns in the training corpus. We, therefore, could incrementally choose those texts of Inisfallen, Ulster and Loch Cé, which could be dated correctly by using the learned dating model, add them to the training corpus, and train new dating models on the extended corpus. The detailed steps for building a large medieval Irish dating corpus are given in Algorithm 4.1.

Any of the dating methods we proposed in Section 2.4 can be implemented in Algorithm 4.1 to build a large medieval Irish corpus for general dating purposes. We chose FTI, which costs the least computing time among our solutions, to build our present training corpus. Values for dating tolerance were set as $\delta = 3, 6, 10$ and 25, and $m = 1$. The extending process found the FTI temporal parameters $\delta' = 4, 7, 8$ and 12 for Inisfallen, $\delta' = 4, 5, 8$ and 11 for FTC+Ulster, and $\delta' = 3, 5, 9$ and 11 for FTC′+Loch Cé. The final dating performance estimated on the established large corpus is given in Table 4.1. It shows that our method of FTI significantly outperformed the basic UCD_{NBM} classifiers of the state-of-the-art method (Szymanski and Lynch, 2015), with a t-test p-value of

ALGORITHM 4.1 Building a larger and more datable medieval Irish corpus

---

Input: 827 Inisfallen texts covering 1092-1309; 6,368 Ulster texts covering 500-1588; 5,600 Loch Cé texts covering 1000-1652.

Output: *FTC''*, a large dating corpus of 8,627 typical texts, including 816 from Inisfallen covering 1092-1309, 4,437 from Ulster covering 728-1588, and 3,374 from Loch Cé covering 1014-1599.

Steps:

1. For n given values of dating tolerance δ, learn n dating models of a dating method on the corpus of Inisfallen, i.e. tune a set of respective temporal parameters for that dating method;
2. Date the Inisfallen texts by using the n trained dating models with the tuned temporal parameters, and for further training corpus *FTC* select those texts dated correctly at least by m of the n trained models;
3. For the same n given values of dating tolerance δ, learn n dating models of the same dating method on the training corpus of *FTC*+Ulster, i.e. tune a new set of respective temporal parameters for that dating method;
4. Date the Ulster texts by using the n trained dating models with the tuned temporal parameters, and extend *FTC* to be *FTC'* with those Ulster texts dated correctly at least by m of the n trained models;
5. For the same n given values of dating tolerance δ, learn n dating models of the same dating method on the training corpus of *FTC'*+Loch Cé, i.e. tune one more set of respective temporal parameters;
6. Date the Loch Cé texts by using the n trained dating models with the tuned temporal parameters, and further extend *FTC'* to be *FTC''* with those Loch Cé texts dated correctly at least by m of the n trained models;
7. For dating new texts with a given tolerance of δ, a new dating model of any dating method can be learned on the final extended training corpus *FTC''*.

0.0015. Thus, our method can guess the date of an annal to within ±25 years with an accuracy rate of just over 75%, and to ±50 years with an accuracy rate of nearly 85%. In other words, it will correctly guess the date of a record to within half a century three times in every four and to within a century in 17 out of 20 cases. The performance is not even across the entire range, however, as can be seen from Figure 4.1 which shows accuracy rates for 50-year spans.

The model produces negligible predictive power for the early period 500-699 and is only marginally effective for the period 700-749. Results are uneven between 750 and 999, but the accuracy rate never falls below 65.65% for the entire period after 1000 CE, usually remaining at 70% or higher. For the final three half-centuries (1450-1599), accuracy rates exceed 80%.

The greater consistency and accuracy after 1000 CE may be due in no small part to the fact that the annals are more likely to be contemporary records but also because the quantity of training data increases during this period. Figure 4.2 shows the number of entries in the annals increases substantially

TABLE 4.1 Dating performance (%) estimated by 10-fold cross-validation on the extended large medieval Irish corpus

δ	δ'	Our FTI method	Basic UCD$_{NBM}$
3	4	36.43	32.69
6	4	48.17	42.43
10	5	58.38	50.49
25	7	75.89	66.07
50	10	84.76	78.62

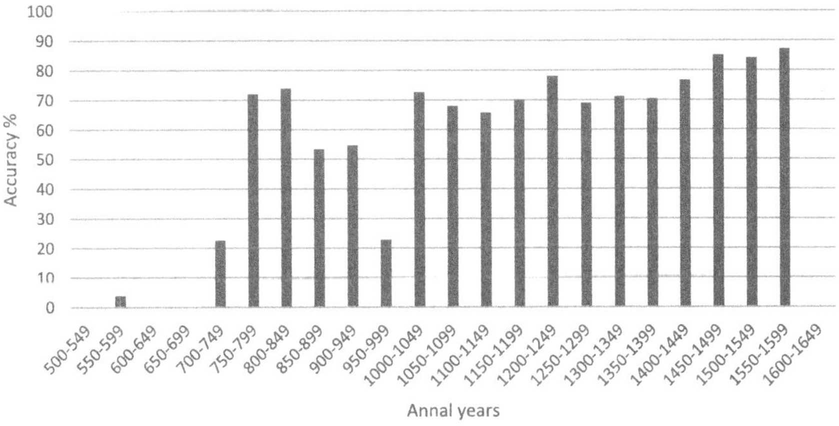

FIGURE 4.1 Accuracy rates by time for annals with $\delta = 25$

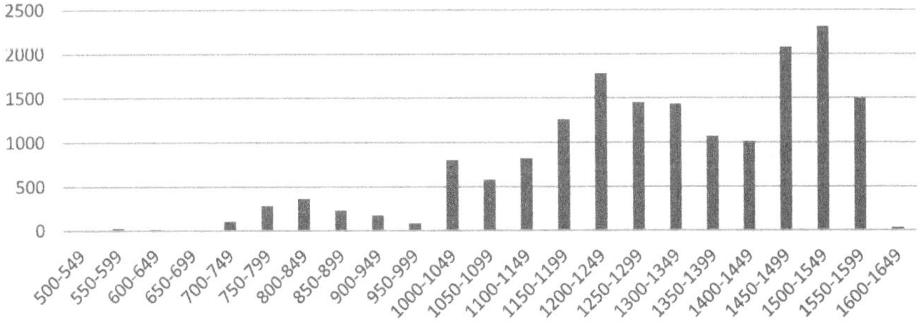

FIGURE 4.2 Number of entries in the annals by half century

from 1000 CE, to which we must add that the length of individual entries is generally much greater than in previous centuries.

The number of entries is negligible before 700 CE and remains low between then and 1000 CE. This period is shown in more detail in Table 4.2. Where the number of entries falls near or below 100, we see accuracy rates plummet to

TABLE 4.2 Accuracy of dating 700-999 relative to size of training corpus annals with δ = 25

Range	Total entries	Proportion of all annals (%)	Accuracy (%)
700-749	102	0.59	22.55
750-799	285	1.64	71.93
800-849	360	2.07	73.89
850-899	233	1.34	53.22
900-949	174	1.00	54.60
950-999	79	0.45	22.78

22%. Accuracy rates are much higher for the century 750-849 and rival accuracy rates for later periods, but we will see below that the data may be overfitted and proves difficult to transfer beyond this context.

4.2 Dating Long Documents

While the dating of the annals is of limited practical utility, the dating of long documents, such as stories, religious texts, and historical accounts, is a much more pressing problem for scholars in the humanities. In this section, we propose a method of using the dating models learned from the annals corpus to date non-annalistic texts. We will see that the model derived from the annals is valid when applied to a variety of texts from various genres, including prose, metrical and prosi-metrical texts.

4.2.1 *Test Data and Pre-Processing*

For the experiment of dating long texts by models trained on the extended corpus of annals described in Section 4.1, we collected 22 longer medieval Irish texts from the CELT corpus (www.ucc.ie/celt) and these are listed in Table 4.3. These texts cover the period c.700-c.1500, with as much of a spread as could be achieved from those texts that have widely accepted dates. For full details on how these dates were established see the discussion of the scholarly arguments in Appendix A. In most cases, only a date range can be proposed by traditional methods such as linguistic dating, internal evidence and the manuscript date (see Chapter 1). These are indicated in the table as absolute date ranges so that they can be compared with the output of our experiments. For example, a date range 750-800 indicates that the balance of evidence favours a date of composition in the second half of the eighth century. We have endeavoured to provide date ranges of fifty years or less in order to make

TABLE 4.3 Test data of long medieval Irish texts

	Title	Given date	Length
1	Táin Bó Fraích	750-800	3530 words
2	Aislinge Óengusso	750-800	1340 words
3	Bethu Brigte	800-850	3574 words
4	Treatise on the Psalter	800-852	2563 words
5	Monastery of Tallaght	831-840	6708 words
6	Echtra Láegaire	850-900	476 words
7	Fingal Rónáin	900-950	1905 words
8	Saltair na Rann	950-988	27545 words
9	Betha Adamnáin	961-1000	2060 words
10	Aided Nath Í	1050-1100	1163 words
11	Genemain Áeda Sláine	1050-1100	327 words
12	Tucait Indarba na nDessi	1050-1102	263 words
13	Aided Guill	1100-1160	3889 words
14	Cogadh Gaedel	1103-1170	2202 words
15	Cath Catharda	1140-1170	58853 words
16	Cath Ruis na Ríg	1150-1166	6154 words
17	Bórama	1151-1181	11579 words
18	Acallamh na Senórach	1200-1225	80020 words
19	Cath Maige Léna	1250-1325	19403 words
20	Caithréim Cellacháin	1330-1360	52063 words
21	Guy of Berwick	1452-1500	31467 words
22	Maundeville	1475	23100 words

the test as rigorous as possible but in some cases it must be acknowledged that the ranges appear to give a level of certainty and precision that is not warranted by the evidence. In addition, at this stage we are only considering the supposed date of composition rather than the dates of subsequent revisions which can be even more difficult to establish. At a later stage below (4.4), we will also consider the relationship between the date of the manuscript in which each text appears and the dates produced by our method.

The CELT texts have been digitally captured from published editions, including in some case diplomatic editions, and marked up there in accordance with TEI guidelines for structural markup (pages, sections, etc.), language, dates, places and personal names. For the purposes of the test texts, we removed all extraneous tagging, as well as words and phrases tagged as Latin. Numbers have been removed as with the annals texts. We have removed brackets indicating letters supplied by the editor(s) but we have allowed the inserted letters to stand. Where diplomatic editions were used, we allowed the punctuation of the manuscript to remain unchanged and did not add stops where these might be required in modern punctuation. Where direct speech is marked off with stops rather than quotation marks we allowed this to stand.

Our training texts from the annals are generally very short: the shortest one consists of five words, the longest one of 464 words, and the average length is 23.6 words. Therefore, we cut each long text into chunks of 20+ words; very long sentences were divided using punctuation marks (commas, semicolons) as in the editions, and sentences of less than 20 words were grouped to create chunks of over 20 words.

4.2.2 *Dating Long Documents with the Most Frequent Predict*

A very straightforward method for estimating the date of a long document would be to select the most frequent predicted date for all the chunks in the document. First, the dating model of a given δ value and learned temporal parameters, such as those FTI δ' values in Table 4.1, can be used to date the chunks individually, then we rank the dates and take the most frequently occurring one as the final estimation. In this and the next few experiments on long texts, we employ the FTI model of $\delta = 50$ (See Table 4.1). This is an appropriate duration for dealing with dates based primarily on the linguistic evidence such as these although we will experiment with smaller tolerances in a subsequent experiment. For evaluating the dating performance, we adopted the same method as employed for short texts, namely, a text is regarded as being dated correctly if the estimated date falls in the tolerable area of $[t'-\delta, t'+\delta]$, where t' is the gold standard date. Therefore, our dating is counted as successful for this experiment if it is within fifty years of the range of dates supplied by traditional scholarship.

Table 4.4 gives the established date for each text in the test (the given date) together with the most frequently predicted estimation generated by our method. For a dating tolerance of 50 years, seven out of the 22 texts were dated correctly, that is, the dating accuracy is 31.82%. Dates within the 50-year tolerance are shown in bold.

4.2.3 *Dating Long Documents with Multiple Choices*

The low success rate of the previous experiment (4.2.2) may be due to a number of factors. We shall see below that there is a high correlation between the date of the manuscript and dates supplied by this method, suggesting perhaps that orthography may be one of the most influential factors in producing the most frequent estimation of the date of a text. Furthermore, as we have seen, the majority of the texts with which we are dealing have long periods of transmission and may comprise multiple strata, so a single estimated date may ref-

TABLE 4.4 Dating long medieval Irish texts by estimation with the most frequent predict

	Title	Given date	Most frequent predict
1	Táin Bó Fraích	750-800	$1208_{\pm 50}$
2	Aislinge Óengusso	750-800	$914_{\pm 50}$
3	Bethu Brigte	800-850	$914_{\pm 50}$
4	Treatise on the Psalter	800-852	$1208_{\pm 50}$
5	Monastery of Tallaght	831-840	$1208_{\pm 50}$
6	Echtra Láegaire	850-900	$1124_{\pm 50}$
7	Fingal Rónáin	900-950	$1208_{\pm 50}$
8	Saltair na Rann	950-988	$\mathbf{914}_{\pm 50}$
9	Betha Adamnáin	961-1000	$1523_{\pm 50}$
10	Aided Nath Í	1050-1100	$1208_{\pm 50}$
11	Genemain Áeda Sláine	1050-1100	$1208_{\pm 50}$
12	Tucait Indarba na nDessi	1050-1102	$1208_{\pm 50}$
13	Aided Guill	1100-1160	$\mathbf{1208}_{\pm 50}$
14	Cogadh Gaedel	1103-1170	$\mathbf{1208}_{\pm 50}$
15	Cath Catharda	1140-1170	$1229_{\pm 50}$
16	Cath Ruis na Ríg	1150-1166	$\mathbf{1208}_{\pm 50}$
17	Bórama	1151-1181	$\mathbf{1208}_{\pm 50}$
18	Acallamh na Senórach	1200-1225	$\mathbf{1208}_{\pm 50}$
19	Cath Maige Léna	1250-1325	$\mathbf{1229}_{\pm 50}$
20	Caithréim	1330-1360	$1544_{\pm 50}$
21	Guy of Berwick	1452-1500	$1229_{\pm 50}$
22	Maundeville	1475	$1229_{\pm 50}$

erence any stage in the development of a text, not necessarily its date of composition. When human scholars attempt to date a text, they most frequently look for the date of composition, so a digital method must be developed to help separate out the different strata. Instead of making a single guess, we can provide multiple choices as computer assistance for domain experts to choose from. Our classification method can actually reveal some linguistic strata in the query document, which may help domain experts analyse the underlying temporal structure.

4.2.3.1 Top-n Most Frequent Predicts as Multiple Choices

The prediction of the date of composition of a long text could be based on the wider distribution of the estimated dates for its chunks rather than focussing solely on the most frequent one. Indeed, for dating short Arabic texts the top-*n* predictions have been counted to improve the recall ratio (Belinkov, Magidow, Romanov, Shmidman, and Koppel 2016). For dating a long text, after making predictions for all its chunks, the top-*n* most frequently predicted dates for the

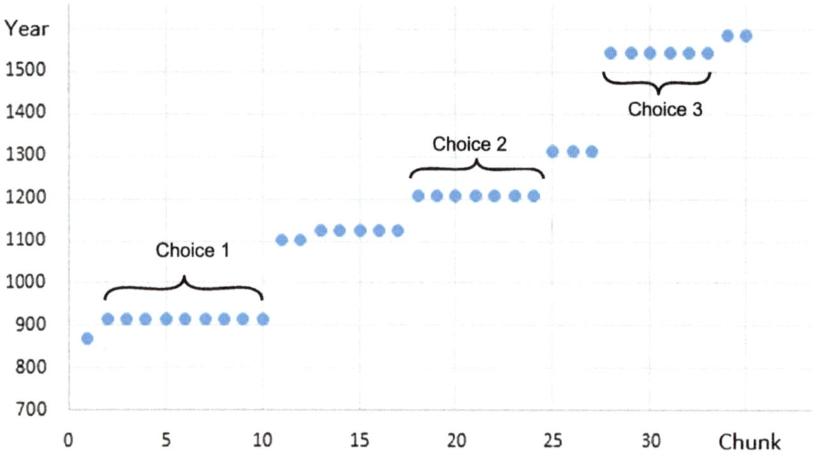

FIGURE 4.3 Chunk dating results and multiple choices for dating *Aislinge Óengusso*

chunks could be selected as possible dates for composition and revision, as illustrated by the example in Figure 4.3.

To ensure statistical significance, for the top-*n* choices we only choose a predicted date with frequency equal to or larger than the first quartile frequency. Table 4.5 reports the top-3 most frequently predicted dates for each long text. There might be fewer choices for some texts, such as **6, 11-12**, which are not long enough to support three statistically significant predictions. The correct estimations are also printed in bold font. It shows that the top-3 most frequent multiples achieved a precision of 24/63 = 38.1%, a recall ratio of 15/22 = 68.18%, and a F-measure of 48.88%, while both the precision and recall for Choice 1, which is the equivalent of the estimation in Table 4.4, is only 7/22 = 31.82%, which equals the F-measure and dating accuracy.[1]

4.2.3.2 Top-n Multiple Choices by Reinforcement and Adaptive Learning

The long texts that we are testing are believed to have been written in the period c.750-c.1500. For reasons discussed in Chapter 1, the development of the language as represented in texts during such a long period is unlikely to be linear. Dialects are a largely unknown quantity for the medieval period, although they must have existed. Certain dialects would have preserved various archaic features which in other dialects would have long been replaced

1 Compare a recall ratio of 71.14% for Arabic texts in Belinkov, Magidow, Romanov, Shmidman, and Koppel (2016) 50. Note, however, that texts are there assigned to century-long buckets, so each predicted date belongs to a different century: the top three choices, therefore, cover 300 years, whereas here overlapping and non-contiguous results are permitted.

TABLE 4.5 Top-3 most frequently predicted dates as multiple choices

	Text	Given date	Choice 1 ±50	Choice 2 ±50	Choice 3 ±50
1	Táin Bó Fraích	750-800	1208	914	1124
2	Aislinge Óengusso	750-800	914	1208	1544
3	Bethu Brigte	800-850	914	1166	1124
4	Treatise on the Psalter	800-850	1208	914	1523
5	Monastery of Tallaght	831-840	1208	914	1229
6	Echtra Láegaire	850-900	1124	**914**	
7	Fingal Rónáin	900-950	1208	**914**	1523
8	Saltair na Rann	950-988	**914**	1208	872
9	Betha Adamnáin	961-1000	1523	1124	1544
10	Aided Nath Í	1050-1100	1208	1313	**1103**
11	Genemain Áeda Sláine	1050-1100	1208	**1124**	
12	Tucait Indarba na nDessi	1050-1100	1208	1313	
13	Aided Guill	1100-1160	**1208**	**1124**	914
14	Cogadh Gaedel	1103-1170	**1208**	**1124**	**1103**
15	Cath Catharda	1140-1170	1229	**1208**	**1124**
16	Cath Ruis na Ríg	1150-1166	**1208**	**1124**	1313
17	Bórama	1151-1181	**1208**	**1124**	**1103**
18	Acallamh na Senórach	1200-1225	**1208**	1523	**1229**
19	Cath Maige Léna	1250-1325	**1229**	1523	**1208**
20	Caithréim	1330-1360	1544	1229	**1313**
21	Guy of Berwick	1452-1500	1229	1208	**1418**
22	Maundeville	1475	1229	**1523**	1208

by more innovative features (see 1.7.2). Particular scribes or schools may have been very conservative in their use of language or have introduced deliberate archaisms, and they may have attempted to reproduce prestige styles of writing. Conversely, some scribes appear to have been more innovative. Moreover, there are clear differences in genre between the training corpus of annals and the long query texts which may make a lot of short training texts irrelevant for dating a long text. The annals are, particularly in the early medieval period, brief accounts of current events focussed on a small number of topics such as the deaths of prestigious individuals or battles, whereas the long texts we are considering may include dialogue, a wider variety of tenses, considerably more adjectives and lengthy descriptive passages, poems and a much greater diversity of theme and material.

We, therefore, propose in Algorithm 4.2 a method to improve the top-*n* multiple choices by means of reinforcement and adaptive machine learning. Reinforcement learning (Kaelbling et al., 1996) is an area of machine learning, in-

ALGORITHM 4.2 Improving the multiple choices by reinforcement and adaptive learning

---

Input: A large training corpus FTC_0 of short texts that covers a long period, and a corpus L of a few long narrative texts.

Output: A set of possibly biased dates $\{t_1, t_2, t_3, \ldots\}$, and n multiple dating choices for each long text.

Steps:

1. Train a dating model M_0 of classification with any solutions described in Section 2.4 on FTC_0;
2. **For** each long text in L, cut it into chunks of at least 20 words or independent sentences of 20 plus words;
3. Date the chunks by using the trained model M_0, and add to the set B of possible biases top-n most frequently predicted dates for chunks of the long text;
4. **End for;**
5. Select from B the m dates with largest frequencies as possibly biased dates $\{t_1, t_2, t_3, \ldots\}$. We can set $m \geq 2n$ such that the top-n most frequently predicted dates for a long text may have retrieved some biases;
6. **For** each long text l in L:
7. **For** each possibly biased date t_i, which belongs to l's top-n most frequently predicted dates by Step 3:
8. Remove any short text from FTC_0 with time stamp t such that $t \geq t_i$, achieve $FTC_{<i}$, train a classifying model $M_{<i}$ on $FTC_{<i}$, date chunks of the long text by $M_{<i}$, and add the most frequently predicted date into the candidate choice set C;
9. Remove any short text from FTC_0 with time stamp t such that $t \leq t_i$, achieve $FTC_{>i}$, train a classifying model $M_{>i}$ on $FTC_{>i}$, date chunks of the long text by $M_{>i}$, and add the most frequently predicted date into the candidate choice set C;
10. **End for;**
11. Select from C top-n most frequently predicted dates as multiple dating choices for the long text;
12. **End for.**

---

spired by behaviourist psychology, concerned with how an algorithm or model ought to take actions in an environment so as to maximise some notion of cumulative reward. Adaptive learning for computer science is also called domain adaptation (Ben-David et al., 2010), which is a field associated with machine learning and transfer learning. This scenario arises when we aim at learning from a source data distribution a well performing model for a different (but related) target data distribution.

This procedure to improve the top-n multiple choices actually selects relevant short training texts using our dating method to detect possible dating biases in the trained model. Our theoretical assumption consists of two points: Firstly, the most frequently predicted date can either be correct or a biased

TABLE 4.6 Possibly biased dates

Frequency	Biased date
18	1208
10	1124
9	914
7	1229
6	1523
4	1313

date due to stylistic/genre differences, if the learned dating model has reasonably captured enough characteristics of the temporal distribution for all the training texts (corresponding to Step 5 in Algorithm 4.2); Secondly, only the training corpus either earlier than or later than a biased date is relevant and compatible for dating the long text (corresponding to Steps 8 and 9 in Algorithm 4.2). The reinforcement part of the procedure consists of Steps 1-5, which learns online a set of possible biases, and the adaptive part consists of Steps 8-9, which belongs to the reweighting method for domain adaptation and gives 0 weightings to short training texts considered irrelevant.

We again applied the FTI model of $\delta = 50$ (See Table 4.1) to Algorithm 4.2 to get improved top-n multiple choices for dating the 22 test documents (See Table 4.3). We set $n = 3$ such that the possibly biased dates could be gathered from Table 4.5 by sorting the multiples' frequencies. The $m = 6$ most possibly biased dates and corresponding frequencies are listed in Table 4.6. This corresponds to the reinforcement part, i.e. Step 1-5 of Algorithm 4.2.

After applying the adaptive part of Step 8-9 in Algorithm 4.2 for each test document, we got the improved top-3 multiple dating choices as listed in Table 4.7, where the correct estimations are again printed in bold font. It shows that the improved top-3 multiples achieved a precision of 26/64 = 40.63%, a recall ratio of 17/22 = 77.27% and a F-measure of 53.26%, which significantly outperformed the baseline results in Table 4.5 with a single-tailed pairwise t-test p value of 0.04263

Figure 4.4 illustrates an example of how we have estimated the composition date of a long medieval Irish text (*Aislinge Óengusso* here) by providing multiple choices via Step 7-11 of the procedure in Algorithm 4.2. The three most frequently predicted dates, namely 914, 1208 and 1544 (see Table 4.5), by the full dating model M_0 (Step 3 in Algorithm 4.2) are all selected as possibly biased dates (see Table 4.6). Removing the possible biases could be conducted by two complementary ways of cutting the training corpus of short texts. For

TABLE 4.7 Improved top-3 multiple dating choices

	Text	Given date	Choice 1 ±50	Choice 2 ±50	Choice 3 ±50
1	Táin Bó Fraích	750-800	1208|61	914|42	851|42
2	Aislinge Óengusso	750-800	1544|16	872|15	1124|15
3	Bethu Brigte	800-850	914|84	1166|59	**851|44**
4	Treatise on the Psalter	800-850	**872|38**	1208|33	914|23
5	Monastery of Tallaght	831-840	1313|83	1208|77	**851|62**
6	Echtra Láegaire	850-900	1208|7	**914|5**	
7	Fingal Rónáin	900-950	1544|43	**851|21**	1523|18
8	Saltair na Rann	950-988	**914|313**	872|301	1313|252
9	Betha Adamnáin	961-1000	1544|51	1103|31	1124|20
10	Aided Nath Í	1050-1100	**1019|19**	1313|18	1208|14
11	Genemain Áeda Sláine	1050-1100	**1124|6**	1313|3	**1103|3**
12	Tucait Indarba na nDessi	1050-1100	1523|4	**1124|4**	
13	Aided Guill	1100-1160	***1103|61***	**1208|52**	***1124|52***
14	Cogadh Gaedel	1103-1170	***1103|39***	**1208|31**	914|27
15	Cath Catharda	1140-1170	1229|1091	**1103|931**	**1208|851**
16	Cath Ruis na Ríg	1150-1166	**1103|112**	**1208|90**	**1124|64**
17	Bórama	1151-1181	**1103|202**	**1208|185**	1019|157
18	Acallamh na Senórach	1200-1225	1544|2232	***1208|1347***	1523|983
19	Cath Maige Léna	1250-1325	1544|533	**1208|465**	**1229|242**
20	Caithréim	1330-1360	1208|1055	1544|441	1229|384
21	Guy of Berwick	1452-1500	1229|505	**1418|473**	1166|463
22	Maundeville	1475	1544|653	1208|550	1229|384

example, to remove the bias of 914, we can keep only the short texts composed either earlier than or later than 914 for training a new Classifier $M_{<i}$ or $M_{>i}$. For training $M_{<i}$, we need to keep only the training corpus earlier than 914, namely to remove those short texts composed at 914 and later (Step 8 in Algorithm 4.2). Figure 4.4(1) shows the sorted predictions of chunks in *Aislinge Óengusso*. For training $M_{>i}$, we need to keep only the training corpus later than 914, namely to remove those short texts composed at 914 and earlier (Step 9 in Algorithm 4.2), and Figure 4.4(2) shows the resulting sorted predictions. Figure 4.4(3-6) shows the sorted predictions respectively after removing the biases of 1208 and 1544. Finally, we got six dating choices for *Aislinge Óengusso*, and the top-3 multiples are 1544, 872 and 1124.

4.2.4 *Evaluation of Bias Compensation*

While there is an overall marginal improvement in performance following the offset for bias (4.2.3.2), the results are not evenly achieved and in several cas-

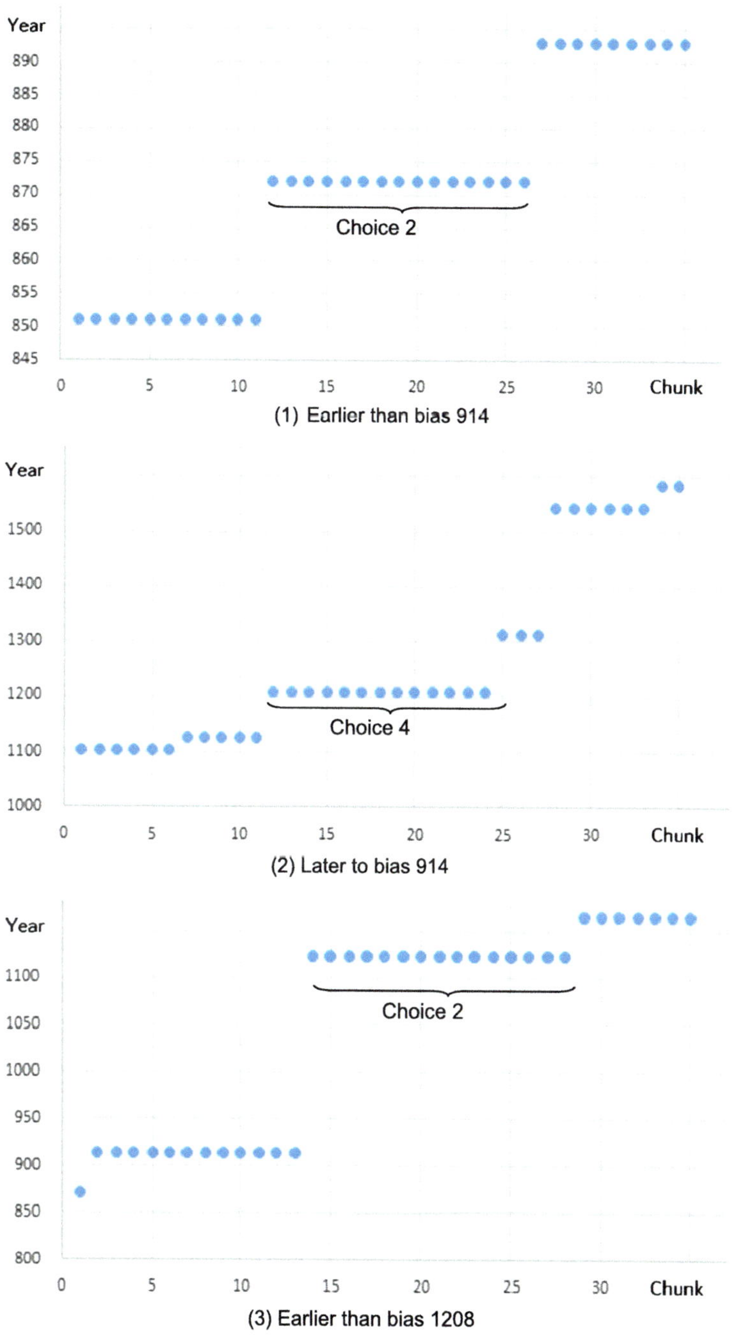

FIGURE 4.4 Example for providing improved multiple choices for dating Aislinge Óengusso

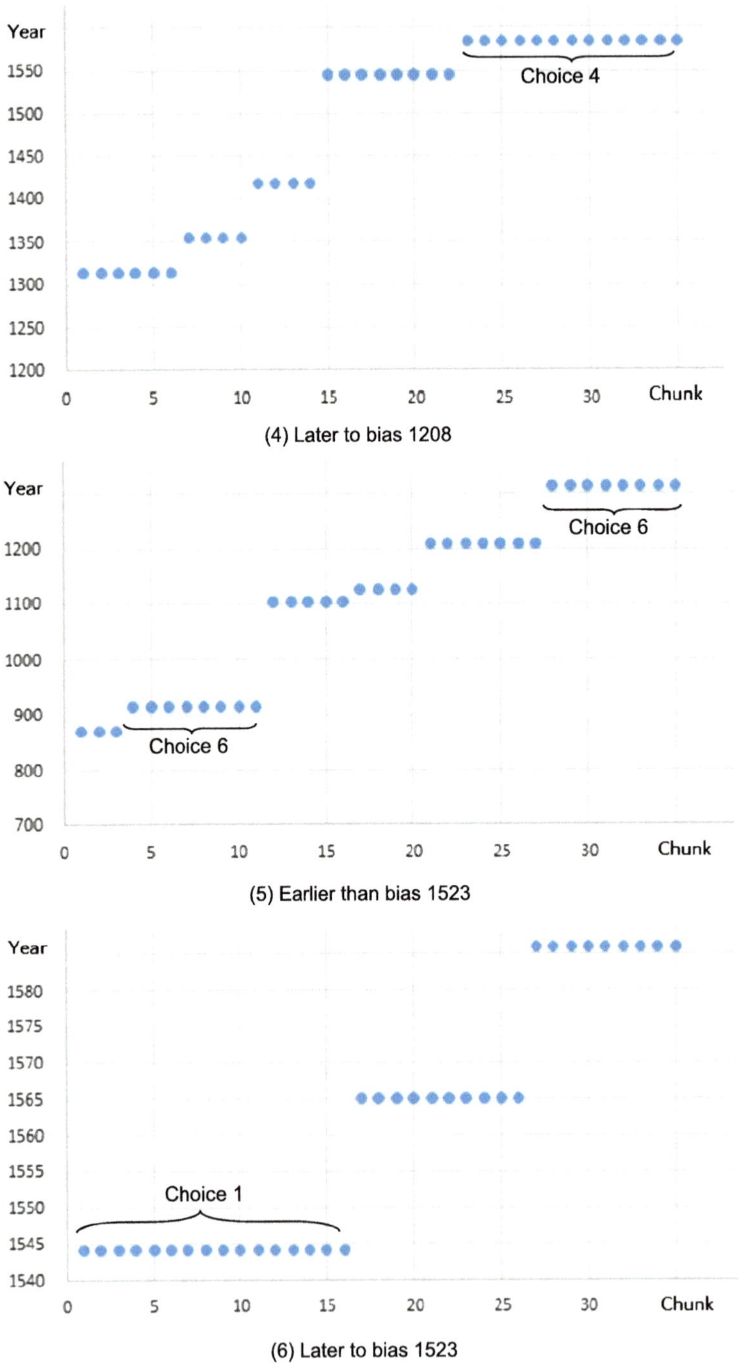

FIGURE 4.4 Example for providing improved multiple choices for dating Aislinge Óengusso (*cont.*)

es produces worse results. We see improvements in texts 3-5, all written before 900 CE and all now provided with one date within the margin of error. In general, we see that the tendency is for at least one date to move earlier, bringing it closer to the known date of composition even if it does not succeed in identifying the correct date (e.g. 1-2). However, texts written after c.900 CE often have a worse outcome. The twelfth-century texts 14 and 17 are the most severely affected, producing anomalous dates of 914 and 1019 respectively after compensation. There are some improvements in this period: text 12 produces one acceptable date after compensation, and texts 11 and 13 produce a better range of dates after compensation, including the removal of one very early date from 13. Other texts are adversely affected without being entirely corrupted. Text 7 has a correct date of 914 before compensation but after the correction is pushed back to 851 which is just inside the acceptable range of 900-950 CE. Similarly, text 10, conventionally dated 1050-1100, has a close match at 1103 but bias compensation produces an earlier date of 1019 which is within the permitted tolerance but clearly further away from the expected date.

Bias compensation, therefore, appears to affect texts of different date in different ways. While improvements are notable for the pre-900 period, the situation deteriorates considerably after that date, with four texts showing some improvement but providing less accurate results. Broadly speaking, where raw chronometric dating is unsuccessful before c.900, bias alleviation produces positive results, but where raw dating is most successful, the compensation method often incorrectly identifies biases and introduces new errors.

4.3 Establishing the Date of Composition

We have seen that texts potentially have multiple dates of revision, and we might expect these to leave some trace on the language, orthography and style of different sections of a given text. Multiple dates in our experiments may reflect distinct strata within a text although this is difficult to prove because we lack sufficient texts for which layers have been accurately dated by traditional scholarly means. We will argue below that there is a correlation between our results and the date of the earliest manuscript in which the text occurs, but first of all we will try to establish the correlation between our results and the date of composition of texts. We will begin with a more detailed assessment of the accuracy of the results in an attempt to determine where the methods described so far are most reliable and where there are weaknesses.

TABLE 4.8 Long-text dating with bias compensation ±50 years. Bold = date within dating tolerance = 50 years; bold italic = within the given date range

	Text	Given date	Baseline top 3			Unbiased top 3		
			D1	D2	D3	D1	D2	D3
1	Táin Bó Fraích	750-800	914	1124	1208	851	914	1208
2	Aislinge Óengusso	750-800	914	1208	1544	872	1124	1544
3	Bethu Brigte	800-850	914	1124	1166	**851**	914	1166
4	Treatise on the Psalter	800-850	914	1208	1523	**872**	914	1208
5	Monastery of Tallaght	831-840	914	1208	1229	**851**	1208	1313
6	Echtra Láegaire	850-900	**914**	1124		**914**	1208	
7	Fingal Rónáin	900-950	***914***	1208	1523	**851**	1523	1544
8	Saltair na Rann	950-988	872	**914**	1208	872	**914**	1313
9	Betha Adamnáin	961-1000	1124	1523	1544	1103	1124	1544
10	Aided Nath Í	1050-1100	**1103**	1187	1208	**1019**	1208	1313
11	Genemain Áeda Sláine	1050-1100	**1124**	1208		**1103**	**1124**	1313
12	Indarba na nDessi	1050-1100	1208	1313		**1124**	1523	
13	Aided Guill	1100-1160	914	***1124***	**1208**	***1103***	***1124***	**1208**
14	Cogadh Gaedel	1103-1170	***1103***	***1124***	**1208**	914	***1103***	**1208**
15	Cath Catharda	1140-1170	**1124**	**1208**	1229	**1103**	**1208**	1229
16	Cath Ruis na Ríg	1150-1166	**1124**	**1208**	1313	**1103**	**1124**	**1208**
17	Bórama	1151-1181	**1103**	**1124**	**1208**	1019	**1103**	**1208**
18	Acallamh na Senórach	1200-1225	***1208***	**1229**	1523	***1208***	1544	1523
19	Cath Maige Léna	1250-1325	**1208**	**1229**	1523	**1208**	**1229**	1544
20	Caithréim	1330-1360	1229	**1313**	1544	1208	1229	1544
21	Guy of Berwick	1452-1500	1208	1229	**1418**	1166	1229	**1418**
22	Maundeville	1475	1208	1229	**1523**	1208	1229	1544

4.3.1 *Correlation between the Results and the Accepted Date of Composition*

The bias compensation experiments show that, on the whole, the compensation routine produces earlier dates than the uncompensated method, with beneficial results for the dates of texts written before 900 CE but negative or neutral for texts composed after that date. For that reason, we provide both sets of dates here for analysis but we will largely ignore the compensated dates except for the pre-900 texts. Texts are sorted according to their accepted date of composition as before, but for ease of discussion the results, here labelled D1, D2 and D3, are presented in chronological order rather than in the order in which they are produced by the algorithm (as in Table 4.7).

Of the three dates supplied for each text, we see that the best-fit date is usually the earliest of the three. Table 4.8 shows that for 10 out of the 22 texts

(45.45%), the earliest predicted raw date is correct to within 50 years, although in a few cases a slightly later date may provide a better fit with the date proposed by scholars. In those examples in which the earliest candidate date (D1) is not correct, the second candidate date (D2) proves to be correct in just three cases; the third choice (D3) provides correct dates on only two occasions if it has not already been established by either D1 or D2. As D1 is most likely to represent the date of composition, we will focus on that in the following analysis.

The method is clearly inaccurate for texts written before c.850 (1-5), with all these texts being dated to 914. The training corpus can achieve high degrees of accuracy in this period (71.93% for 750-799; see Figure 4.2) but clearly this is not transferable to longer, non-annalistic texts such as those being considered here. It may be that the corpus for this period is not sufficiently large or representative of the language more generally. The early annals are particularly formulaic and limited in scope, and are especially prone to modernisation and revision, so it may not be possible to derive sufficient linguistic features from it for our purposes. At the very least, we can state that the model derived from the annals is not compatible with narrative texts for this period. Even with bias compensation, we cannot achieve a date any earlier than 851, suggesting that the most serious weakness in our model stretches back from c.850. Nevertheless, it is noteworthy that no Old Irish (c.700-c.900) text is given a D1 later than 914, so that the model is clearly good enough to pick up on the Old Irish material, although this is not an unambiguous marker of an Old Irish text as tenth-century texts can also exhibit this D1 (7 and cf. 8, discussed below).

There is also a problem with texts written after 1300. We have five Early Modern (c.1200-c.1650) texts (18-22). The first two are dated correctly, each producing two dates within the acceptable range. The later three texts produce a correct date only at D2 (20) or D3 (21-22), and bias compensation only confuses the matter further. Unfortunately, although at least one correct date is ascertained for each of these three texts, they do not do so in a predictable way and are not precisely datable by this method. Having said that, the method does successfully distinguish Early Modern texts from older ones: no text written after 1200 is dated before 1208 and all proposed dates lie within the Early Modern period. We might possibly distinguish between the thirteenth-century texts (18-19) and the later texts as the former are marked by two dates close together in the early 1200s but we shall see (4.3.2) that a similar profile is also attached to a later Early Modern text in a separate trial.

For the Middle Irish period (c.900-c.1200), D1 correctly predicts the date of a text in 7 out of 11 cases (63.64%), and a further two texts are correctly dated by D2 (8, 13). D3 does not produce any correct dates if they have not been already determined by D1 or D2. The grouping of dates for texts 13-19 is particularly marked – two or more dates for each of these texts fall within the acceptable range – indicating the robustness of the model for this period. It is surely significant that all these are found primarily in manuscripts of the late-11th or 12th centuries, that is, close to their date of composition, so there can have been little room for later revision and modernisation. It will be noticed that this group of texts also produces some of the most precise dates. Texts 7, 13 and 14 are all dated squarely within the range suggested by scholars, and the central dates for 10, 11 and 15 are placed within 25 years of the terminal date of composition by D1. In other words, six of the seven correct D1 dates for this period are within 25 years of the range suggested by scholars. Coupled with the limited divergence between D1, D2 and D3 for the twelfth century, this suggests a highly robust model.

The model is not uniformly predictive, however. Two Middle-Irish texts (9, 12) do not produce a correct date at all, and a further two (8, 13) produce an incorrect D1. Text 12 is very short (<250 words) and its incorrect dating may be partially related to this. Text 9 has been dated to the second half of the tenth century, yet our model shows no hint of such an early date. Although the conventional dating is primarily based on internal evidence, there is also sufficient linguistic evidence to support a tenth-century date of composition. However, it is clear also that the text was much modernised at a later period and we might postulate that the algorithm has picked up the later layers of revision but was unable to detect the smaller proportion of tenth-century features. Text 8 is also incorrectly dated by D1, although on this occasion a correct date is supplied by D2. It is true that one scholar would place its composition around 870 (see Appendix), which matches nearly perfectly with D1, but the consensus remains that it belongs to the second half of the tenth century. The fact that it is a metrical text in its entirety (the only such text in our corpus), composed on a biblical theme, might have something to do with the earlier than expected dating but it is likely that weaknesses in the training data have contributed to the early dates for both of these tenth-century texts.

There appear to be weaknesses in the model for the tenth and eleventh centuries that impact upon our ability to date texts from this period with greater consistency. It is noteworthy that not a single text is placed in the entire period between 914 and 1103. In the training set, the period 850-999 has a lower than average accuracy and plummets to 22.78% in the latter half of the tenth century (see Figure 4.2 above). We may postulate, therefore, that there are insufficient diagnostic features to produce a completely robust model for the tenth century. Some weaknesses may extend beyond that into the eleventh century. We have no texts for the first half of that century in this test but those assigned by scholars to the period 1050-1100 (**10-12**) are dated, at the earliest, to 1103 ± 50. While this falls neatly within the tolerance, the date for text **11** (1124) fits a little less comfortably. Text **12** misses the target completely as we have seen. The process of bias reduction produces considerably better results for these three texts and so its effectiveness might be extended into the eleventh century (but see text 29 in Table 4.9).

4.3.2 *Extending the Range of Texts*

Following the previous experiment, we conducted the same test on another set of texts, many of which have a more complicated textual history including texts that have a long period of transmission and show signs of modernisation, and texts that may have multiple strata. The results are presented, sorted in chronological order by text, in Table 4.9.

Overall, the earliest date before bias compensation proves correct in six out of fourteen cases (42.86%). All but one of the correct examples lie in the period c.900-c.1300 CE, so that 50% (5/10) are correctly dated within this zone, still somewhat lower than the 63.64% in the first batch. This batch confirms the conclusion drawn from the first experiment that the unadjusted model struggles to cope with texts composed before c.1000 CE with only two correct dates for texts **23-28**. Text **28** is dated within the tolerance but, as with the first

TABLE 4.9 Long-text dating with bias compensation ±50 years. Bold = date within dating tolerance = 50 years; bold italic = within the given date range

	Text	Given date	Baseline top 3			Unbiased top 3		
			D1	D2	D3	D1	D2	D3
23	Tochmarc Emire A	700-800	914			851	1124	
24	SMMD	750-850	1103	1124	1208	914	1103	1124
25	Mesca Ulad A	800-900	**914**	1124	1208	**914**	1208	1229
26	Táin A	800-900	1103	1124	1208	1019	1103	1208
27	Derbforgaill	900-1000	1103	1124	1208	***914***	1208	1229
28	Cath Almhaine	900-1000	**1019**	1124	1229	**1019**	1229	1313
29	Mac Conglinne	1075-1100	**1103**	**1124**	1208	1019	**1103**	1208
30	Mesca Ulad B	1100-1150	914	***1124***	1208	872	***1103***	1208
31	Táin B	1100-1150	***1124***	1208	1523	***1103***	1208	1544
32	Bruiden Da Choca	1100-1150	914	***1124***		914	***1124***	1229
33	Betha Colmáin	1130-1180	**1208**	1250	1523	**1187**	**1208**	1544
34	Merugud Ulix	1175-1225	***1208***	**1229**	1523	***1208***	**1229**	1544
35	Regimen na Sláinte	1400-1450	1208	1229	1544	1187	1208	***1418***
36	De Dosibus	1459	1229	**1418**	1586	1208	**1418**	1586

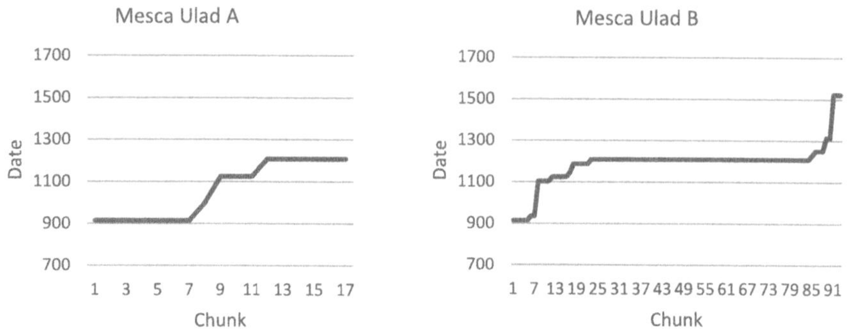

FIGURE 4.5 Uncorrected datings for Mesca Ulad A and Mesca Ulad B (texts 25 and 30)

batch, at the higher end of the range rather than comfortably within it. After c.1075 CE (29-34) until the middle of the thirteenth century, dating becomes more consistent with at least one correct prediction at D1 or D2 for all texts in this group.

The D1 produced in two texts written before the Early Modern period (30, 32) is too early: this is roughly comparable to three cases in the larger first batch. Text 30 is a complex text as it is a twelfth-century revision of text 25. It is possible, therefore, that the D1 of 914 represents this early stratum in the later text. We should note that, despite the similarity in the headline results for these two versions of the same text, there is a considerable difference in the quantity of chunks assigned the early date in the two versions, with 914 much better represented in the early version (Figure 4.5):

It is clear that the 914 dating for Mesca Ulad B is poorly represented in the results: in fact, the date of 1124 is so dominant that any D2 or D3 that is subsequently selected is statistically insignificant.

No such explanation can be offered for text 32 which also produces an unexpected early date at D1. There was an older version, probably at least as old as the tenth century, but it is not thought that the extant version is based on it. The tale does contain occasional quotations from earlier tracts and quite a number of rhetorical compositions which are based on older material but the latter were removed before testing. Figure 4.6 shows that it contains a much higher proportion of material dated to 914 than is found in 30 and so the dating is not easily dismissed and it is noteworthy that bias compensation does not remove the anomalous date. It is true that this graph shows that the balance of dates for each chunk favours a twelfth-century date: 63 out of 104 chunks (60.58%) are dated between 1124 and 1166. A more sophisticated approach, therefore, might amalgamate these results before attempting to produce final dates.

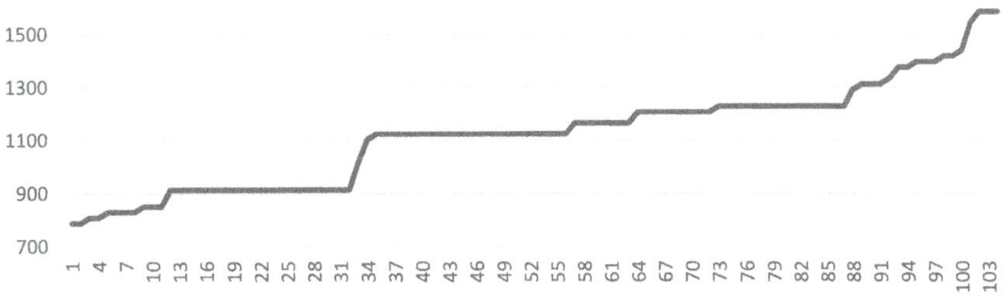

FIGURE 4.6 Uncorrected datings for Bruiden Da Choca (32)

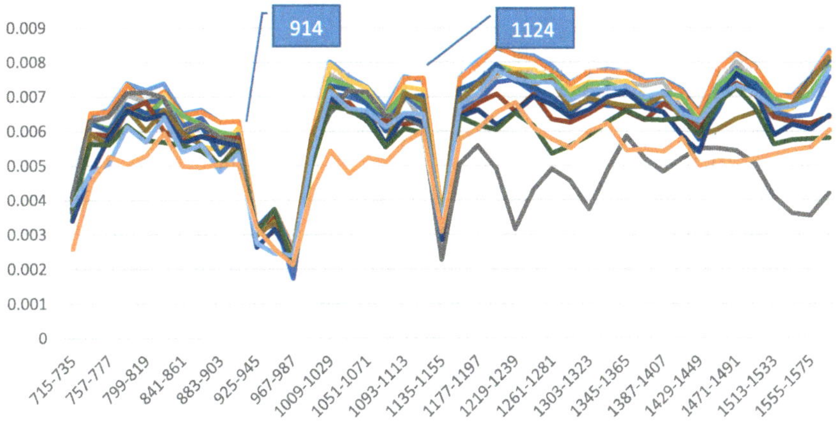

FIGURE 4.7 Top dating features in Bruiden Da Choca (32) over time

Nevertheless, the data still appears to suggest a date of 914 ± 50 years for at least a sizeable portion of the text. We suggest that this reflects a further weakness in the data model. Figure 4.7 shows the distribution over time of the most significant features in our model used to produce the dating for this text: the pattern is similar for the top 50 features but we show only the top 15 features for the sake of clarity. It shows that the frequency of each of the top features behaves similarly across almost the entire range but that there are two significant drops just after 914 and after 1124. As our dating algorithm compares the before and after periods, the drop may be the most significant pattern here producing an equivalence between the two dates that causes them to be confused.

The 'before and after' is a key innovation in our algorithm, enabling us to significantly improve the overall accuracy of the method, but here it seems to have a detrimental effect on the performance. The troughs do not reflect a real distinction in the data but rather gaps in our records. The sudden drop after 1124 (= 1114-1134) occurs during the period 1135-1155 during which we have a large lacuna in our training data. Similarly, but less dramatically, the drop after

914 reflects the poorer collection of annal entries at this time. If we were to amend these gaps, either by supplementing the training set with another set of annals, or by filling the gap digitally, these anomalies may well disappear.

Bias compensation for this batch produces slightly better results in general but more mixed results when we look at the specifics. Just 11 (28.21%) of the 39 dates generated are correct before compensation, rising to 13 (31.71%) after compensation. We see improvements in the dating of texts **27**, **33** and **35**, but deterioration in that of **29** which loses one good date and produces an anomalous D1. Therefore, there are improvements in the dating of one text in each of the periods up to 1000 CE (**27**), 1000-1200 CE (**33**) and after 1200 CE (**35**), but a worsening of the dating of a text (**29**) that lies in the middle period which has been shown to be the most robust part of the model in 4.3.1.

4.3.3 *Conclusion*

Tests on both sets of texts suggests that the model produced from the annals can be applied to long narrative texts of various genres. The raw chronometric results clearly distinguish between Old Irish, later Middle Irish and Early Modern Irish texts. Old Irish texts are generally dated to 914 – to an extent that this is nearly a marker of an Old Irish text – but bias compensation enables us to date some of these more accurately within the ninth century although not before that. Later Middle Irish texts are the most accurately dated, and where they appear in near-contemporary manuscripts we witness close clustering of two or more suggested dates. Bias compensation produces slightly worse results for this period: there are some improvements for the eleventh century but degradation elsewhere. The model can successfully distinguish Early Modern texts from late Middle Irish ones but there is little evidence for the capacity to more accurately date texts within the Early Modern period.

The current method of date selection, choosing simply the three most frequently occurring dates among the figures generated for each chunk, is generally effective but creates some anomalies. We saw from Mesca Ulad (see Figure 4.5) that the two versions produce similar profiles if we only look at the top three dates, but a closer examination of the broader profile shows that they are, in fact, clearly distinguished from each other in chronological terms. We may note in particular that it may be desirable to consider closely aligned dates as a single series so as to give due weight them. Treating them as discrete dates, as we currently do, can lead to greater emphasis being put on one date which happens to be coherent rather than on a broader series of dates that lie very close to one another. A further problem arises from gaps in our training data leading to the confusion of the dates 914 and 1124, as well as some less serious distortion in twelfth-century dates. This could be addressed by supplementing the training data with additional material covering the lacunae, or by compensating for the gaps algorithmically.

4.4 Transmission and Manuscript Dates

We have already suggested that some of the later dates supplied by the experiment may point towards later transmission. Table 4.10 below shows the texts analysed in the previous section but here they are sorted according to the date of the earliest manuscript in which they appear. Predicted dates that are less than 50 years from the date of the manuscript, that is, within the tolerance, are shown in blue. Dates that are more than 50 years after the date of the manuscript are shown in grey. As the last four texts occur in manuscripts that were written outside the range covered by our training corpus, that is, after 1588, we will omit them from this discussion.

Only 9 of the 32 texts (28.13%) produce a date more than 50 years after the date of the manuscript (shown in grey) and of these only about three are more than a century too late. In the case of our two oldest manuscripts, the Book of the Dun Cow and Rawlinson B502, the date 1208 appears in each of the six occurrences. For texts 10 and 26, this is an acceptable date for the work of the scribe known as H, but in the other four cases we must consider the scribal work to have been completed by c.1130. The date of 1208, therefore, is approximately only 70 years too late and we may wonder whether it was adversely affected by the lacuna in the middle of the twelfth century in our training data.

Texts from the Book of Leinster are usually dated no later than the known date of the manuscript, that is, at 1208 ± 50, and might have been dated even earlier were it not for the mid-twelfth-century lacuna. Three texts, however, are placed beyond the acceptable range, as late as 1523 in two cases. This is a somewhat surprising result, indicating that the early sixteenth-century annals may bear some similarity to these twelfth-century manuscripts. We have seen (1.7.4) that some sixteenth and seventeenth-century scribes indulged in a form of archaism which may be producing a false signal here, although we currently have no method for determining whether this is true, and it is noteworthy that it does not impinge more widely on the dating of texts from this manuscript. Further investigation would be required to establish what it is about the annals in the century around 1523 that prompts our algorithm to supply that date for these Book of Leinster texts. Only two other texts (from the Book of Ballymote and Harley 546) produce a date later than the date of the manuscript, in both cases about a century too late. In total, therefore, only

TABLE 4.10 Texts sorted by date of manuscript

	Text	Baseline top 3			Earliest manuscript(s)	Date of manuscript(s)
		D1	D2	D3		
25	Mesca Ulad A	**914**	1124	1208	Dun Cow (M)	11c.^{ex}/12c.^{i}
11	Genemain Áeda Sláine	**1124**	1208		Dun Cow (M)	11c.^{ex}/12c.^{i}
10	Aided Nath Í	**1103**	1187	1208	Dun Cow (M/H)	11c.^{ex}/12c.
26	Táin A	1103	1124	1208	Dun Cow (M/H)/ Yellow Book of Lecan	11c.^{ex}/12c./14c.
8	Saltair na Rann	872	**914**	1208	Rawl. B 502	12c.^{1}
12	Indarba na nDessi	1208	1313		Rawl. B 502	12c.^{1}
6	Echtra Láegaire	**914**	1124		Book of Leinster	12c.^{2}
1	Táin Bó Fraích	914	1124	1208	Book of Leinster	12c.^{2}
13	Aided Guill	914	***1124***	**1208**	Book of Leinster	12c.^{2}
14	Cogadh Gaedel	***1103***	***1124***	**1208**	Book of Leinster	12c.^{2}
17	Bórama	**1103**	**1124**	**1208**	Book of Leinster	12c.^{2}
24	SMMD	1103	1124	1208	Book of Leinster	12c.^{2}
27	Derbforgaill	1103	1124	1208	Book of Leinster	12c.^{2}
30	Mesca Ulad B	914	***1124***	1208	Book of Leinster	12c.^{2}
16	Cath Ruis na Ríg	**1124**	**1208**	1313	Book of Leinster	12c.^{2}
7	Fingal Rónáin	***914***	1208	1523	Book of Leinster	12c.^{2}
31	Táin B	***1124***	1208	1523	Book of Leinster	12c.^{2}
34	Merugud Ulix	**1208**	1229	1523	Book of Ballymote	14c.^{1}
29	Mac Conglinne	**1103**	**1124**	1208	Speckled Book	15c.^{i}
33	Betha Colmáin	**1208**	1250	1523	Rennes 598	15c.
35	Regimen na Sláinte	**1208**	1229	1544	RIA 24 P 26	15c.
18	Acallamh na Senórach	**1208**	1229	1523	Book of Lismore etc.	15c.
21	Guy of Berwick	1208	1229	**1418**	Mac an Leagha	15c.^{2}
5	Monastery of Tallaght	914	1208	1229	RIA 3 B 23	15c.^{2}
36	De Dosibus	**1229**	1418	1586	Harley 546	15c. (?)
3	Bethu Brigte	914	1124	1166	Rawl. B.512	15c./16c.
23	Tochmarc Emire A	914			Rawl. B.512	15c./16c.
4	Treatise on the Psalter	914	1208	1523	Rawl. B.512/ Harl. 5280	15c./16c.
22	Maundeville	1208	1229	**1523**	Rennes 598 / Eg. 1781	15c.^{ex} /16c.^{ex}
2	Aislinge Óengusso	914	1208	1544	Eg. 1782	15c.^{i}/16c.
15	Cath Catharda	**1124**	**1208**	1229	various	15c./17c.
19	Cath Maige Léna	**1208**	1229	1523	Franciscan A/ Phillipps' 10266	16c.
32	Bruiden Da Choca	914	***1124***		H.3.18	16c./17c.
20	Caithréim	**1229**	1313	1544	23 Q 16/ H.1.18	16c./18c.
9	Betha Adamnáin	**1124**	1523	1544	Brus. 4190-4200	17c.
28	Cath Almhaine	**1019**	1124	1229	Brus. 5301-20	17c.

about three texts (**12**, **7**, **31**) are dated much more than a century after their earliest manuscript, and the brevity of the first of these may be partially responsible for the error.

For a significant number of texts, the latest date precedes the date of transcription by quite some margin. Rawl. B.512, for example, is a fifteenth/sixteenth century manuscript which contains three texts, two of which are dated no later than 1166 (**3**, **23**). Although all three texts are thought to belong to the ninth century, our results indicate that the scribe of at least these two was conservative in his transcription.

4.5 Focussed Dating Predictions

The previous experiments have dated the texts with a tolerance of ±50 years, producing date ranges of 101 years (the central year ±50). It should be possible to narrow this range to indicate approximately where in that 101-year period a text belongs. The confidence in the resulting date must be considerably less than for longer periods – no dating method derived from linguistic cues could produce results with that degree of accuracy – but it should indicate approximately at which part of a longer range a text may be situated. Therefore, we subsequently ran the algorithm with a 10-year tolerance but only permitting responses within the 101-year period determined by the previous step. This two-stage process is more secure than a simple one-step 10-year dating which, due to the lack of robustness at that scale would likely produce many anomalous results. The results are shown in Tables 4.11 and 4.12 and Figure 4.8.

As the focussing is confined by the dates achieved already in the previous stage, there is little impact on major errors in our dating. If there is a problem with the broader date, the refinement cannot compensate for that and merely shifts the suggested date around within that period by a maximum of approximately fifty years. The focussed date, therefore, is invalid if the original longer-term date range is incorrect to start with.

Generally, the refined granularity tends to shift proposed dates closer to those established by scholars in the field. We may disregard the Old and Early Modern Irish texts in Table 4.11 as the chronometrics for these periods has proved unreliable even at ±50 years so variation within those epochs after focussing is unlikely to tell us anything useful. For Middle Irish (texts **11**-**29**), we may disregard those texts for which an accurate date was not achieved in the ±50-year experiment. Of the remainder, nine register some improvement (texts **13**-**14**, **16**, **17**, **25**-**29**) in D1, as against two that move further away from the date suggested by its editor (**19**, **24**). Two further texts (**11**, **21**) show some

TABLE 4.11 Dates adjusted to ±10-year tolerances before bias adjustment; texts sorted by given date

		Text	Given date	Focussed prediction		
				D1	D2	D3
1	23	Tochmarc Emire I	700-800	922<-914		
2	1	Táin Bó Fraích	750-800	922<-914	1120<-1124	1208<-1208
3	2	Aislinge Óengusso	750-800	922<-914	1208<-1208	1538<-1544
4	24	SMMD	750-850	1120<-1103	1131<-1124	1197<-1208
5	4	Treatise on the Psalter	800-850	922<-914	1208<-1208	1571<-1523
6	3	Bethu Brigte	800-850	922<-914	1120<-1124	1120<-1166
7	25	Mesca Ulad-A	800-900	922<-914	1120<-1124	1208<-1208
8	26	Táin A	800-900	1098<-1103	1098<-1124	1197<-1208
9	5	Monastery of Tallaght	831-840	922<-914	1208<-1208	1208<-1229
10	6	Echtra Láegaire	850-900	**922**<-914	1120<-1124	
11	7	Fingal Rónáin	900-950	***922***<-914	1197<-1208	1516<-1523
12	27	Derbforgaill	900-1000	1120<-1103	1120<-1124	1197<-1208
13	28	Cath Almhaine	900-1000	**1010**<-1019	1131<-1124	1219<-1229
14	8	Saltair na Rann	950-988	**922**<-914	**922**<-872	1208<-1208
15	9	Betha Adamnáin	961-1000	1120<-1124	1538<-1523	1538<-1544
16	10	Aided Nath Í	1050-1100	***1098***<-1103	1208<-1187	1208<-1208
17	11	Genemain Áeda Sláine	1050-1100	***1098***<-1124	1208<-1208	
18	12	Indarba na nDessi	1050-1100	1208<-1208	1307<-1313	
19	29	Mac Conglinne	1075-1100	**1120**<-1103	**1120**<-1124	1208<-1208
20	30	Mesca Ulad-B	1100-1150	922<-914	***1120***<-1124	1208<-1208
21	31	Táin-B	1100-1150	***1120***<-1124	1208<-1208	1527<-1523
22	32	Bruiden Da Choca	1100-1150	922<-914	**1175**<-1124	
23	13	Aided Guill	1100-1160	922<-914	***1120***<-1124	**1197**<-1208
24	14	Cogadh Gaedel	1103-1170	**1098**<-1103	***1120***<-1124	**1197**<-1208
25	33	Betha Colmáin	1130-1180	**1208**<-1208	**1208**<-1250	1516<-1523
26	15	Cath Catharda	1140-1170	**1175**<-1124	1230<-1208	1230<-1229
27	16	Cath Ruis na Ríg	1150-1166	**1131**<-1124	**1197**<-1208	1318<-1313
28	17	Bórama	1151-1181	**1120**<-1103	**1120**<-1124	1208<-1208
29	34	Merugud Ulix	1175-1225	***1208***<-1208	***1208***<-1229	1516<-1523
30	18	Acallamh na Senórach	1200-1225	**1197**<-1208	**1197**<-1229	1516<-1523
31	19	Cath Maige Léna	1250-1325	**1230**<-1208	**1230**<-1229	1527<-1523
32	20	Caithréim	1330-1360	1241<-1229	**1318**<-1313	1571<-1544
33	35	Regimen na Sláinte	1400-1450	1208<-1208	1208<-1229	1538<-1544
34	21	Guy of Berwick	1452-1500	1230<-1208	1230<-1229	**1428**<-1418
35	36	De Dosibus	1459	1219<-1229	**1428**<-1418	1593<-1586
36	22	Maundeville	1475	1230<-1208	1230<-1229	**1516**<-1523

TABLE 4.12 Dates adjusted to ±10-year tolerances with bias reduction; texts sorted by given date

		Text	Given date	Focussed unbiased prediction		
				D1	D2	D3
1	23	Tochmarc Emire I	700-800	867<-851	1120<-1124	
2	1	Táin Bó Fraích	750-800	856<-851	922<-914	1208<-1208
3	2	Aislinge Óengusso	750-800	922<-872	1120<-1124	1538<-1544
4	24	SMMD	750-850	922<-914	1120<-1103	1131<-1124
5	4	Treatise on the Psalter	800-850	922<-872	922<-914	1208<-1208
6	3	Bethu Brigte	800-850	*834*<-851	922<-914	1120<-1166
7	25	Mesca Ulad-A	800-900	**922**<-914	1208<-1208	1208<-1229
8	26	Táin A	800-900	1120<-1103	1208<-1208	1516<-1544
9	5	Monastery of Tallaght	831-840	*834*<-851	1208<-1208	1307<-1313
10	6	Echtra Láegaire	850-900	**922**<-914	1197<-1208	
11	7	Fingal Rónáin	900-950	**867**<-851	1516<-1523	1516<-1544
12	27	Derbforgaill	900-1000	**922**<-914	1197<-1208	1197<-1229
13	28	Cath Almhaine	900-1000	**1010**<-1019	1219<-1229	1318<-1313
14	8	Saltair na Rann	950-988	**922**<-872	**922**<-914	1296<-1313
15	9	Betha Adamnáin	961-1000	1120<-1103	1120<-1124	1538<-1544
16	10	Aided Nath Í	1050-1100	**1010**<-1019	1208<-1208	1318<-1313
17	11	Genemain Áeda Sláine	1050-1100	*1098*<-1103	*1098*<-1124	1296<-1313
18	12	Indarba na nDessi	1050-1100	**1120**<-1124	1516<-1523	
19	29	Mac Conglinne	1075-1100	1010<-1019	**1120**<-1103	1208<-1208
20	30	Mesca Ulad-B	1100-1150	922<-872	**1120**<-1103	1208<-1208
21	31	Táin-B	1100-1150	1010<-1019	**1098**<-1103	**1197**<-1208
22	32	Bruiden Da Choca	1100-1150	922<-914	**1175**<-1124	1219<-1229
23	13	Aided Guill	1100-1160	*1120*<-1103	*1120*<-1124	1197<-1208
24	14	Cogadh Gaedel	1103-1170	922<-914	1098<-1103	1197<-1208
25	33	Betha Colmáin	1130-1180	**1208**<-1187	**1208**<-1208	1516<-1544
26	15	Cath Catharda	1140-1170	**1120**<-1103	1230<-1208	1230<-1229
27	16	Cath Ruis na Ríg	1150-1166	**1131**<-1103	**1131**<-1124	**1197**<-1208
28	17	Bórama	1151-1181	1010<-1019	**1120**<-1103	**1208**<-1208
29	34	Merugud Ulix	1175-1225	*1208*<-1208	*1208*<-1229	1516<-1544
30	18	Acallamh na Senórach	1200-1225	**1197**<-1208	1516<-1523	1516<-1544
31	19	Cath Maige Léna	1250-1325	**1230**<-1208	**1230**<-1229	1527<-1544
32	20	Caithréim	1330-1360	1241<-1208	1241<-1229	1571<-1544
33	35	Regimen na Sláinte	1400-1450	1208<-1187	1208<-1208	*1428*<-1418
34	21	Guy of Berwick	1452-1500	1197<-1166	1230<-1229	**1428**<-1418
35	36	De Dosibus	1459	1219<-1208	**1428**<-1418	1593<-1586
36	22	Maundeville	1475	1230<-1208	1230<-1229	**1516**<-1544

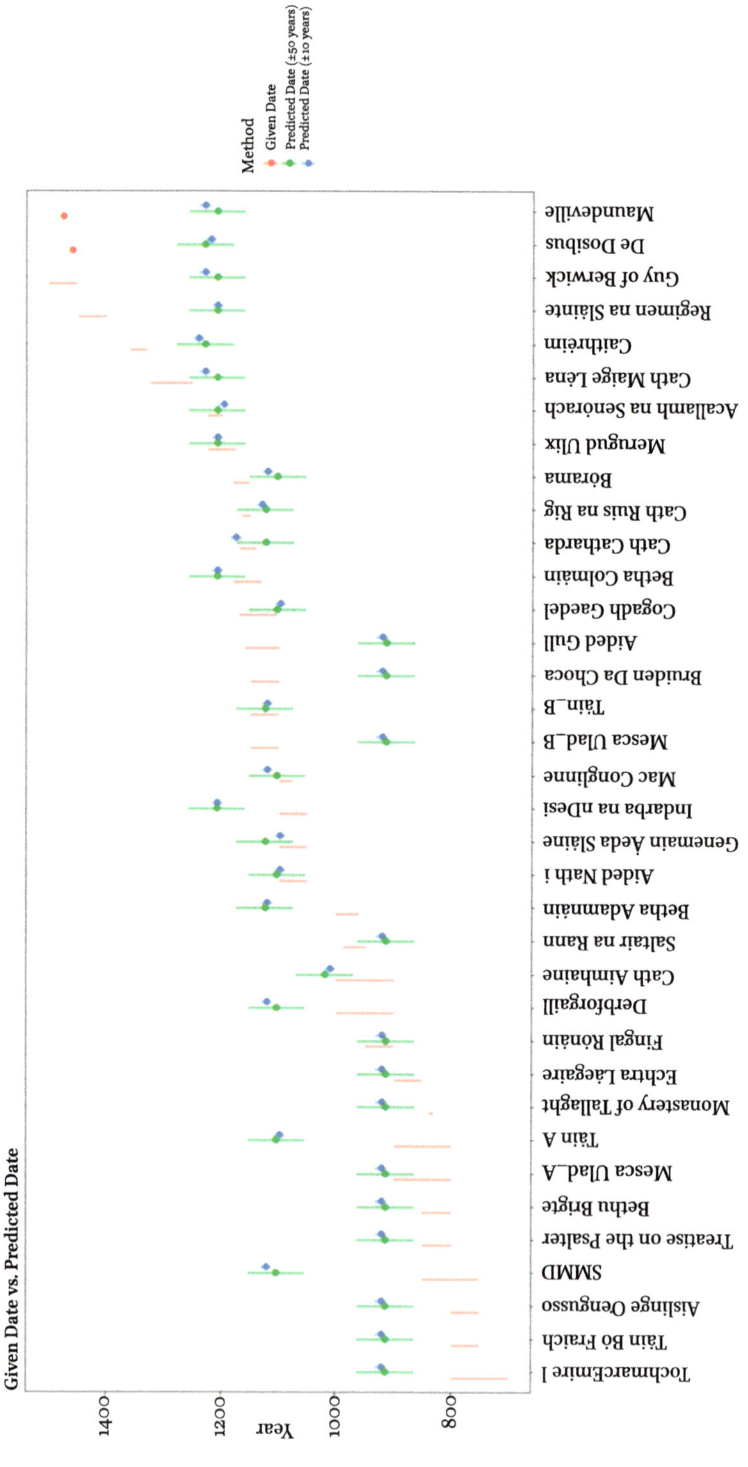

FIGURE 4.8 Dating by traditional method v. our method (without bias reduction). Texts are arranged by the conventional date. With thanks to Tom Toner for producing this graph

change but only within the timespan suggested by scholars so that we are not in a position to judge whether they are better or worse.

Focussing compensates to some extent for the lacuna in our training materials in the middle of the twelfth century as it allows texts to be placed closer to the hiatus. Text **26** flips from one side of the lacuna (1124) to the other (1175), which fits slightly better with the suggested date of 1140-1175. Text **27** is traditionally dated towards the end of the lacuna at 1150-1166. The results here include two focussed dates of 1131 (D1), which sits immediately before the gap, and 1197 (D2), both of which are closer to the expected date than the dates supplied at the 50-year tolerance. This is perhaps the pattern that we would expect to see if its actual date lay within the lacuna.

One further feature that is worth noting is that distinct dates from the previous experiment here sometimes coalesce to form a single date. This happens when two 100-year periods overlap, allowing the possibility that the same 20-year period will be suggested for both after focussing. Thus, text **29** produces a focussed date of 1208 at D1 and D2, strongly suggesting that this is a good approximation of its actual date. For text **28**, the original D1 and D2 of 1103 and 1124 combine to give a focussed date of 1120 in both positions. Goverts (2014) has suggested that it was composed 1151-1181, thus falling in or just after the twelfth-century lacuna, so that the focussed 1120 is perhaps the best approximation that our algorithm could make. Text **19** shows a focussed date of 1120 at D1 and D2 for which its editor had suggested a date in the last quarter of the eleventh century, although he does not rule out a 'very early' twelfth-century date (Jackson 1990: xxiii). We have counted this here as a worse result than the unfocussed attempt, but the double dating at 1120 suggests a strong correlation with the annals at this period that cannot easily be dismissed. Text **14** was dated at the coarser granularity at 872 and 914 for D1 and D2, the earlier of which is almost certainly too early. The date that we have used for testing is 950-988 where the upper limit is supplied by verses which, it is thought, were appended to the poem no earlier than 988 (see Appendix A). Beyond that, the poem remains insecurely dated. We may note that Carney argued that it was a century older than the more generally accepted dating. The focussed dating renders both D1 and D2 as 922, adding weight to the possibility that it was composed at the end of the Old Irish and into the beginning of the Middle Irish period.

We saw in 4.2.3.2 that reinforcement and adaptive learning could be used to improve the results for Old Irish texts, although with very mixed results for later periods. Table 4.12 shows the results of focussing combined with bias reduction at described in 4.2.3.2. For Old Irish texts (**1-10**), focussing does little to improve the results obtained at ±50 years and generally makes things worse.

Overall, D1 is moved further away from the accepted date for 8 out of the 10 texts, and we see improvements only in two cases (6, 9), although both of these show results moving exactly into the traditional date ranges. If we count only those texts which are correctly dated within a tolerance of ±50 years, the same two texts figure here as improved and the number of texts whose date suffers adversely is reduced to two (7, 10). Nevertheless, the overall effect of focussing on dates that have been adjusted for bias is not encouraging.

4.5.1 *Overall Performance*

Figure 4.8 shows most clearly how the chronometric dating, by and large, follows the scholarly dating achieved by traditional means. Texts belonging to the Old Irish period (c.700-c.900) are not usually dated quite early enough by D1 but they are clearly distinguishable from later texts of the Middle (c.900-c.1200) and Early Modern (c.1200-c.1600) periods. With various exceptions, the two series closely shadow each other until c.1250, so that it is clear that the method successfully places texts within the correct linguistic era (see further 4.6) and, in general, successfully sorts them chronologically. After c.1250, the lines diverge markedly, a matter to which we shall return below.

The results are summarised in Table 4.13 and broken down by century. D1 is correct to ±50 years in 50% of cases, but of course there is considerable variation within this. The method fails to detect a correct D1 for any text written before 800 or after 1300. However, for the period 800-1300, the overall accuracy is 66.67%.

D2 is correct in just 38.89% of cases (Table 4.14), primarily due to the fact that D1 is too early for many of the twelfth-century texts: only four of the nine texts correctly dated by D2 were also dated correctly by D1, leaving five texts correctly dated only by D2.

Focussing may help to explain more clearly why our method cannot effectively date texts composed before 900 before the introduction of bias re-

TABLE 4.13 Accuracy of focussed dating by century using D1 only

Period	Text no.	D1 = correct	D1 correct (%)
-800	1-4	0	0
800-900	5-10	4	66.67
900-1000	11-15	4	80.00
1000-1100	16-19	3	75.00
1100-1200	20-29	5 (6)	50.00 (60.00)
1200-1300	30-31	2	100.00
1300+	32-36	0	0
Total	1-36	18 (19)	50.00 (52.78)

TABLE 4.14 Accuracy of focussed dating by century using D2 only

Period	Text no.	D2 = correct	D2 correct (%)
-800	1-4	0	0
800-900	5-10	0	0
900-1000	11-15	1	20.00
1000-1100	16-19	2	50.00
1100-1200	20-29	9	90.00
1200-1300	30-31	1	50.00
1300+	32-36	1	20.00
Total	**1-36**	**14**	**38.89**

duction. It will be observed that 8 out of 10 Old Irish texts (1-10 in Tables 4.11 and 4.12) are dated to 914 before reinforcement and adaptive learning is used, and that these are all converted to 922 after focussing. In other words, focussing is pointing to 914 ± 10 years as the effective horizon for dating by our method. We noticed in Figure 4.2 that the number of annals before c.1000 CE is very small, although there are clearly enough records in the period 750-950 to enable the algorithm to learn how to date the annals themselves with an impressive level of accuracy. When we look at the annals around 914 and 922 in more detail, we see that the length and detail in these records increases substantially, particularly from 913 onwards. We suggest, therefore, that this period would produce the only substantial amount of material from which a transferable temporal model could be constructed and that this would be the closest thing to Old Irish that the model would produce. As 914 is a very clearly biased date, therefore, reinforcement and adaptive learning is very successful in removing it from texts and allowing us to see slightly further back in time.

4.6 Periodisation

While the method struggles to assign accurate dates to texts belonging to the Old and Early Modern periods, it is noteworthy that it generally succeeds in placing texts in the correct linguistic period (see Table 4.15).

Table 4.15a shows focussed dates before bias reduction is implemented; Table 4.15b shows focussed dates after the bias reduction has been performed. In both cases, they are here sorted by their predicted earliest date (D1). In addition, texts have been colour-coded to indicate whether they are thought by scholars to be Old Irish (green), Middle Irish (yellow) or Early Modern (amber). There is a marked tendency for texts to be placed in their correct period by both methods. There is slight confusion at the boundary between Middle

TABLE 4.15a Focussed dates from Table 4.11 sorted by D1 (before bias reduction)

	Text	Given date	D1
1	Tochmarc Emire I	700-800	922
2	Táin Bó Fraích	750-800	922
3	Aislinge Óengusso	750-800	922
5	Treatise on the Psalter	800-850	922
6	Bethu Brigte	800-850	922
7	Mesca Ulad-A	800-900	922
9	Monastery of Tallaght	831-840	922
10	Echtra Láegaire	850-900	**922**
20	Mesca Ulad-B	1100-1150	922
22	Bruiden Da Choca	1100-1150	922
23	Aided Guill	1100-1160	922
11	Fingal Rónáin	900-950	***922***
14	Saltair na Rann	950-988	**922**
13	Cath Almhaine	900-1000	**1010**
16	Aided Nath Í	1050-1100	***1098***
17	Genemain Áeda Sláine	1050-1100	***1098***
24	Cogadh Gaedel	1103-1170	**1098**
8	Táin A	800-900	1098
4	SMMD	750-850	1120
19	Mac Conglinne	1075-1100	**1120**
21	Táin-B	1100-1150	***1120***
28	Bórama	1151-1181	**1120**
12	Derbforgaill	900-1000	1120
15	Betha Adamnáin	961-1000	1120
27	Cath Ruis na Ríg	1150-1166	**1131**
26	Cath Catharda	1140-1170	**1175**
30	Acallamh na Senórach	1200-1225	**1197**
18	Indarba na nDessi	1050-1100	1208
25	Betha Colmáin	1130-1180	**1208**
29	Merugud Ulix	1175-1225	***1208***
33	Regimen na Sláinte	1400-1450	1208
35	De Dosibus	1459	1219
31	Cath Maige Léna	1250-1325	**1230**
34	Guy of Berwick	1452-1500	1230
36	Maundeville	1475	1230
32	Caithréim	1330-1360	1241

TABLE 4.15b Focussed dates from Table 4.12 sorted by D1 (after bias reduction)

	Text	Given date	D1
6	Bethu Brigte	800-850	***0834***
9	Monastery of Tallaght	831-840	***0834***
2	Táin Bó Fraích	750-800	0856
1	Tochmarc Emire I	700-800	0867
11	Fingal Rónáin	900-950	**0867**
3	Aislinge Óengusso	750-800	0922
4	SMMD	750-850	0922
5	Treatise on the Psalter	800-850	0922
7	Mesca Ulad-A	800-900	**0922**
10	Echtra Láegaire	850-900	**0922**
12	Derbforgaill	900-1000	**0922**
14	Saltair na Rann	950-988	**0922**
20	Mesca Ulad-B	1100-1150	0922
22	Bruiden Da Choca	1100-1150	0922
24	Cogadh Gaedel	1103-1170	0922
13	Cath Almhaine	900-1000	**1010**
16	Aided Nath Í	1050-1100	**1010**
19	Mac Conglinne	1075-1100	1010
21	Táin-B	1100-1150	1010
28	Bórama	1151-1181	1010
17	Genemain Áeda Sláine	1050-1100	***1098***
8	Táin A	800-900	1120
15	Betha Adamnáin	961-1000	1120
18	Indarba na nDessi	1050-1100	**1120**
23	Aided Guill	1100-1160	***1120***
26	Cath Catharda	1140-1170	**1120**
27	Cath Ruis na Ríg	1150-1166	**1131**
30	Acallamh na Senórach	1200-1225	**1197**
34	Guy of Berwick	1452-1500	1197
25	Betha Colmáin	1130-1180	**1208**
29	Merugud Ulix	1175-1225	***1208***
33	Regimen na Sláinte	1400-1450	1208
35	De Dosibus	1459	1219
31	Cath Maige Léna	1250-1325	**1230**
36	Maundeville	1475	1230
32	Caithréim	1330-1360	1241

Green = Old Irish; Yellow = Middle Irish; Amber = Early Modern. Text 29 (maroon) straddles the Middle/Early Modern boundary.

and Early Modern Irish, but the difference separating them is just eleven years (between 1197 and 1208). For the Old and Middle Irish boundary, we see that only two texts by each method are incorrectly placed. It must be stressed that Old Irish texts are dated to 922 without bias reduction (Table 4.15a), so that they are not distinguished from early Middle Irish texts, but only in two cases (4, 8) are Old Irish texts placed later than this. With bias reduction (Table 4.15b), we start to see a gap opening up between the Old and Middle Irish texts, although the date 922 remains persistent preventing us from using this as definitive tool for labelling texts according to period. Clearly, any improvement in the training corpus for the Old Irish period may help to improve the capacity of the algorithm to discriminate between the two periods.

4.7 Stratification

We have already observed (4.3.2) that the algorithm has the capacity to detect different phases of revision and writing within a text and that this may be reflected in the stratified dating of chunks. This provides the possibility for a further use for the method: the detection and dating of strata. The method clearly distinguishes between two different versions of the same tale in Fig. 4.5 above: the earlier version (A), which it dates predominantly to 914, and the later version (B), which it places emphatically at 1208 (about half a century too late). When we first ran the experiment, we inadvertently tested the two versions together (as they are printed together in the edition that we used) but the algorithm was still able to date the two parts of the text correctly. Fig. 4.9 shows the dating of the two versions as found in the composite edition but unlike the data in Fig. 4.5 we have plotted the chunks here in narrative order. The bulk of the text, from the beginning to near the end, is supplied from the later version (B), while the material at the end, enclosed in the rectangular box, comes from the older version (A).

It should be emphasised, however, that the method cannot be relied on for the dating at the micro-level as individual chunks may amount to little more than a single sentence. These are simply too short be dated robustly and we can only be confident in the dating where it is consistent across a large portion of the text. Moreover, if a particular chunk, say #102 in Fig. 4.9, is dated to 914, for example, it would be wrong to conclude that it necessarily belongs to a tenth-century layer. There is a margin of error in all datings and they are only valid in the aggregate.

We need to differentiate between what we might term discrete and non-discrete strata. Discrete strata would describe those layers in texts which were

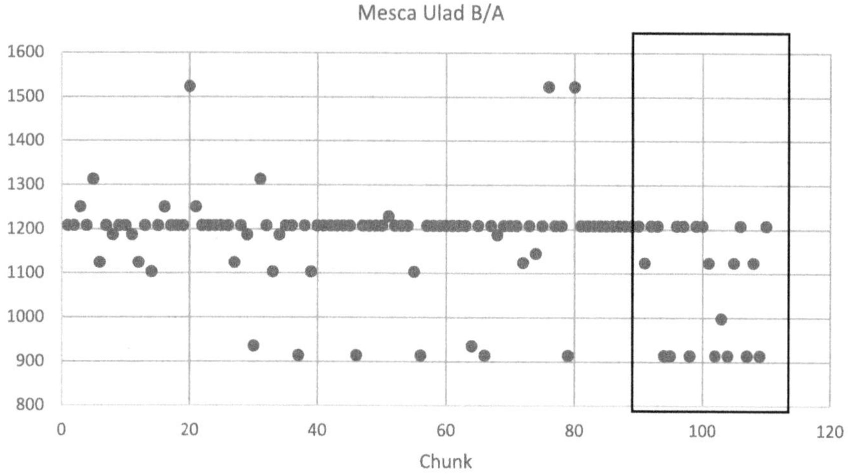

FIGURE 4.9 Mesca Ulad version B (chunks 1-92) and A (chunks 93-109) in narrative order. Box indicates extent of version A

contributed quite separately by different redactors, or parts of a text taken over from other texts by a single author with little or no change. Non-discrete strata are probably more common, however, and surely include to a greater or lesser degree all texts that are not preserved in contemporary manuscripts. Non-discrete stratified texts may be defined as those that have suffered scribal interference across all or most of a text, perhaps by way of calculated modernisation. While discrete strata can, it seems, be distinguished and dated, it does not follow that the dating of non-discrete layers is accurate. Unfortunately, while we can test that the method works with discrete strata by feeding in different versions of the same text and observing the results as we have done in Fig. 4.9, we have no way of independently and unambiguously verifying its functionality for non-discrete strata as secondary layers are rarely accurately dated, if at all, by traditional methods. With our algorithm, it may be the case that the mixture of different linguistic forms confuses it, causing it to assign incorrect dates to a chunk. However, against this supposition, we may point out that we know that we can detect the earliest stratum reflecting the original composition in most Middle Irish texts: if it were the case that the algorithm gets confused by later layers, then it would not be possible ever to detect the earliest. Moreover, we have seen a correlation between the date of the manuscript and the D3 date of the text (4.4), suggesting that this is being distinguished as a separate layer. On balance, therefore, we suggest that the algorithm can date non-discrete strata.

4.8 Conclusion

The methodology described in this chapter has had to address several practical problems associated with the data set. The training corpus is derived from the annals which are more or less continuous for the whole of the medieval period but are only rarely preserved in contemporary manuscripts such as the Annals of Inisfallen from c.1092-1309. The majority of our training corpus, therefore, is taken from much later copies, with the risk of contamination, revision and modernisation. The annals for the early period, though invaluable, are particularly difficult because the records tend to be much briefer and are frequently bilingual or wholly in Latin, a great number of entries have been either translated from Latin or retrospectively inserted, and by their very nature they have suffered a much longer period of transmission. Nevertheless, our method of extending the annals has produced a clear temporal model which changes over time and can be highly effective in dating both the annals themselves and other non-annalistic texts. Tests on the annals reveal that the levels of accuracy increase over time and remain consistently high from c.1000 CE until the end of the sixteenth century. The quantity of data available for training is a major factor in the algorithm's ability to generate good results and the larger the corpus, the more confident we can be in the model's robustness. However, a high degree of accuracy can be obtained with quite a small number of records. Levels of accuracy exceeding 70% are reported for 750-849 with as few as 285 records per 50-year period. Accuracy rates drop significantly, however, where the number of records falls below 250. While we cannot entirely separate this from the other complicating factors discussed here, this may nevertheless suggest a threshold for this corpus.

The longer non-annalistic texts suffer from many of the same problems as the annals, notably long delays between the initial composition of a text and the writing of the manuscripts in which they are preserved leading to opportunities for revision and modernisation. Scribes and redactors frequently introduced extraneous material, often from a variety of sources, sometimes older than the date at which they were working. These are not monolithic texts, therefore, but once-living organisms that accreted new material with the passage of time. Finally, the dating method must deal with the problems of dialect and register, although both are very difficult to pin down in individual texts and may be obscured through lengthy transmission. Little is known of the distinctions between dialects in early medieval Ireland because texts are rarely explicitly associated with one place of composition, and it must be conceded that a text could be incorrectly dated if dialect forms played a large role. However, given the nature of our approach, it is probably less likely that dialect would impinge on our dating than, for example, a traditional approach which focusses on a small number of evolving linguistic features which might be geographically contingent. Register is a greater problem, as can be seen from the case of Early Modern texts which tend to produce dates at the turn of the thirteenth century regardless of when they were actually composed. Whether this is also a factor in other periods remains to be seen.

Notwithstanding these problems, we have seen that it is possible to apply the temporal model derived from the annals to long non-annalistic texts with convincing results. We have seen that the annals-based model maps well onto long texts for the period c.800-c.1300. At the higher end of the scale, for texts of the thirteenth century, we have seen that we can distinguish between those texts written at the end of the twelfth century/beginning of the thirteenth, and those texts that were written later in the period. The most convincing results come from texts that were composed close to the date of the manuscript, with two or three dates being tightly grouped together. This supports the idea, explored elsewhere in this chapter, that a lengthy period of transmission, with greater opportunity for revision, is reflected in our data. It seems likely that had we better texts from the earlier period in contemporary manuscripts then we would be able to produce clearer and more closely clustered dates. There is an apparent tendency for the algorithm to date texts slightly later than traditional methods would suggest, and this may be due to distortions in the annalistic record with much fuller accounts and more data emanating from later years. As it stands, there are various blind spots in this period, so that for example, no text is dated to the first half of the ninth century, and a gap in the annalistic record in the middle of the twelfth century seems to be skewing some of the dates for texts of this period, forcing them into either the earlier or later parts of the century. The latter problem could be readily addressed by introducing some other annals into the training set, such as the Annals of Tigernach. The difficulties relating to the ninth century are more difficult to deal with as the problem seems to lie with the quality of the data that we have for that period rather than a simple gap in the record. Theoretically, we could supplement the annals with non-annalistic material in contemporary manuscripts – such as some of the longer glosses – but there is great uncertainty about the dating attached to most potential texts in this category. It is to be hoped that further advances can be made at this end of the scale but clearly the method is restricted to those periods for which there is ample training material of acceptable quality and reliable intrinsic dating. We also have problems in dating Early Modern Irish texts precisely, although they are invariably placed within or on the cusp of that period (see Table 4.15a). This shows that the model is strong enough to recognise Early Modern texts but not sufficiently granular to date them more precisely.

Our experiments with bias compensation produced mixed results. We found that the method generally produces better results for the period before c.1000 CE, but little improvement or worsening of performance for the later periods. We might surmise that it is most effective for the earlier period because it is starting from a lower base, but the most likely reason is that there is a greater distinction between the annals of this period and narrative text or continuous prose. As we have already noted, the annals tend to be much shorter at this date, amounting often to little more than notices of battles and deaths, with limited verbal forms and vocabulary. Moreover, in order to generate as much text from the very earliest years as possible, we abstracted a lot of material from a bilingual context which, by and large, is not found in the longer texts examined. We removed the Latin from the sentences in the training corpus, and the resulting disjointed text hardly represents real linguistic use in all cases. One option that we considered was including the Latin in the training. However, while this would have allowed us to deal with actual sentences, and probably would have increased the accuracy for the training phase, it would not have been particularly transferable in a robust way and may have led to the dating of any text that contained Latin to the early period, regardless of when it was written.

Our tests on non-annalistic texts were conducted at the scale of ±50 years as we viewed this as a realistic time span for dating by linguistic means (see also Belinkov, Magidow, Romanov, Shmidman, and Koppel 2016: 49). Linguists and textual editors will frequently attempt to date texts to the nearest half century with convincing results, but any finer granularity proves far from convincing. However, we propose that we can refine the dates further by a process that we have called focussing. Starting with the ±50-year dating which is a robust measure which is likely to contain the correct date, we then used our analysis of the annals at ±10-year intervals to narrow this century-long period. Rather surprisingly, we found that this tended to improve the accuracy of the results as evidenced by closer correspondence with the established dates of composition.

As we observed in the Introduction, a simple date is not always possible for texts that have undergone lengthy transmission and subsequent revision. It is much more difficult to prove that our method is actually uncovering later redactions as these are rarely dated with any degree of accuracy or confidence by editors and linguists in the field. However, there are indications that this is probably the case, namely, the fact that there is a correlation between D1 and the date of composition (the earliest stratum) and between D3 and the date of the manuscript.

CHAPTER 5

Conclusion

The problem of dating texts with no explicit internal dating is central to the historical study of ancient and medieval literatures and societies, but it is a contentious and challenging area. However, it is now clear that machine learning can facilitate the development of viable methods to assist in the determination of the calendrical dating of texts, what we have termed here 'chronometrics'. We have been able to build a temporal model for medieval Irish based on a more or less unbroken series of annals that continues up until the end of the seventeenth century and to use this, with varying degrees of success, to establish dates for non-annalistic texts. While other language-based dating systems are based on word n-grams which are effective but highly susceptible to genre differences, the system explored here, employing character n-grams, appears to be successful across different genres as well as being able to deal with texts exhibiting a high degree of linguistic inflection and non-standardised orthography.

In the Introduction we discussed the necessary collaboration between humanities and computational researchers to tackle complex problems, and it follows that any new method must satisfy both computational experts and scholars working in the relevant humanities disciplines. Significant progress is unlikely to be made unless cutting edge methodologies, much of it with relevance to industry, are developed by IT specialists, but we have argued that the humanities scholar has a key role to play in assuring that valid and representative data is used as input. In our case study, the training material is essential to the construction of the temporal model on which the dating is subsequently based, and it cannot be left to non-specialists to select this. Weaknesses in the training data may only become fully apparent when tested in a real-life situation, and so the humanities scholar must be involved in the iterative improvement and refinement of training data. However, we need to be aware of what the computer can do for us in this regard. The temptation might be to cleanse the training data of perceived imperfections, but this may not be necessary and, indeed, could be counterproductive. We know, for example, that the Annals of Ulster exist only in late copies and that many of the earlier annals show signs of modernisation during the transmission process. However, this 'dirty data' does not affect the algorithm's ability to create a functional model. Its only concern is to identify those features that are diagnostic of particular intervals and so it can identify an early record if

 | DOI:10.1163/9789004410046_007

it contains enough genuinely contemporary features, regardless of any modernisation that may have occurred since. It is the domain expert's job, therefore, to supply it with the best possible training materials and then let it learn.

The humanities scholar is also essential in the interpretation of the results. As Ramsay and Rockwell (2012: 79) acknowledge, a 'digital artifact that transparently shows you something else might convey knowledge, but it doesn't intervene as an explanation or argument'. In the trials set out in this book, the results point towards certain dates for texts, but it is the job of the language specialist or textual historian to evaluate those results against other criteria. As we have seen, many of the texts that we are dealing with have multiple strata that can be hard for the human researcher to detect or date accurately. The algorithm appears to succeed in doing this well but it cannot of itself evaluate or explain its results. That remains a job for the domain expert.

5.1 A Temporal Model

The reader will have noticed that we have used the term 'temporal model' rather than 'linguistic model' throughout to describe the products of our algorithms. This is quite deliberate, for although the success of the algorithm depends on it detecting a linguistic pattern which is contingent on chronology, we cannot be sure that it does this all the time. Indeed, it is likely that it is simply finding the most straightforward route to achieving maximum accuracy in the training texts. That it is partially transferable to texts in other genres indicates that the model is probably largely linguistic, but this may not be the case for other eras where it is less successful. The problem of 'black boxing' has been raised in the Introduction. While we can describe the different steps involved in our algorithm, it is less clear how it is actually arriving at its results and, as we shall see, this probably varies according to the nature of the training data.

We know that our algorithm is identifying the relative frequency of 1, 2, and 3-letter n-grams at different time intervals, thereby building up a model that can correctly date other texts. However, the algorithm proposed here cannot 'understand' any of the texts that it reads in anything like the way a human does. It cannot abstract any meaning from the texts, it does not even distinguish parts of speech, and it is unlikely in most cases to be able even to lemmatise words in its model. Moreover, it has no understanding of the historical development of the language so it will not know that Old Irish *ad-cí* 'sees' becomes *at-chí* in Middle Irish, then *do-chí*, although it may well recognise that these forms exist at, and are characteristic of, different periods without knowing that they are linked in any way. In some ways, this is the algorithm's strength too, because it may be largely immune to an author's attempt to produce a patina of archaism in order to dupe the reader.

It is clear, therefore, that the model generated by our algorithm can hardly be described as a linguistic model as we would understand it – that is merely a metaphor for what it is doing because that is what we, as humans, are accustomed to using to date otherwise undated texts. Given that it is using character n-grams, it is reasonable to conclude that orthography has a large part to play in the creation of the model, so for example it might recognise that *ea* starts to appear in the twelfth century where earlier scribes used *e*. That orthography is indeed important in the model is confirmed by the fact that there is a close correlation between the latest predicted date (D3) and the date of the earliest manuscript in which the text is found (see 4.4). In fact, this may be one of the major reasons why the signal corresponding to the date of composition is sometimes comparatively weak – it is being drowned out by the more dominant orthographical component.

That the algorithm works with non-linguistic criteria is clear from experiments which achieved over 40% accuracy in dating items from Freecycle to within ±10 days (see 3.1.3.3). Evidently, this cannot reflect linguistic or even orthographical change over such short periods of time, and we would posit that it is modelling topics here as items for sale will reflect seasonal changes. This suggests that the nature of the input affects the nature of what the algorithm identifies as diagnostic. If presented with more or less standardised orthography and no linguistic variation across an entire data set, the algorithm will rely more on topic modelling. In fact, we can demonstrate this for the Irish annals by dating the translations of the original Irish-language texts that we used in the training. As an experiment, we ran the same algorithm on the English translations of the annals produced by their modern editors.[1] Despite the lack of linguistic variation, the algorithm was able to date annals to the correct year with an accuracy rate of 51.51% with a tolerance of 50 years (compared to 85% for the Irish text) as shown in Figure 5.1.

This success may be due partially to linguistic data encoded within the Gaelic names of people and places in the translations, but as these were largely

1 In principle, a modern translation should not show any linguistic or orthographical variation across time, but for the Annals of Ulster we have had to use two different translations, a twentieth century one covering the beginning until 1131 CE, and a nineteenth-century one covering the years from after the lacuna in the original until 1588 CE (see Appendix A). Within each of these translations, however, there should be no linguistic variation, and so what we argue here is certainly valid for these two broad periods.

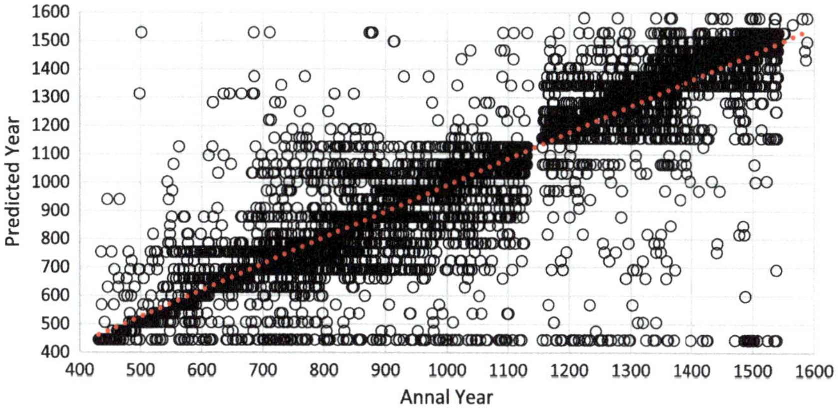

FIGURE 5.1 Dating of the translations of the Annals of Ulster with δ = 50

normalised in the editions minor variations over time would have been largely excised. True, a name such as *Tigernach* might be rendered as such by the editor for the Old and Middle Irish periods but as *Tighearnach* when translating an Early Modern annal, and it is likely that the importance of such variation in the spelling of names increased dramatically when the algorithm was starved of other linguistic clues. However, it is also likely that it started to behave more as a topic modeller, just as with Freecycle. As the Gaelic originals are non-standard and unlemmatised, it would be difficult for our algorithm to identify topics, but this does not apply to the English translations. Here, without significant or meaningful linguistic change, the algorithm must have relied much more on changes in topic. Names would have played an important role but as they are normalised it is not their varying form that would have been significant but their presence/absence. The appearance of a particular individual, dynasty, or place would have been what most differentiated one period from another.

It should not be concluded from this that 50+% of the success in dating the annals in Irish is to be attributed to topic modelling. If the algorithm adapts to different data sets, as seems likely, then we cannot know for certain what it is measuring – orthographic change, language development, or variation in topic. In practice, it is likely to always be a combination of these, with the emphasis shifting from one factor to another depending on what is most helpful for dating. When we eliminate normalisation from the balance of material available to it, the algorithm will naturally turn to those elements which are more amenable to dating, such as changes in the language. Therefore, as the degree to which the model is dependent on language is unknown, and because there is probably at least some element of non-linguistic modelling, we prefer to refer to it as a temporal model rather than a linguistic model. In other words, it is a model of how particular texts change over time which may be partially but not wholly linguistic.

This has important implications for the performance of our model on non-annalistic texts. We have noted that it performs poorly on Early Modern texts, so how are we to reconcile this failure with the fact that the algorithm works exceptionally well for annals during this period? We might conclude that the language of the annals continues to change at a more or less consistent rate but that Early Modern prose texts were written in the de facto standard and thus cannot be related to the linguistic changes in the annals. In support of that interpretation, we may note that all the Early Modern texts in this trial produce an earliest date (D1) very close to 1200 CE, that is, at the very same time at which Early Modern Irish was codified, so we might argue that developments in the spoken language were reflected in the annals but not in the literary language more generally. Indeed, Murray (2012b: 46) asks whether it is likely that annal writers would use the same language register as found in literary narrative texts. Our experiments would appear, at first glance, to support his scepticism for the Early Modern period but not for Middle Irish where the success of the model suggests sufficient identity between the two. For the Early Modern period, Ó Catháin (1933) has traced several linguistic developments in the annals which would suggest that they do capture some change in the language over time. However, he also finds corresponding developments in a variety of prose texts, indicating that they too are not wholly monolithic. While current scholars would be loath to date a text solely based on Ó Catháin's criteria (see 1.7.4), it shows that prose writers were open to some linguistic variation.

Another interpretation of our results for Early Modern texts is possible, namely, that the annals are written in the standardised register and that the algorithm, as a result, is treating them in the same way as the translations into English or the Freecycle texts, that is, it is using topic modelling, particularly proper names, to date them. As Kulkarni, Tian, Dandiwala and Skiena (2018: 202) note, features such as this are not generalisable across different domains, so that the model which was successful for dating the annals proves largely inept when it comes to dating texts from other genres. However, the truth may lie somewhere in between these two interpretations. We may note, for example, that none of the Early Modern texts are confused with Old or Middle Irish (allowing for some leeway at the Early Modern boundary) – enough transferable patterns are emerging to enable the algorithm to invariably place them in their correct linguistic period. But the much higher degree of success in dating the annals may be due more to topic modelling rather than linguistic modelling, and this part of the model is not transferable to the texts used in our testing. If this is the case, then names are actually disrupting the generalisability of the model.

If topic modelling is occurring in Early Modern Irish, then it is also possible that it is being exploited for the earlier phases of the language. However, the success of the algorithm with relation to Middle Irish texts suggest that it has captured something more generic than topics, and that it has constructed for this period a temporal model that is primarily, if not wholly, linguistic.

5.2 Towards a Tool: Computational Chronometrics

What has been discussed so far demonstrates that a computer algorithm can generate a temporal model that enables the dating of previously unseen texts. In the tests described in Chapter 4, we have been concerned with evaluating the accuracy of the model against dates already established by traditional scholarly methods, but it is quite another thing to apply it to undated or insecurely dated texts. In order to use the model as a practical tool, we need to understand how and when it can be used effectively.

The model works extremely well at the macro-level and could be used as a tool for assigning texts to a linguistic period (see 4.6). The distinction between Old and early Middle Irish is not clear cut, however, with both Old Irish and early Middle Irish texts being dated to 914. Bias compensation can help to identify those texts that belong to the Old Irish period, although not consistently and not without creating some errors (see 4.3.3). As we have seen, there is only a very minor overlap in our results between the Middle and Early Modern periods, so that this can be considered a robust distinction. While acknowledging the difficulties with the earlier material, we can conclude that the method can divide material into the following categories with a high degree of accuracy and consistency: Old/Early Middle Irish (to c.1000 CE), Middle Irish (c.1000 CE - c.1200 CE), and Early Modern Irish (c.1200 CE - c.1600 CE).

The ultimate goal must be to produce a tool that will facilitate a full chronometric analysis of texts – that is, to provide precise, absolute dates, rather than assign them to broad linguistic periods. This is not yet possible for Old or Early Modern texts for the reasons discussed above, although this may become feasible, at least in part, in the future. For Middle Irish, the system works very well but there are problems. In this book, we have used the top three datings in order to systematise and evaluate the results more effectively, but a more nuanced assessment of the complete distribution, and the relative proportion of particular datings, is necessary. To that end, graphs showing the spread of dating of each individual chunk, such as Fig. 4.5 and 4.6, need to be produced and analysed. A quirk of gaps in the training data has probably caused some inaccuracy that must be taken into consideration by users. If the underlying model is weak for any time interval, then texts belonging to this period are very likely to be dated incorrectly (see 4.3.2). Most particularly, a small gap in the twelfth-century record leads to imprecision in the dating of texts from that period with the algorithm being forced to choose in some cases an incorrect early or late twelfth-century dating for texts that properly belong to the middle of the century. Moreover, there appears to be an anomaly in the model caused by other gaps in the training data (see Fig. 4.7) which causes a small number of texts to be dated too early. Therefore, a thorough analysis of the dates of individual texts will require the researcher to take cognisance of these dissonant features and evaluate the consequences.

We have shown that we cannot assume a single date of writing for a text and that we must allow for the possibility of several revisions. The algorithm allows us to distinguish between discrete strata and probably also to identify the existence of non-discrete strata (see 4.7). While the former can be tested on separate versions or on known and clear compilations, the latter cannot, although it would seem reasonable to conclude that, on balance, this too is possible. One particularly useful facet of this feature is that it enables us to visualise the extent to which a text has been modernised – the tendency of much twentieth-century scholarship in the field was to determine the date of composition and then to treat the text as belonging to that date, regardless of later revision. It must, of course, be borne in mind that our results can be unduly influenced by minor orthographical variation, and we have seen a strong correlation between the date of the manuscript and the latest predicted date (see 4.4). Nevertheless, the revelation of multiple strata by our algorithm must sound a warning note to scholars engaged with texts that they may not be dealing with a version of the text close to the original.

As for detecting discrete strata, we have noted that we can only have limited confidence in the dating of individual chunks, but where there is some consistency in the grouping of dates then we may be more assured that we are dealing with distinctive contributions to the text. Of course, our inability to distinguish different sections chronologically does not mean that they were written by the same author – this is not author attribution software – and human scholars have the same difficulty when confronted by what appears to be a textual compilation but for which there is no obvious or consistent linguistic separation (see 1.7.1). To some extent, a consideration of strata can set aside problems with absolute chronology as we can focus rather on the relative chronology of different sections. We have experimented, for example, with a tool that will shade a text according to its relative date, from which it can become apparent which sections are later and which are earlier. Graphs can be displayed with chunks sorted by narrative order (as in 4.7), and the raw data, including texts, can be displayed as a table showing either chronological or narrative order.

It is clear that adjustments could be made to the method to improve the robustness and precision of the results and to create a more effective tool. We have already suggested that expanding the training corpus, and addressing, in particular, the gaps in the current corpus, would obviate some of the current difficulties with the model. The gap in the twelfth-century, for example, could easily be filled by records from the Annals of Tigernach (Stokes 1993). The options for the Old Irish period are more restricted. We could use some non-annalistic texts to bolster the data derived from the annals. The natural choice would be to select material in contemporary manuscripts, although this tends to be restricted to glosses and occasional verse. The problem in general with Old Irish sources is that they lack sufficiently precise dating from which to construct a fine-grained and consistent chronology. Other methods may have to be developed to deal with material that does not have an annual date. It may also be possible to use narrative texts in non-contemporary sources, employing the same incremental technique as with the early annals, but again we are faced with a lack of precisely dated texts.

We have suggested that the inclusion of names in the training material may lead to the occurrence of topic modelling and that although this can improve the performance in training, it is not transferable to the wider corpus. We deliberately retained names because they encode valuable linguistic information and are sometimes the only form of language available for very early annals. To have omitted them would have greatly reduced the extent of the early training corpus and therefore the possibility of using it for dating. It might be desirable in the future to remove names altogether or, more cogently, to replace them with generic tokens that would preserve the natural order of the language.[2] This would allow other features of a linguistic nature to emerge as stronger diagnostic features and might improve the dating functionality for certain periods. We have attempted here to construct a universal model for temporal change in Irish, but a further possibility that must be considered is the introduction of distinct models for different purposes or periods. For the Early Modern period, we could develop a separate model with names removed. We have not, so far, tested any bardic material from the Early Modern period as

2 Removing names entirely creates abnormal sentence structures. At its most extreme, we would reduce sentences like 'Flaithbertach son of Conchobor, king of Ailech, made a raid in Dál Araidi and plundered Condaire' to 'son of, king of, made a raid in and plundered' (see Mac Airt & Mac Niocaill 1983: 403 s.a. 963.1).

we have generally tried to avoid using verse in the testing.[3] A separate model for bardic verse could be developed using examples from the many closely dated bardic compositions from the period, and in such a case, the inclusion of names is likely to be a distinct advantage.

In the tests that we have discussed in this book, we have refrained from providing the algorithm with any knowledge about the texts with which it is dealing other than the date of the training annals. However, it would be possible to introduce further information about the permissible dates to be assigned to a text. For example, if we know that a text to be tested occurs in a mid-twelfth-century manuscript, then we could instruct the algorithm to ignore any dates after 1200 CE. We have already used a similar technique successfully in our focussing experiments (see 4.5) although in that case we only employed boundaries generated by the algorithm in the first place without any human intervention. The user-directed concatenation of the chronology would force the algorithm to reassign chunks to the period of interest before the cut-off point. Our hypothesis is that chunks are placed too late in the chronology through simple errors in the model or because there is some overlap between the patterns being used at the two dates due, perhaps, to later imitation of an earlier style or register. By concatenating the chronology, we would eliminate this kind of error and enable more contemporary features to be forefronted. Similarly, if we have a terminus post quem for a text, then this could be used as a further concatenation boundary. Theoretically, concatenation could also be applied to texts that are known to be Middle Irish but found only in much later texts. This approach must be used with caution, however. A later copy may well contain Early Modern features, and we do not know how they would be treated by the algorithm. Rather than allowing Middle Irish features to be forefronted, concatenation may well corrupt the dating in such texts. This is testable, however, for example by using two copies of a text, one from a Middle Irish manuscript and one from a later manuscript. If concatenation produces similar results for the two copies, then it would appear to be valid.

5.3 Applicability to Other Literatures

Although we have used English and Irish in our experiments, the method could be extended to any language, including those with non-Latin-based

3 We did opt to use Saltair na Rann (text 8) in testing as it is one of the few texts from the tenth century with a relatively secure date. Many of the prose texts also contain sometimes lengthy poems which were included in the tests unless excluded on other grounds (see Appendix A for details).

character sets, so long as a suitable training corpus is available. It is clear that the reliability of the method is dependent on the quality and quantity of the input data, although we have seen that in the Irish situation, as few as 250-300 records per 50-year-period was sufficient to produce significantly high levels of accuracy (see 4.1). Annals have proved a fertile training source, and with suitable data the resulting model appears, with certain limitations, to be effective across genre boundaries. The construction of a reliable model along these lines is reliant on a continuous or near-continuous set of closely dated training texts such as the annals, and we have seen that gaps in the record generate wider problems in the dating. Whether the method is entirely dependent on annals or similar kinds of continuous records remains to be seen, but it is possible that the algorithm could be adjusted to work with non-serial records or even with approximately dated sources. We would hope that by extending the use of the algorithm to other historical literatures that not only would it assist scholars in other disciplines in their work but that the validity of the method would be tested and proved. As in the sciences, a digital method should be able to demonstrate its merit by being replicated in other experiments. Furthermore, we have seen that setting the algorithm to work on alternative data sets provides insights into how it is working and we would hope that further experiments in other corpora would produce new insights into the development of a set of tools for all languages.

Artificial Intelligence offers the potential of significant advances in humanities research by performing certain tasks that are beyond the capacity of the human brain and by providing new ways of analysing texts. What we have proposed here attempts to answer a question which is superficially empirical – the date of text – but which we have seen is in fact intricate and multifaceted. Ramsay proposes in relation to the vexed field of digital literary criticism that literary critics need to 'create tools – practical, instrumental, verifiable mechanisms – that enable critical engagement, interpretation, conversation, and contemplation', and that digital humanities must 'endeavor to assist the critic in the unfolding of interpretative possibilities' (Ramsay 2011: x, 10). Elsewhere, Ramsay & Rockwell (2012: 79) advocate the use of digital tools as 'hermeneutical instruments' and liken them to '"telescopes for the mind" that show us something in a new light.' While the tools proposed here may provide definitive answers to some questions, in most cases we are dealing with the creation of instruments that will assist, not replace, scholars in the dating of ancient and medieval literary artefacts.

APPENDIX A

Conventional Dating of Texts Used in This Study

This section presents the conventionally accepted dates of texts used in this study. As outlined in Chapter 1, we are dependent on manuscripts ranging from the late eleventh century through to the sixteenth or seventeenth centuries for examples of continuous texts in medieval Irish. Although we have a number of contemporary or near-contemporary manuscripts containing glosses and commentary from the Old Irish period (c.700-c.900), the earliest manuscripts containing extensive continuous texts in Irish belong to the late eleventh and twelfth centuries. Three eleventh/twelfth-century manuscripts in particular are important repositories of literature in Irish, namely, 1) the Book of the Dun Cow (*Lebor na hUidre*), preserved in the Royal Irish Academy, Dublin, 2) Rawlinson B 502, held in the Bodleian Library, Oxford, and 3) the Book of Leinster, which is preserved in Trinity College Dublin. Other later manuscripts are also of significance, sometimes preserving better or older versions than these twelfth-century codices, the earliest of which date from the fourteenth century.

A.0.1 *Book of the Dun Cow*

The manuscript known as The Book of the Dun Cow (*Lebor na hUidre*) is the earliest of the three. Traditionally, two primary scribes have been identified (A and M). The scribe known as M wrote the majority of the manuscript in collaboration with A. M appears to have signed his name Máel Muire grandson of Conn who has been identified as a monk who was murdered in the monastery of Clonmacnoise in 1106. There has been some questioning of aspects of the identification (Oskamp 1966 67: 130; Ó Concheanainn 1973-74), but it is still accepted by most commentators (see Oskamp 1975-76; Jackson 1983: 4; Mac Eoin 1994; Duncan 2012b: 20; Ó Corráin 2015: 1). Therefore, we are on relatively secure ground in dating the work of M, and that of scribe A with whom he collaborates, to some time before 1106.

Another scribe or scribes wrote several new texts but also erased portions of the manuscript and inserted other material. This was agreed to be a single scribe designated as H whom Thurneysen (1921: 31) dated to the thirteenth century, but a twelfth-century date for these sections now seems generally accepted among linguists (Oskamp 1966-67: 128; Mac Eoin 1994: 41; Breatnach 2015).[1] Gearóid Mac Eoin (1994), largely on the basis of his orthography, suggests that H was working in the mid- to

1 We may set aside Ó Concheanainn's assessment of the identify of Máel Muire which would place H in the late twelfth century.

 DOI:10.1163/9789004410046_008

late twelfth century.[2] Liam Breatnach (2015) argues on linguistic grounds that H is not much later than either of the principle scribes of the manuscript, and suggests a date in the first quarter of the twelfth century (2015: 76-7). Recently, Duncan (2015) has proposed that H is actually the work of at least six different but closely related hands. She would date the 'heavier and clumsier' specimens (H4-H6) to the last quarter of the twelfth century or the first quarter of the thirteenth (2015: 47).[3] In a recent unpublished paper, Caoimhín Breatnach (DIAS, 2017) has disputed Duncan's discrimination between different hands, suggesting that the need to adjust his script to fit the available space and the use of erased parchment are the reasons for the variability in writing style of H. Duncan's dating of the later stints of H (H4-H6) to the end of the twelfth century or beginning of the thirteenth century revives, to some extent, Thurneysen's original dating for H as a whole.

A.0.2 *Rawlinson B 502*

Rawlinson B 502, housed in the Bodleian Library, Oxford, is a composite manuscript consisting of two originally independent vellum sections and later paper sections. It is described in detail by Ó Cuív (2001: 163-200) from which this description derives. Section B (ff. 19-89), is the work of a single scribe which Ó Cuív dates on palaeographical and linguistic grounds to about the end of the eleventh century or the beginning of the twelfth' (Ó Cuív 2001: 171, 174), but internal evidence would place it no earlier than 1123×1138 (Ó Cuív 2001: 175). Section A (ff. 1-12), contains an incomplete copy of the annals sometimes called the Irish World Chronicle and edited by Stokes as part of the Annals of Tigernach (Stokes 1993: i, 5-49). It is the work of several scribes (Ó Cuív 2001: 165). Best (1913-14) identifies one of the glossators as scribe H of 'The Book of the Dun Cow' which would suggest that it was compiled at Clonmacnoise in the twelfth century.

A.0.3 *The Book of Leinster*

The Book of Leinster is preserved in the library of Trinity College, Dublin (MS. 1339). Best, Bergin & O'Brien (1954, xv-xvi) identify the entire manuscript as the work of Áed úa Crimthaind, who signed himself 'Aed mac meic Crimthaind' on f. xxxii, and they suggest that he worked between 1151 and 1201. However, the work of O'Sullivan (1966) and Duncan (2012a) confirms the presence of multiple hands, not all of whom worked contemporaneously.[4] An examination of the notices of contemporary kings in

2 This is emphatically rejected by Caoimhín Breatnach (1996: 206-7).

3 Duncan (2012b: 22) dates hands H and M on palaeographical grounds to the twelfth century. Hand A, she states, is more like specimens from the eleventh century.

4 The hands identified by O'Sullivan are laid out with admirable clarity by Schlüter 2010: 226-43.

the genealogies suggests that scribe A, most commonly identified as Áed, was working in the 1150s and early 1160s (Duncan 2012a: 53). Áed is described in the manuscript as the head (*coarb*) of the monastery of Terryglass which was destroyed in 1164, suggesting a possible terminus ante quem for his work (Best, Bergin & O'Brien 1954: xvi). The manuscript also contains a letter addressed to Áed from a certain Find who has been identified as Find Ua Gormáin, bishop of Kildare, whose death is recorded in the Annals of Ulster in 1160. Bhreatnach (2002) has shown that Find Ua Gormáin has been confused with the Find mac Máel Muire meic Cianáin, also bishop of Kildare, who attended the Synod of Kells in 1152, and she suggests that either of these two bishops could have been the author of the letter.

According to Duncan, nearly all the scribes worked in the 1150s and 1160s. T2 is the latest dateable scribe and is assigned on internal grounds to between 1181 and 1224 (Duncan 2012a: 55). The latest regnal notices record the death of Rúaidrí mac Con Ulad meic Conchobuir (+1201) and the reign but not the death of Cathal Crobderg mac Toirdelbaig (1189-1224). He is unlikely, therefore, to have been working after 1224 but it is most likely that he had completed his work not long after 1201.

A.1 Texts

The following provides a summary of the main arguments for the conventional dating of the texts examined in Chapter 4.

A.1.1 *Acallam na Senórach*

'The Dialogue of the Ancients' (*Acallam na Senórach*) exists in three recensions, the earliest of which concerns us here. It survives in several manuscripts, none continuous, including Bodleian Library Laud Miscellany 610, ff. 123r-146v, dated 1410×1452, Bodleian Library Rawlinson B.487 ff. 12r-52v (15th century), and Chatsworth House, Book of Lismore ff. 201r-242v (15th/16th century).

Nuner's (1958-59) examination of the verbal system of the prose suggests a date in the first quarter of thirteenth century. Dooley (2004) discusses some key internal evidence that points towards a similar conclusion, notably the renaming of Dub as Radub and the appearance of the phrase 'a beautiful triumvirate in one place' (*triar álaind a n-aenbaili*). The suggestion is that the former must be linked to the fortunes of Radub's descendants, Uí Raduib, who suffered decline after the death of Cathal Croibderg in 1224, providing us with a rough terminus ante quem. The latter apparently relates to John de Courcy's aim of establishing the cult of three national saints in the mid-1180s which would provide us with a terminus post quem. Dooley's arguments have been widely accepted (e.g. Murray 2012b: 44-47; Connon 2014). It should be noted, however, that the text contains several poems that probably predate the prose (Parsons 2009).

A.1.2 *Aided Derbforgaill*

The earliest copy of 'The death of Derbforgaill' (*Aided Derbforgaill*) is to be found in the Book of Leinster, pp. 125a-125b. Ingridsdottir (2009: 67) concludes from her linguistic examination that it belongs to the tenth century. The text is brief, comprising a short prose introduction (35 lines) followed by two poems. The second poem is not as rich in ornamentation as the first and Ingridsdottir (2009: 63) suggests that it might be later, although she concedes that there is no linguistic support for this. Notable linguistic features are the preservation of the neuter and some instances of hiatus, which would, in conjunction with other conservative elements, support Ingridsdottir's dating. We may note, however, some instances of the suffixed pronoun which Breatnach (1977: 103) says is obsolete by the tenth century.

A.1.3 *Aided Echach mac Maireda*

This death-tale is found in its entirety only in the Book of the Dun Cow, pp. 39a22-41b8 where it has been inserted by an interpolator or interpolators. The text is a composite one which de Vries believes was compiled by the scribe himself (2012: 15-19) and which she divides into three sections as follows:

1) §§1-7: The deaths of Echu and his brother (prose)
2) §§8-10: Three poems on the survivors of the bursting forth of Lough Neagh (verse)
3) §§11-18: The life of Lí Ban after the creation of Lough Neagh (prose)

The existence of independent copies of some of the verse material suggests an autonomous existence for at least two of the poems.[5] The internal dating evidence is limited, the only substantial element being a reference in the poem in §9 to the king of Loch Léin which suggests a terminus post quem of the beginning of the ninth century (de Vries 2012: 181-2).

De Vries concludes from her linguistic analysis as follows:

- The poem *Fo Loch Echach* (§9) was written at 'the end of the ninth century or the beginning of the tenth century' (2012: 191)
- The poem *Muirgein is gein* (§10) is 'slightly later' than *Fo Loch Echach* and is to be dated, tentatively, to the eleventh century (2012: 192), although there are few truly diagnostic features (existence of non-augmented preterite forms, loss of hiatus, *noco* for *co*, one example of univerbation and *sein* for OIr. *sin* guaranteed by rhyme).

---

5 See de Vries 2012: 178-80. Eleven quatrains from the poem *Fo Loch Echach adba dam* also appear in two later manuscripts, the sixteenth-century National Library of Ireland MS G7, col.12,12-col.13,11 and Royal Irish Academy MS 23 L 14 p.24m ff. Other verse material from the same poem and from *Murgein is gein* is found in four of the manuscripts of *Félire Óengusso* (see de Vries 2012: 173-6).

- The poem *Ticid, ticid* (§8) is 'extremely difficult to date' because it consists of only two quatrains, and she wavers between the ninth century and the eleventh/twelfth (2012: 193).
- The prose of §§1-7 is more conservative than the prose introductions to the poems and the final prose section (§§11-18) (2012: 193). Of particular note is the use of independent object pronouns in the final section, although otherwise the text is almost entirely lacking pronouns with the exception of an infixed 3 sg. fem. (*coros-bāid*, §4).

The terminus ante quem for the text as a whole is provided by its appearance in the Book of the Dun Cow, although the identity and date of the scribe are unknown (see above). Duncan (2015: 51-52) assigns the writing of this text to two hands: H1 (pp. 39a22-40a, 40b4-18) and H5 (pp. 40b1-3, 40b19-41b8). Thus, according to Duncan, §§1-10 (with the exception of a single stanza at the end of the poem in §9) were transcribed by H1, while §§11-18 (de Vries's third section) were transcribed by H5. This would require us to conclude that the tale is not the work of a single author, but it is not incompatible with de Vries' more general conclusion on the division of sections and the relative dating of the prose. It is notable that H5's portion is dated later by de Vries on linguistic grounds: Duncan (2015: 47) would date H5 on palaeographical grounds to the end of the twelfth century or beginning of the thirteenth century.

A.1.4 *Aided Guill maic Carbada*

The earliest copy of this tale is found in the Book of Leinster, pp. 107b-111b, where it is transcribed by scribe U who belongs to the earlier phase of the transcription and so provides a terminus ante quem in the 1160s. The text is generally dated to the twelfth century (see Ó Corráin 2017: 1286; Thurneysen 1921: 485). It does not appear in either of the saga lists, and Ó hUiginn (1996: 223) views it as a fresh composition not based on earlier material. Stokes (1893: 397-9) provides a brief description of the language but offers no date.

A.1.5 *Aided Nath Í*

This text ('The Death of Nath Í') is found in the Book of the Dun Cow pp. 38a-39a with the text primarily in the hand of M but the end (= p. 39a) is in the hand of H1. The text is also found independently in Trinity College Dublin H.2.16 (olim 1318 = the Yellow Book of Lecan) cols. 909-911 (1391×1392), and the Royal Irish Academy 23 P 12 (olim 512 = the Book of Ballymote), ff. 136va42-137ra30 (1383×1397), and an abridged version is found in Royal Irish Academy 23 P 2 (535 = Book of Lecan), ff. 70v-b (1397-c.1418) (Ó Concheanainn 1991: 2). Ó Concheanainn (1975-76) argues that these later manuscripts were derived from the Book of the Dun Cow but this has been comprehensively rejected by more careful considerations (West 1990, 84-9, Herbert 2015: 90-97). As they provide independent evidence of the Book of the Dun Cow's exemplar, we may conclude that, although the final page of the text is in a different hand, it may be treated as of the same approximate date as the text in hand M. Herbert (2015: 98) accepts that a date in the second half of the eleventh century is appropriate for the prose.

A.1.6 *Aislinge Óengusso*

This short tale ('The Dream of Óengus') is preserved only in one independent manuscript, British Library Egerton 1782, ff. 70r-71v which was compiled in 1517 (Meid 2017: 27). Shaw (1934: 32) describes the text as 'Old Irish with a very strong leaven of early and late Middle Irish forms'. He notes a number of 'very old forms' (p. 35) and would date the text to the eighth century (p. 37). Meid (2017: 48-9) objects to Shaw's specific dating criteria but nevertheless reaches a similar conclusion 'daß der Text ein eher frühes Altirisch reflektiert', although he does not provide any additional evidence.

Shaw's text, which is used in this study, is heavily restored to classical Old Irish, although he has made some exceptions (compare the manuscript transcription in Meid 2017: 34-37). Notably, he made no attempt to normalise the text to the language of the eighth century, following the authority of the manuscript where it appeared to be Old Irish. Thus, while he has cleansed the text of Middle Irishisms, it would be incorrect to assume that it accurately reflects the language of the eighth century.

A.1.7 *Aislinge Meic Conglinne*

On the basis of a comprehensive analysis of the language Jackson (1990: xxvi) places 'The Dream of Mac Conglinne' in the last quarter of the eleventh century. Among the features he refers to are (p. xxiii): survival of the dative plural of the adj. (§xxvi), lack of pronouns as subject of verbs other than the copula (§xxx), the use of infixed pronouns (§xxxvii f.), lack of *-th-* forms of prepositions, absence of confusion of *fri* and *la*, absence of *mar* as a conjunction (§xliv), lack of confusion of preverbs, *ro* and *do* do not replace *no* (§xlv), infixed versus prefixed *ro* (§§xlvi-xlix), *nícon*/*nochon* (§li), a relative absence of deponents (§lvi), the proportion of surviving deuterotonic forms (§lxxiv), and the lack of encroachment of the s-preterite (§lxxxix). The tale exists in two manuscripts where the narration is substantially different. The older (used by Jackson as the basis for his edition) is found in 'The Speckled Book' (Royal Irish Academy 23 P 16), pp. 213-29 where it was copied 1408×1411 (Jackson 1990: xi). The younger manuscript, Trinity College Dublin H.3.18 (1337) pp. 732-42, contains a shorter version that Jackson believes is anterior but not significantly earlier in language (1990: xxx).

A.1.8 *Bethadh Bibuis*

The Irish Life of Bevis of Hampton (Robinson 1908) is derived from the Anglo-Norman *Boeve de Haumtone* through a lost Middle English version with which it shares some unique material (Poppe 1992: 77-8). It is found in a single fifteenth-century manuscript,

Trinity College Dublin H.2.7 (1298), part 2, pp. 348a-363b, which was penned by Uilliam Mac an Leagha. Quin (1939: xl) suggests that Mac an Leagha was the translator of both this story and Guy of Warwick (A.1.23 below), as well as several other texts in the manuscript. Ó Corráin (2017: 1682) notes that English loan words are freely admitted.

A.1.9 *Betha Adamnáin*

'The Life of Adamnán' is preserved in Brussels, Bibliothèque Royale de Belgique, MS. 4190-4200 (3409), ff. 29-33, a seventeenth-century manuscript. Ó Riain dates it on the basis of internal evidence to 956×964 or more particularly 961×964 (Herbert & Ó Riain 1988: 4-8) which is accepted by Sharpe (1990). C. Breatnach (1992: 180) is convinced by the terminus post quem of 961 but not by the 964 terminus ante quem which is based on the apparent lack of reference to the rise of the Dál Cais. He draws attention to a possible coded mention of the slaying of Fógartach mac Tolairc in 972 (C. Breatnach 1992: 181) and would allow for the possibility of composition up until the end of the tenth century (see also Ó Briain 1993; Clancy 2011: 100-101).

Ó Riain characterises the language of the text as Middle Irish (Herbert & Ó Riain 1988: 5). He notes in particular 'the largely correct use of infixed pronouns, the absence of independent pronoun objects, the preservation of early forms of the article, the correct use of masculine and feminine forms of the adjectives, the generally correct case-usage after prepositions and the retention of the verbal prefixes *ro-* and *no-*' as indications of an early Middle Irish date (ibid. 5-6). Unfortunately, he does not provide any detail to substantiate this analysis. Mac Donncha (1976) places its composition much later and attributes it to Máel Ísa Ó Brolcháin (+1086).

A.1.10 *Betha Colmáin*

'The Life of Colmán' is preserved in Bibliothèque de Rennes Métropole, MS. 598 (15489), ff. 75r-89v. The manuscript is dated to the end of the fifteenth century (http://www.tablettes-rennaises.fr/app/photopro.sk/rennes/detail?docid=48917#sessionhistory-ready) but our story is contained in a separate, undated section. Meyer (1911: vii) states that the discovery of St Colmán's relics in 1122 is 'not unlikely' to have been 'the immediate cause of the composition' of the Life. He produces no argument for this statement but finds that the language, 'may well be that of the first half of the twelfth century' (ibid.). Paul Walsh (1912: 568-9) argues on topographical grounds that it cannot have been composed any earlier than the date proposed by Meyer. Ó Riain (2011: 197), however, notes that there are 'many features of the Life, including its excessive concern with grants of land and alliances, its tendency to confuse homonyms, its anachronisms, and what appears to be its use of the late twelfth-century Midlands version of the Martyrology of Aonghas as a source that point to a later date'.

A.1.11 *Bethu Brigte*

'The Life of Brigit' (*Bethu Brigte*) occurs in a single independent manuscript, Rawlinson B.512 ff. 31r-35v in the Bodleian Library, Oxford (Ó hAodha 1978: ix) which is a composite manuscript dating to the fifteenth and early sixteenth centuries (Ó Cuív 2001: 223). The transcription features a distinctive half-uncial *d* which may suggest a ninth-century exemplar (Ó Cuív 2001: 231). Linguistic dating places the composition of the text firmly in the first half of the ninth century although there is evidence of some modernisation (O'Brien 1938-39: 345; Ó hAodha 1978: 66-87).

A.1.12 *Bórama Laigen*

'The cattle-tribute of the Leinstermen' is preserved in the Book of Leinster pp. 294b-308b. Duncan (2012a: 59) would date the scribe, S, around 1160 and certainly before 1181. Another version is extant in Dublin RIA 23 P 2 (olim 535 al. Book of Lecan), ff. 295r-304v, 305v-310r, but it is the former copy that is examined here. Mac Eoin (1968: 28-30) asserts that the tale is derived from earlier materials but took on its current form in the eleventh century. He thinks the language is eleventh century but concedes that no linguistic analysis had been done at that stage (p. 28) and no internal evidence is advanced. Murphy (1955: 54) places it in the early twelfth century, although again without substantiation. A recent detailed linguistic analysis by Goverts (2014: 259) leads the author to assign it to between 1151 and 1181 'possibly during the first decade'. She holds that it is similar in date to *Cath Ruis na Ríg* and *In Cath Catharda* (see below) but concedes that it may occasionally incorporate some earlier textual material.

A.1.13 *Bruiden Da Choca*

Internal and linguistic evidence points to the first half of the twelfth century for the date of composition for this tale (Toner 2007: 3, 90). The tale is known to have existed in some form before this date, perhaps as early as the eighth century, but there is little evidence that the extant tale drew on that. The earliest surviving version is found in a portion of Trinity College Dublin MS H.3.18 (1137), pp. 708-724 which was written in the sixteenth or seventeenth century. One interesting feature of the tale is that it frequently draws on earlier verse sources, effectively forging some archaic looking *roscad* passages out of material from the eighth, ninth and tenth centuries (Toner 2007: 98-9). Because of their artificial nature, these have been omitted from the experiments in Chapter 4.

A.1.14 *Caithréim Thoirdhealbhaigh*

It is generally accepted (Ó Corráin 2017: 1644; G. Ó Riain 2012: 56-7) that this is the work of Seaán Mac Craith whose father, Ruaidhrí, died in 1343. The exact date of composition is unknown but is placed c.1330 × c.1360 (Ó Riain 2012: 57). It was edited by

O'Grady (1929) from two manuscripts, the early sixteenth century Royal Irish Academy 23 Q 16 (89) and Trinity College Dublin H.1.18 (1292), which was written in 1721 (Ó Riain 2012: 54). The text of the older manuscript is incomplete due to the loss of leaves. O'Grady's edition is mainly based on this older manuscript, with the Trinity College manuscript used to make good the lacunae. Ó Riain concludes from his examination of the manuscript that O'Grady reproduces the text of 23 Q 16 'quite faithfully on the whole' but that he seems to have taken a freer approach with the later manuscript where that is used (2012: 55-6).

A.1.15 *Cath Almaine*

'The Battle of Allen' (*Cath Almaine*) (Ó Riain 1978) is extant in four manuscripts, including primarily the Yellow Book of Lecan (Trinity College Dublin MS. H.2.16 olim 1318), cols. 939.9-942.35, compiled in late fourteenth/early fifteenth century, the Book of Fermoy (Royal Irish Academy 23 E 29 (1134)) pp. 128b1-130b13, compiled in the fifteenth century, and Brussels, Bibliothèque Royale MS. 5301-20, pp. 8-12, which was written after 1643. The Brussels manuscript is a separate recension and is the one used in our experiments. Ó Riain (1978: xxvii) notes seventeenth-century modernisation, including orthography and morphology, but holds that it belongs to the early Middle Irish period and is to be identified with the source text for the version found in the other manuscripts. He dates the later version on linguistic evidence to about the beginning of the twelfth century and would place its redaction at Lismore, Co. Waterford (Ó Riain 1978: xxiv).

A.1.16 *In Cath Catharda*

'The Civil War' is an adaptation of Lucan's *Bellum Civile*. It is found in several manuscripts, four of which form the basis for Stokes' edition (1909) which is used in this study. They are Trinity College Dublin MS. H.2.7 (olim 1298), pp. 376-390, 390-415, 416-41 (fifteenth century), Royal Irish Academy MS. D iv 2 (olim 1223), ff. 2ra-23va (15th century), University College Dublin MS. Franciscan A 17, ff. 1-139 (dated 1616), and Royal Irish Academy C vi 2 (olim 466) (dated 1633).

Sommerfelt (1916-21) provides a detailed description of the verbal system. He suggests a date of 1100 (1920-21: 38) but as Jackson (1990: xxii) points out, he was misled in this by the very early date that had then been assigned to 'The Colloquy of the Ancients' (*Acallam na Senórach*). Jackson therefore reassigns it to c.1150 which is probably closer to its true date.

A.1.17 *Cath Maighe Léna*

The version of the 'Battle of Moylena' used here is the long version edited by Jackson (1938). The earliest copies are found in two sixteenth-century manuscripts, University College Dublin, Franciscan MS. A 6, ff. 1r-14r and National Library of Ireland Phillipps'

MS 10266, pp. 5-18 (Jackson 1938: ix-xi). Based on various linguistic forms such as the use of infixed pronouns, the retention of the accusative of feminine nouns and adjectives, and the verbal system, Jackson dates the text to the second half of the thirteenth century or the 'earlier part' of the fourteenth (1938: xxiv), and he would place it earlier than the Gaelic Maundeville.

A.1.18 *Cath Ruis na Ríg*

'The Battle of Rosnaree' (*Cath Ruis na Ríg*) is extant as two separate versions. The version that is used in this study is the Middle Irish version found in the Book of Leinster, pp. 171a-178a. Mac Gearailt (1989) places this version in the second half of the twelfth century, and possibly midway through that 50-year period (1991: 129) or in the last two decades of the century (2004: 63). However, while the language of the tale is clearly late for a twelfth-century manuscript, such a late date is incompatible with the date of the scribe, A, who was active in the 1150s and early 1160s (see A.0.3 above). Mac Gearailt views the Book of Leinster version as an original composition, probably composed by the scribe. He argues (1991: 137) that it contains a peculiar mixture of language comprising an admixture of a) archaic, obsolete or obsolescent forms, b) current forms, and c) invented forms, and suggests that the author is trying to give the text an erudite appearance. He has modelled his texts on other sources, notably the version of the Cattle-Raid of Cooley also found in the Book of Leinster, which Mac Gearailt (1991: 140) would view as a work by a different author. Similarity in style may suggest that author of 'The Battle of Rosnaree' was more familiar with Fenian tales than the Ulster Cycle to which it formally belongs (Mac Gearailt 1988: 350).

It is likely, therefore, that our text was written in the 1150s or early 1160s, but it is worth bearing in mind that if the author is Áed úa Crimthainn, as Mac Gearailt suggests, then he must have been an established scholar by the 1150s when Bishop Find addresses him as successor of Colum mac Crimthaind, the *fer légind* of the high king of Leth Moga and the chief historian (*phrimsenchaid*) of Leinster (Best, Bergin and O'Brien 1954: xvi). We may assume, therefore, that he was born early in the twelfth century. In this study, we use the diplomatic edition from the Book of Leinster.

A.1.19 *Cogadh Gaedel re Gallaib*

There are two recensions of 'The War of the Gaels and the Galls' (*Cogadh Gaedel re Gallaib*). A fragment only of Recension 1 is contained in the Book of Leinster pp. 309a-310b, which is the version that concerns us here. It represents only about 1/7 of the full text (Ní Mhaonaigh 1992: 138-9). Ní Mhaonaigh (1995) observes that the verbal system resembles those of the Book of Leinster 'Cattle-Raid of Cooley' and 'The Civil War' (*In Cath Catharda*), and concludes that the language points to the second half of the eleventh or first half of the twelfth century. On the basis of internal evidence Ní Mhaonaigh (1995: 356, 377) would date the original text to 1103-13.

A.1.20 *De Dosibus Medicarum*

This medical tract is a translation of Walter de Agilon's text. It is extant in several manuscripts, including British Library, London, Harley 546, ff. 1-11 in which it is stated that it was translated by Cormac Mac Duinnshléibhe in Cloyne, Co. Cork, in 1459. O'Grady (1992: 171) takes the manuscript to be contemporary with the translation but Sheahan's analysis (1938: 32) of the stemma suggests that this cannot have been the case.

A.1.21 *Echtra Láegaire*

There are two copies of 'The Expedition of Láegaire' (*Echtra Láegaire*), namely, the Book of Leinster pp. 275b22-276b2 and the fifteenth-century Book of Lismore ff. 167ra24-va31 held in Chatsworth House, Derbyshire. Jackson (1942: 377) states the language of the prose is 'good Old Irish, probably of the second half of the ninth century' and that its state is much the same as 'The Tripartite Life of Patrick' (c.900) 'or somewhat earlier', a text believed to have been written in the late ninth or tenth century but revised in the eleventh (Mac Donncha 1980-83: 370, Jackson 1986). The neuter article is 'fully preserved', and the superlative *-em* still exists, pointing to a terminus ante quem of 'hardly much later than about 900'. Jackson (1942: 378) dates the verse to slightly later, describing it as 'very early Middle Irish rather than late Old; older however than *Saltair na Rann*' (on which see below), and would place it in the second quarter or middle of the tenth century. The Book of Lismore version is not copied from the Book of Leinster and provides independent evidence of the archetype. Jackson (1942: 379) describes the modernisation common to both copies as 'minor', and notes that Leinster has 'very little extra modernization on its own account'. Jackson's edition is not available electronically so we have used the copy from the diplomatic edition of the Book of Leinster. The text is rather short (130 lines in Jackson's edition).

A.1.22 *Fingal Rónáin*

The tale of 'The Kin-slaying of Rónán' (*Fingal Rónáin*) is preserved in two manuscripts, the Book of Leinster ff. 271-3 and Trinity College Dublin H. 3.18 (1337), pp. 749-54. It appears be to an original composition which is not based on an earlier text. Greene (1975: 2) observes that the language is consistent throughout and points to the end of the Old Irish period (c.900), although he provides no details, and he concludes that it dates to 'early in the tenth century'. This is generally accepted (e.g. Mac Gearailt 2006-7: 63), although it surely warrants further investigation. Uhlich (2006: 19) states that 'the case for an Old Irish date has not been made, and that on the other hand the text contains a substantial proportion of Middle Irish features common to both manuscripts, which appear to suggest at least an early Middle Irish date of composition.' We use here the diplomatic edition of the Book of Leinster text which contains some modernisation not found in the later manuscript (Uhlich 2006: 16-17).

A.1.23 *Guy of Warwick*

This story was translated in the second half of the fifteenth century by Uilliam Mac an Leagha and is written in a late Irish style with many loanwords admitted (Quin 1939: xl; Ó Corráin 2017: 1681). The only edition is that of Robinson 1908. It is preserved in Trinity College Dublin MS. H.2.7 (olim 1298) part 2, pp. 300a-347b.

A.1.24 *Genemain Áeda Sláine*

'The Conception of Áed Sláine' is preserved in two manuscripts, the Book of the Dun Cow ff. 52a-53a and Bibliothèque Royale de Belgique, MS. 5100-5104, ff. 14b-15b, written in 1630. The verse only is also found in the Book of Leinster f. 145b.

The text of the Book of the Dun Cow is in the hand of M with very minor corrections by H1. The poem is by Flann Mainistrech (d.1056) and is omitted in this study. Herbert (2015: 81-84) distinguishes two components in the prose, namely, the miracle of St Ciarán (ll.4206-34) and the birth of Áed Sláine (ll.4272-334). She thinks that the origin of the prose birth tale is unlikely to be earlier than the mid-eleventh century (that is, during Flann's lifetime). She describes the miracle story as an 'insertion… as a foretale to the birth' (p. 82). She thinks the language of the two parts is consistent, but if the miracle tale is an insertion as she suggests, then we should perhaps date it slightly closer to the date of the manuscript.

A.1.25 *Maundeville*

This Irish translation of *The Buke of John Maundeville* was made by Fínghin Ó Mathghamhain in 1475 (Stokes 1898: 1-2). It is preserved incomplete in two manuscripts, Bibliothèque de Rennes Métropole, MS. 598 (15489), ff. 52r-69v, dated 1586, and in British Library MS Egerton 1781, ff. 129a-146b, which may be dated c.1484-87 (Flower 1926: 526), with a further fragment in British Library Additional 33993, ff. 6r-7r (16th century). Stokes' edition, which is used in this study, is based on the Rennes manuscript so far as it goes, supplemented by the last folio in the Egerton copy. The translation lacks the archaisms that we see in some other texts of the period: the infixed pronoun is never used, there are no examples of perfective *ro-*, and the pret. 3 pl. ending *-atar* is generalised (Ó Catháin 1933: 17). Ó hUiginn (2013: 94) suggests that it was deliberately written in a register close to the spoken language.

A.1.26 *Mesca Ulad*

'The Intoxication of the Ulstermen' exists in four manuscripts representing three versions. The oldest version is partially preserved in the Book of the Dun Cow pp. 19a-20b where it was written by the scribe M with minor corrections by H. Only the ending survives. A later version is preserved in the Book of Leinster pp. 261b25-268b49, where the ending is lost. The two incomplete copies overlap slightly, so that it is possible to see that the revision was thorough. The earlier version is dated to the Old Irish period 'but has suffered a good deal of modernisation in transmission' (Watson 1941: xxxiii). Watson concludes, drawing on Thurneysen's analysis of the text, that the later version dates 'to the first third, perhaps the first quarter of the twelfth century' (Watson 1941: xx).

A complete text of the tale is preserved in two manuscripts: National Library of Ireland MS G.4 (Phillipps MS. 8214), cols 959-972 and National Library of Scotland MS 71.1.40 (formerly Gaelic MS. XL) ff. 49-67. The relationship between this version and the earlier versions is disputed. Mac Gearailt (1986: 153-5) points to several instances where the Edinburgh manuscript exhibits apparently older readings than the Book of Leinster, and he proposes a common ancestor for these two manuscripts which he dates to c.1100, dating the copy in the Book of Leinster to c.1160. See also Ó Concheanainn (1987).

A.1.27 *Merugud Uilix*

This tale, based on the story of Ulysses, is found in three manuscripts: Royal Irish Academy, 23 P 12 (536 = the Book of Ballymote), pp. 445a-447b, Royal Irish Academy Stowe MS. D iv 2 (992), ff. 59b-61a (15th century), and Dublin, King's Inns' Library, MS. 12, ff. 41v-43v, which was written c.1491×1493.

Kuno Meyer (1886) attempted a critical edition from Ballymote and Stowe. Robert Meyer (1958) edits from the Book of Ballymote where it was, he thinks, transcribed by Manus Ó Duigenan (d. 1452). He dates the text on linguistic grounds to the early thirteenth century (1958: xiii) but the discussion is cursory and contains non-diagnostic as well as conflicting evidence. Mac Niocaill (1958: 135) agrees with R. Meyer's analysis but adds that a date in the last quarter of the twelfth century would be equally acceptable. Hillers (2014: 83) dates it c.1200, calling it late Middle Irish (cf. Hillers 1992: 64). There is evidence of some isolated archaisms (*teach* as a neuter and an example of the dative plural of the adjective (R. Meyer 1958: xiii)). We use Robert Meyer's edition here.

A.1.28 *Monastery of Tallaght*

The oldest recension of this text survives incomplete in Royal Irish Academy MS 3 B 23 (1227), pp. 33-47, 51-52, and various other fragments are to be found elsewhere. The manuscript is dated to the fifteenth century. Gwynn and Purton (1911-12: 121-2) suggest on internal grounds that the text was written after the death of Máel Ruain (d. 792) and during the lifetime of his pupil, Máel Díthruib (d. 840), with a single paragraph added after his death. A reference to Díarmait, abbot of Iona 815-831 (or later) provides a terminus post quem, and so they conclude that the text was written 831×840 (ibid. 122). The language is certainly Old Irish but according to Gwynn and Purton (1911: 124) it 'has undergone a good deal of alteration'. The edition used here is Lash's electronic edition in POMIC which follows Gwynn and Purton (https://www.ucd.ie/tlh/text/gp.pria.29.001.text.html).

A.1.29 *Regimen na Sláinte*

This medical tract, a translation of *Regimen Sanitatis* by Magninus of Milan, is preserved in two primary manuscripts, Royal Irish Academy 24 P 26 (474), pp. 353-486, dated to 1469, and Trinity College Dublin H.2.13 (1315), pp. 126-186 dated to 1486 (Ó Ceithearnaigh 1942: xxv-xxvi). The date of the translation has not been established with certainty but its editor provisionally places it in the first quarter of the fifteenth century (Ó Ceithearnaigh 1942: xxviii).

A.1.30 *Saltair na Rann*

'The Psalter of the Verses' (*Saltair na Rann*, ed. Stokes 1883) is a versified account of the Bible, mostly concerning events from the Old Testament. The oldest manuscript in which it is found is Rawlinson B 502, ff. 19ra-40vb, which is dated to c.1130 (see above A.0.2). The poet identifies himself in the final canto as Óengus, *céile Dé* (l.8009), who is generally recognised as Óengus macc Óengobann, otherwise Óengus the Culdee (fl. c.800). The ascription was rejected by Stokes (1883: i) who notes the Middle Irish character of the language and various historical events and persons belonging to the end of the tenth century (ll.2337-2376) which appear in a canto dealing with chronology. Lines 2337-40 state that it was a thousand years less twelve (= 988) from the birth of Christ to the great destruction of cattle (*co hár cétach na cethra*).

A list of near-contemporary kings is given, including: Cináed mac Máel Cholaim of Scotland (reigned 971-995), Máel Sechnaill mac Domnaill (980-1002), Brian of Munster (976-1002), Donnchad of Leinster (984-999), Cathal of Connacht (973-1010), Eochaid of Ulster (972-1004), Fergal mac Conaing meic Néill, king of Ailech and Cenél nÉogain (974?-1001), Dub da Letha of Síl Érimon (965-998), Otto II (973-983), Hlothair (= Lothair) of the Franks (954-986), Edgar of the Saxons (959-975), and Máel Cholaim mac Domnaill mac Éogain (died AU 997). The kings are referred to in the past tense, suggesting that this section was written after their reigns, so their inclusion provides a terminus post quem of 1010 (the death of Cathal), although the centrality of the cattle murrain of 988 suggests it could not be long after 1010. Both Mac Eoin (1960-61: 57) and Carney (1982-83: 212-214) suggest, therefore, that this section is an interpolation, so any conclusions on dating can only relate to this section.

Mac Eoin (1960-61: 57-8; 1982b) views only the date of the cattle disease in 988 as relevant to the date of composition of the main text and accepts the traditional date of composition, arguing that it was written by Airbertach mac Cosse Dobráin (d. 1016). He takes the reference to Óengus, céile Dé, as a literary conceit, used by the poet to suggest that even the most brilliant of men could not understand God's ways (Mac Eoin 1982b: 14-15). Airbertach's authorship is rejected by Carney (1982-83: 207-16), rightly in our opinion. Rather, Carney takes the ascription as genuine but argues that it is not Óengus Mac Oíbleán, the author of 'The Calendar of Óengus' (*Félire Óengusso*) (c.800). Instead, he takes him to be Óengus, a monk of Clonenagh, who wrote a poem which gives a short biography of the author of the Calendar (Carney 1982-83: 184-5). On the basis of this, he would date the work as a whole to c.870. This dating has not received general approval.

It will be noted that once the evidence of the king lists is rejected, this text is basically without secure internal dating evidence, and so it need not be anchored to the end of the tenth century conventionally ascribed to it. Carney (1982-83: 211) notes that the language 'is at times so peculiar that one might seem justified in saying that it was *sui generis*, and belonged to no period'. He views the author as a gifted and innovative writer who was not followed by his contemporaries who 'wrote to a great extent in a dull, uniform, inexpressive, and verbally poor Irish' (ibid. 212). Aspects of the orthography and morphology of the poem lead Carney to conclude that 'it can be said with some confidence that [it] was written in what was technically the O. Ir. period, but the author showed his originality by drawing not only on preceding literature but upon the language of the people' (ibid. 212).

In an important contribution, Carey notes that there are clearly distinctive sections, sometimes drawing on earlier sources and sometimes inconsistent with the rest of the text, although he finds no noticeable variation in language and style that would indicate the involvement of different poets (1986: 76-7). He accepts that the poem is the work of a single author, and concludes (1986: 77) that 'the lengthy writing of [*Saltair na Rann*] would have involved the stratified integration of various bodies of material, some of them more successfully incorporated than others'. This has serious implications for our understanding of the language that have not yet been explored. We must assume that parts of the poem may show the influence of earlier texts, while other sections will reflect more closely the language of the poet's own time.

A.1.31 *Scél Mucce Maic Dathó*

The earlier version of 'The Tale of Mac Dathó's Pig' has come down to us in six manuscripts, three of which are of interest to us here. They are the Book of Leinster pp. 743-748 and British Library Harleian 5280, ff. 50, 52, 53r which, according to Thurneysen (1935: iii), best preserves the oldest version. Based on his analysis of the language, Thurneysen places the original composition c.800 AD, and the archetype of the three principal manuscripts in 'the tenth or eleventh century' (ibid. iii-iv). The archetype has some very significant modernisations, for example, in the verbal forms and in the neuter. Although Thurneysen produces a critical edition, which is used in this study, he does not attempt to take us back to the original text and rather selects 'the spelling that seems to be the most archaic' from the extant manuscripts.

A.1.32 *Táin Bó Cúailnge*

'The Cattle-Raid of Cooley' is extant in four versions including two from early medieval manuscripts. The oldest version survives in the Book of the Dun Cow, pp. 55a-82b, and Trinity College Dublin, H.2.16 (1318 = Yellow Book of Lecan), col. 573-644 (written 1391×1392), as well as two later manuscripts (ed. O'Rahilly 1976). The Book of the Dun Cow copy was transcribed by three scribes, A and M, both of whom can be dated to the end of the eleventh/beginning of the twelfth centuries, and an interpolator who is probably twelfth century (see above A.0.1). The Yellow Book of Lecan is a fourteenth-century copy but preserves the better text in many cases.

Thurneysen's analysis of the tale has proved enduring but is not universally accepted. He viewed the first recension as an eleventh-century compilation based on two ninth-century versions (with some earlier material), and while the nature of these versions and their relationship has been questioned, the dates have been widely adopted. O'Rahilly (1976, 1982) portrays a much more complex view of the relationship between the different recensions and argues for the later interpolation of a number of elements not recognised by Thurneysen, although she accepts the dating in broad outline. Tristram (1992) argues that it cannot be earlier than the tenth or eleventh century, although her view is not widely accepted. Charles-Edwards (2015) dates the original composition to the eighth century on internal grounds, but he does not enter into the question of the date of writing of the extant version.

The second recension is preserved in the Book of Leinster from which it is edited by C. O'Rahilly (1982). Duncan (2012a: 57) observes that it was transcribed by two scribes, T1 and F, who were certainly contemporary and probably collaborated. Thurneysen (1921: 113-15) dated the Book of Leinster version to the first third or first quarter of the twelfth century but this is shown by Mac Eoin (1982a: 117) to be based on extremely tenuous grounds. Mac Gearailt's analysis (1992) would require a date of c.1163 for what he determines to be later sections (part of 3 and sections 4-5), that is, at the earlier end of the range when he could have collaborated with T1. More recently, (2010: 26-30) he has argued on linguistic grounds for an eleventh-century date for the composition of Recension II as a whole. The redactor followed his source closely but 'his version is a completely new composition with its own independent verbal system and its own distinctive style and narrative method' (Mac Gearailt 2010: 31). This is relatively well preserved in Mac Gearailt's sections 1, 2 and 3,[6] but the scribe has modernised part of 3 and all of sections 4 and 5 and Mac Gearailt would date this to the middle of the twelfth century (ibid. 32).

A.1.33 · *Táin Bó Fraích*

The story of 'The Cattle-Raid of Fróech' appears in four main manuscripts, all of which are independent of each other according to Meid (1974: xxi). They are the Book of

6 Although he does suggest that parts of the earlier sections may also have been of later date (p. 31).

Leinster pp. 183v-185v, the Yellow Book of Lecan col. 649.47-658.41 in the Royal Irish Academy, British Museum Egerton 1782, pp. 82v21-87v10, and National Library of Scotland Adv. MS. 72.1.40 (olim Gaelic XL) pp. 37b26-45b29. Meid (1974: xxiv-v) dates the original text on linguistic grounds to 700-750. However, there is evidence for an early Middle Irish archetype which, Meid believes, 'apart from some corruptions and a very few Mid. Ir. forms, has faithfully preserved the text and the language of an O[ld] I[rish] original' (1974: xxv). Meid provides no argument for such an early date but rather follows Pokorny's (1921: 120-1) brief list of early forms including *-gloistis* §9 (with unbroken *ō*), *oldaas* §12, *nachimm-éta* §13, *deec* §14, *báu* §§25, 27, and *cichib-foruireth* §28 which he concludes indicate a date of composition before the Würzburg glosses, and so he would not date the text before the last quarter of the eighth century. Whether such an early date can be based on these few words is questionable. The unbroken *ō* is isolated and there are examples in the Annals of Ulster *s.a.* 794 and 844 in any case (Ó Máille 1910: 76) suggesting that it may have persisted later in some areas (see Stifter 2013: 176-7). Disyllabic *deec* is found in the Würzburg glosses (15b1) and *oldaas* is found in Middle Irish (see eDIL s.v. 3 ol). On *nachimm-*, Meid himself (2015: 198) notes that it is characteristic of the Würzburg glosses. The diphthong *áu* was in the process of being lost during the Old Irish period but we may note gen. pl. *báu* in the Táin (Best & Bergin 1929: l.5373) and *bao*, in the St Gall glosses (Stokes & Strachan 1903: 72 (22b11)). While some of these features certainly do point to an Old Irish date, therefore, we may doubt whether a date before the main body of Würzburg glosses has been proven and we must consider possible dates in the middle or second half of the eighth century.

The tale naturally falls into two parts, the first relating to the wooing of Findabair and the second concerning the recovery of Fróech's cattle, wife and sons. The second part does not appear to be any later than the first but Meid (2015: 23) notes that 'part two differs also from the elegantly narrated first part, highlighted by dramatic dialogues, in its style: the narrative is terse and erratic, the dialogues are laconic, so that much remains obscure; apart from textual corruptions there are some remarkable linguistic archaisms'. He suggests, therefore, that the wooing tale absorbed an old tradition about the abduction and recovery of Fróech's family and cattle. This certainly goes back to the archetype and has not been distinguished linguistically from the main body of the text.

Meid (2015) presents a restored Old Irish text but that is not available in electronic format. We have used his 1974 edition in our research. It follows the text of the Book of Leinster, allowing Middle Irish forms to stand even where they could be restored from the other manuscripts. Modernisations in the Book of Leinster text are mostly superficial, relating to orthography, particularly the representation of unstressed vowels. The grammar, including the verbal and pronominal systems, seems well preserved when allowance is made for orthography.

A.1.34 *Tochmarc Emire*

'The Courtship of Emer' (*Tochmarc Emire*) is extant in two separate recensions of which the earlier one concerns us here. Only a fragment is preserved in a single manuscript, Oxford Bodleian Library MS. Rawlinson B.512, ff. 117ra-118rb, which was written in the fifteenth-century (ed. Meyer 1890). Meyer concludes, despite a number of Middle Irishisms, that the Old Irish character of the language 'stands out so clearly that we can safely claim the text of R as a piece of Irish of the 8th century' (1890: 439). Ó Concheanainn (1996: 96-100) argues that R is an archaised Middle Irish text based on the second recension but this is shown to be incorrect by Toner (1998) who reasserts an Old Irish date.

A.1.35 *Treatise on the Psalter*

The Old Irish 'Treatise on the Psalter' survives in two late medieval manuscripts: Bodleian Library Rawlinson B 512, ff. 45r-47v and British Library Harley 5280, ff. 21r-24v9 (Ó Néill 1979: 149). A terminus post quem of c.800 is suggested by its dependence on the *Bibelwerk* (Ó Néill 1979: 162). Meyer concludes on the basis of language that it was written about the same time as the Milan glosses of the late eighth or early ninth century (Meyer 1894 xiii). Ó Néill (1979: 163) points to the lack of assimilation in *mb* and *ln* as evidence that it may be earlier than the Milan glosses, although these are slender grounds for distinguishing between two texts (see Stifter 2013: 182). His final suggested date is a little after 800 or the first half of the ninth century (Ó Néill 1979: 162-3; 2014: 123). Ó Corráin (2017: 104) dates it to the end of the eighth and first half of ninth century. Ó Néill (2014: 132) observes that the tenth-century reviser goes to considerable lengths to make the material of his ninth-century source relevant to his audience, modernising the Irish in the process.

A.1.36 *Tucait Indarba na nDéssi*

The story of 'The Cause of the Expulsion of the Déssi' exists in two versions. Recension 1 is dated to the eighth century (ed. Meyer 1901). Recension 2, which is examined here, is found, lacking the conclusion, in the Book of the Dun Cow pp. 53a33-54b49, as well as Trinity College Dublin H.2.15A (olim 1316), pp. 67a-68b (14th/15th cent.) and H.3.17 (olim 1336) part 6, cols. 720-3 (16th century). It is dated by Ó Corráin (2017: 1498) to c.1050. Hull (1958-59: 15 and note) notes that 'it also preserves a number of Old Irish forms', but concludes that it probably dates to 'at least some fifty or more years previous' to 1106 (the date of the death of the main scribe of the manuscript). There are several minor interpolations by a reviser, but there are also two more substantial interpolations at ll.4388-95 and 4432-37 which differ from the other versions of this text (Hull 1958-59: 16) and so may not belong to the original composition.[7]

7 Duncan (2015: 52) tentatively identifies the scribe as H5.

Ó Cathasaigh (1976) shows that the Book of the Dun Cow text is a compilation. Quite apart from H's interventions, the material in ll.4340-62 is largely unique to that manuscript and is not found in other copies of this version. His linguistic analysis suggests that the main body of the text 'comprises M[iddle] I[rish] innovations distributed through what is otherwise an O[ld] I[rish] text', representing a rewriting of an Old Irish exemplar, but that the section unique to this manuscript represents a new Middle Irish stratum (1976: 153). While he is reluctant to place a date on the new stratum, he is inclined to believe that it might have been contributed by the scribe himself. For testing, therefore, we may consider ll.4340-62 as representative of c.1050-1100, although this leaves us with a very short sample.

APPENDIX B

Machine Learning

This appendix provides a very brief introduction to the most relevant and very basic machine learning principles that are applied in this book. All terms and concepts are described in a non-specialist way aimed at readers from the Humanities with little or no background in computing. Some other concrete techniques that are more complex or advanced but relevant to specific parts of this book are explained briefly in the relevant section or subsection elsewhere in the book. Novice readers or those who want a wider perspective could consider machine learning text books with a more comprehensive coverage of the fundamentals, such as Murphy (2012) or Bishop (2006).

B.1 Classification, Regression and Clustering

Classification and regression are typical examples of supervised learning. Classification is often done when we want to map input to discrete output labels, such as dates, while regression is used when we want to map input to a continuous output space. In both regression and classification, the goal is to find specific relationships or structure in the input data that allow us to effectively produce correct output data. Note that "correct" output is determined entirely from the training data, so while we do have a ground truth that our model will assume is true, it is not to say that data labels are always correct in real-world situations. Noisy, or incorrect, data labels will clearly reduce the effectiveness of the model. Common algorithms for classification and regression include logistic regression, naive Bayes, support vector machines, artificial neural networks, and random forests.

Clustering can be considered the most important unsupervised learning problem, which deals with finding a structure in a collection of unlabelled data. A loose definition of clustering could be "the process of organizing objects into groups whose members are similar in some way". A cluster is therefore a collection of objects which are "similar" to each other and are "dissimilar" to the objects belonging to other clusters. Common clustering algorithms include K-means clustering and hierarchical clustering.

B.1.1 *Text Classification*

Text classification belongs to the field of document classification or categorisation. Also known as text categorisation, text classification attempts to assign a textual document to one or more classes or categories. The classes or categories can be topical, such as ‘sport’, ‘politics’, ‘economy’, etc. for classifying news; or sentimental, such as ‘positive’, ‘neutral’, ‘negative’, etc. for classifying opinions. In this research, the classes will be timestamps, normally periods of time.

B.1.2 *Feature Selection*

Feature selection is the process of selecting a subset of the terms, such as words, characters, or n-grams of words or characters, occurring in the training set of texts and using only this subset as features for classifying other texts. Feature selection serves two main purposes. First, it makes training and applying a classifier more efficient by decreasing the size of the effective vocabulary. This is of particular importance for classifiers that, unlike Naïve Bayes, are expensive to train. Second, feature selection often increases classification accuracy by eliminating noise features. A noise feature is one that, when added to the text model, increases the classification error when applied to new data.

B.1.3 *Training*

After feature selection, texts can be represented as vectors of the features. On this new representation of the training texts, a classifier, i.e. a classification model, can then be trained. By training, we normally mean the process of tuning the weights of features and the values of some model parameters, which often involves a developing set or cross validation. With the method of developing set, the training texts are divided into two parts. The larger part is used for building a model by tuning the feature weights, and the smaller part is held for optimising the classifying performance by tuning the parameter values. Cross validation is extended from the method of developing set, in which the training texts are divided into n parts, and the tuning process will be run n times. Therefore, it is also called n fold cross validation. In each fold, $n - 1$ parts are used for model building, and the remaining one is used for tuning parameters. Finally, the classifier with the best averaged classifying performance will be returned.

B.1.4 *Evaluation*

Evaluation aims to estimate the performance of a classifier or model. This estimation can be implemented on a held-out test set or via cross-validation. Some common measurements include precision, recall and F-measure. For a given set of N texts to be classified, if M texts are finally classified and L of them are classified correctly, the precision is calculated by L/M and the recall by L/N. F-measure is a trading-off combination of precision and recall, which often takes the form of $2 \times \text{precision} \times \text{recall}/(\text{precision} + \text{recall})$. For text classification, classifying accuracy is another popular performance measurement when $N = M$ and, actually, precision equals recall.

B.2 Other Relevant Statistics

Mean: In probability and statistics, mean, also called expected value or mathematical expectation, is used to refer to one measure of the central tendency either of a probability distribution or of the random variable characterised by that distribution.

Median: The median is the value separating the higher half of a data sample, a population, or a probability distribution, from the lower half. For a data set, it may be thought of as the "middle" value. For example, in the data set {1, 3, 3, 6, 7, 8, 9}, the median is 6, the fourth largest, and also the fourth smallest, number in the sample. For a continuous probability distribution, the median is the value such that a number is equally likely to fall above or below it.

Quartile: The first quartile is defined as the middle number between the smallest number and the median of the data set. For example, in the data set {1, 3, 3, 6, 7, 8, 9}, the first quartile is 3.

Deviation: In mathematics and statistics, deviation is a measure of difference between the observed value of a variable and some other value, often that variable's mean. The sign of the deviation (positive or negative), reports the direction of that difference (the deviation is positive when the observed value exceeds the reference value). The magnitude of the value indicates the size of the difference.

Standard deviation: In statistics, the standard deviation is a measure that is used to quantify the amount of variation or dispersion of a set of data values. A low standard deviation indicates that the data points tend to be close to the mean (also called the expected value) of the set, while a high standard deviation indicates that the data points are spread out over a wider range of values.

T-test: The t-test is a kind of statistical hypothesis test, which is most commonly applied when the test statistic would follow a normal distribution if the value of a scaling term in the test statistic were known. The t-test can be used to determine if two sets of data are significantly different from each other.

Bibliography

Abe, Hidenao and Shusaku Tsumoto (2010) 'Text categorization with considering temporal patterns of term usages', in *Proceedings of ICDM Workshops.*

Adam, Kalthoum, Asim Baig, Somaya Al-Maadeed, Ahmed Bouridane, and Sherine El-Menshawy (2018) 'KERTAS: dataset for automatic dating of ancient Arabic manuscripts', *International Journal on Document Analysis and Recognition*, 21.4, 283-90.

Allan, J.R.P. and V. Lavrenko (1998) 'Online new event detection and tracking', *Proceedings of SIGIR'1998*, 37-45.

Altschuler, E.L., A.S. Calude, Andrew Meade, and Mark Pagel (2013) 'Linguistic evidence supports date for Homeric epics', *BioEssays*, 35 (5), 417-20.

Anderson, A. O. and M. O. Anderson (1961) *Adomnan's Life of Columba* (Oxford).

Bakshy, Eytan, Itamar Rosenn, Cameron Marlow, and Lada Adamic (2012) 'The role of social networks in information diffusion', *Proceedings of the 21st international conference on World Wide* Web, ACM 2012, 519-28.

Balasubramanian, Krishnakumar and Guy Lebanon (2012) 'The landmark selection method for multiple output prediction', *Proceedings of the 29th International Conference on Machine Learning*, 983-90.

Belinkov, Yonatan, Alexander Magidow, Maxim Romanov, Avi Shmidman, and Moshe Koppel (2016) 'Shamela: A Large-Scale Historical Arabic Corpus', *Proceedings of the Workshop on Language Technology Resources and Tools for Digital Humanities (LT4DH)*, 45-53.

Ben-David, Shai, John Blitzer, Koby Crammer, Alex Kulesza, Fernando Pereira, Jennifer Wortman Vaughan (2010) 'A theory of learning from different domains', *Machine Learning Journal* 79 (1-2).

Berry, David M. (2012) (ed.) *Understanding Digital Humanities* (Palgrave Macmillan).

Best, R.I. & Osborn Bergin (1929) *Lebor na hUidre: Book of the Dun Cow* (Dublin).

Best, R.I. (1913-14) 'Palaeographical notes', *Ériu* 7, 114-20.

Best, R.I., Osborn Bergin and M.A. O'Brien (1954) *The Book of Leinster, formerly Lebar na Núachongbála* vol. 1 (Dublin).

Bhreathnach, Edel (2002) 'Two contributors to the Book of Leinster: Bishop Finn of Kildare and Gilla na Náem Úa Duinn', in *Ogma: essays in Celtic Studies in honour of Próinséas Ní Chatháin*, ed. Michael Richter & Jean-Michel Picard (Dublin), 105-11.

Bhreathnach, Edel (2005) '*Níell cáich úa Néill nasctar géill*: the political context of *Baile Chuinn Chétchathaig*', in Edel Bhreathnach (ed.), *The kingship and landscape of Tara* (Dublin), 49-68.

Bi, Wei and James Tin-Yau Kwok (2013) 'Efficient multi-label classification with many labels', *ICML (3)*, 405-13.

Bieler, Ludwig & James Carney (1972) 'The Lambeth Commentary' Ériu 23, 1-55.
Bieler, Ludwig (1979) *The Patrician texts in the Book of Armagh* (Dublin).
Binchy, D.A. (1941) *Críth Gablach* (Dublin).
Bisagni, Jacopo (2009) 'The language and the date of *Amrae Coluimb Chille*', in Stefan Zimmer (ed.), *Kelten am Rhein: Akten des dreizehnten Internationalen Keltologiekongresses* = proceedings of the 13th International congress of Celtic studies, 23. bis 27. Juli 2007 in Bonn. Zweiter Teil: Philologie. Sprachen und Literaturen, 1-11.
Bisagni, Jacopo (2013-14) 'Prolegomena to the study of code-switching in the Old Irish glosses', *Peritia* 24/25, 1-57.
Bishop, C. M. (2006) *Pattern Recognition and Machine Learning* (Springer).
Boutsidis, C., M.W. Mahoney and P. Drineas (2009) 'An improved approximation algorithm for the column subset selection problem', *Proceedings of the 20th ACMSIAM Symposium on Discrete Algorithms* (New York) 968-77 .
Boyle, Elizabeth & Deborah Hayden (2014) *Authorities and adaptations: the reworking and transmission of textual sources in medieval Ireland* (Dublin).
Breatnach, Caoimhín (1992) review of Herbert & Ó Riain 1988, *Éigse* 26, 177-187.
Breatnach, Caoimhín (1996), review of Mallory and Stockman 1994, in *Éigse* 29, 200-208.
Breatnach, Caoimhín (2005) 'The significance of the orthography of Irish proper names in the Codex Salmanticensis', *Ériu* 55, 85-101.
Breatnach, Caoimhín (2015) 'The Annals of Ulster: verse, sources and editions', in *Aon don Éigse: essays marking Osborn Bergin's centenary lecture on bardic poetry (1912)*, ed. Caoimhín Breatnach & Meidhbhín Ní Úrdáil (Dublin), 221-38.
Breatnach, Liam (1977) 'The suffixed pronouns in Early Irish', *Celtica* 12, 75-107.
Breatnach, Liam (1980) 'Tochmarc Luaine ocus Aided Athairne', *Celtica* 13, 1-31.
Breatnach, Liam (1984) 'Canon law and secular law in early Ireland: the significance of the *Bretha Nemed*', *Peritia* 3, 439-59.
Breatnach, Liam (1987) *Uraicecht na Ríar: the poetic grades in early Irish law* (Dublin).
Breatnach, Liam (1989) 'An edition of *Amra Senáin*', in Donnchadh Ó Corráin, Liam Breatnach, Kim McCone (eds), *Sages, saints and storytellers: Celtic studies in honour of Professor James Carney* (Maynooth) 7-31.
Breatnach, Liam (1994) 'An Mheán-Ghaeilge', in McCone et al., 221-333.
Breatnach, Liam (1996) 'Poets and Poetry', in *Progress in Medieval Irish Studies*, ed. Kim McCone & Katharine Simms (Maynooth) 65-77.
Breatnach, Liam (2005) *A companion to the Corpus Iuris Hibernici* (Dublin).
Breatnach, Liam (2011) *The early Irish law text Senchas már and the question of its date.* Quiggin memorial lectures, 13 (Cambridge).
Breatnach, Liam (2015) 'Lebor na hUidre: some linguistic aspects', in Ó hUiginn 2015, 53-77.

Breatnach, Pádraig (2017) 'Ornamentation in *Rannaigheacht*', in *Dá dtrian feasa fi-afraighidh: essays on the Irish Grammatical metrical tradition*, ed. Gordon Ó Riain (Dublin), 293-337.

Byrne, F.J. (2005) 'The viking age', in *A new history of Ireland: I Prehistoric and early Ireland*, ed. Dáibhí Ó Cróinín (Oxford) 609-34.

Carey, John (1986) 'Questions of interpolation in the opening cantos of Saltair na Rann', *Proceedings of the Harvard Celtic Colloquium* 6, 69-82.

Carey, John (1996) 'Obscure styles in medieval Ireland', *Mediaevalia* 19, 23-39.

Carey, John (2002) 'The Lough Foyle colloquy texts: *Immacaldam Choluim Chille 7 ind Óclaig oc Carraic Eolairg* and *Immacaldam in Druad Brain 7 Inna Banḟátho Febuil Ós Loch Ḟebuil*', *Ériu* 52, 53-87.

Carney, James (1979) 'Aspects of Archaic Irish', *Éigse* 17, 417-435.

Carney, James (1982-83) 'The dating of early Irish verse texts, 500-1100', *Éigse* 19, 177-216.

Charles-Edwards, T.M. & Fergus Kelly (2008) *Bechbretha*. First published 1983 (Dublin).

Charles-Edwards, T.M. (1995) 'Language and society among the insular Celts A.D. 400-1000', in *The Celtic world*, ed. M.J. Green (London), 703-36.

Charles-Edwards, T.M. (2006) *The Chronicle of Ireland*. Translated Texts for Historians 44: 2 vols (Liverpool).

Charles-Edwards, T.M. (2009-10), review of Mc Carthy 2008, in *Studia Hibernica* 36, 207-10.

Charles-Edwards, T.M. (2015) '*Táin bó Cúailnge*, hagiography and history', in *Sacred histories: a Festschrift for Máire Herbert*, ed. John Carey, Kevin Murray and Caitríona Ó Dochartaigh (Dublin), 86-102.

Christlein, Vincent, Martin Gropp & Andreas Maier (2017), 'Automatic Dating of Historical Documents', in *Kodikologie und Paläographie im digitalen Zeitalter 4/Codicology and Palaeography in the Digital Age 4* (2017), ed. Hannah Busch, Franz Fischer, Patrick Sahle, in collaboration with Bernhard Assmann, Philipp Hegel, Celia Krause (Norderstedt: Books on Demand), 151-64.

Ciobanu, A.M., L.P. Dinu, O.M. Sulea, A. Dinu, and V. Niculae (2013) 'Temporal text classification for Romanian novels set in the past', *Proceedings of RANLP 2013*, 136-40.

Clancy, T.O. (2011) 'Iona v. Kells: succession, jurisdiction and politics in the Columban *familia* in the later tenth century', in *Tome: studies in medieval Celtic history and law in honour of Thomas Charles-Edwards*, ed. Fiona Edmonds & Paul Russell (Woodbridge), 89-101.

Connon, Anne (2014) 'The Roscommon *locus* of *Acallam na senórach* and some thoughts as to *tempus* and *persona*', in *In Dialogue with the Agallamh: essays in honour of Seán Ó Coileáin*, ed. Aidan Doyle and Kevin Murray (Dublin), 21-59.

Corthals, Johan (1990) 'Some observations on the versification of the rhymeless "Leinster Poems"', *Celtica* 21, 113-125.

Cucera, Karel and Martin Stulka (2010) 'Diachronic corpora: see histories of words from another angle', *Webs of words: new studies in historical lexicography*, 1-7.

Dalli, Angelo and Yorick Wilks (2006) 'Automatic dating of documents and temporal text classification', *Proceedings of the Workshop on Annotating and Reasoning about Time and Events*, 17-22.

de Jong, Franciska, H. Rode, and Djoerd Hiemstra (2005) 'Temporal language models for the disclosure of historical text', *Proceedings of AHC2005 (History and Computing)*.

de Vries, Ranke (2012) *Two texts on Loch nEchach: De causis torchi Corc' Óche and Aided Echach maic Maireda* (London).

Dooley, Ann (2004) 'The date and purpose of *Acallam na Senórach*', *Éigse* 34, 97-126.

Drineas, Petros, Michael Mahoney and S. Muthukrishnan (2006) 'Subspace sampling and relative-error matrix approximation: column-based methods', *Proceedings of the 9th International Conference on Approximation Algorithms for Combinatorial Optimization Problems* (Barcelona) 316-26.

Drucker, Johanna (2012) 'Humanistic theory and digital scholarship', in Gold 2012, 85-95.

Dumville, David (1982) 'Latin and Irish in the Annals of Ulster, A.D. 431-1050', in *Ireland in early medieval Europe: studies in memory of Kathleen Hughes*, ed. Dorothy Whitelock, Rosamond McKitterick, and David Dumville (Cambridge), 320-41.

Dumville, David (1997) *Councils and synods of the Gaelic early and central Middle Ages*, Quiggin Memorial Lectures, 3 (Cambridge).

Duncan, Elizabeth (2012a) 'A reassessment of the script and make-up of *Lebor na Nuachongbála*', *Zeitschrift für celtische Philologie* 59, 27-66.

Duncan, Elizabeth (2012b) 'Lebor na Huidre and a copy of Boethius's de re Arithmetica: A Palaeographical Note', *Ériu* 62, 1-32.

Duncan, Elizabeth (2015) 'The palaeography of H in Lebor na hUidre', in Ó hUiginn, 29-52.

Evans, Nicholas (2010) *The present and the past in medieval Irish chronicles* (Woodbridge).

Fitzpatrick, Kathleen (2012) 'The humanities done digitally', in Gold 2012, 12-15.

Flower, Robin (1926) *Catalogue of Irish manuscripts in the British Library [formerly British Museum]* vol. 2 (London).

Garcia-Fernandez, Anne, A.-L. Ligozat, Marco Dinarelli, and Delphine Bernhard (2011) 'When was it written? Automatically determining publication dates', *Proceedings of SPIRE*.

Gold, Matthew K. (2012) *Debates in the Digital Humanities* (University of Minnesota: Minnesota).

Goverts, Disirée Elise (2014) *A linguistic and stylistic analysis of the Bórama* (unpublished Ph.D. thesis, St Catherine's College, University of Cambridge).

Grabowski, Kathryn and David Dumville (1984) *Chronicles and annals of medieval Ireland and Wales* (Woodbridge).

Greene, David (1958) 'The analytic forms of the verb in Irish', *Ériu* 18, 108-12.

Greene, David (1975) *Fingal Rónáin and other stories* (Dublin).

Greene, David (1976) 'The influence of Scandinavian on Irish', *Proceedings of the 7th Viking Congress* (Dublin), 75-82.

Gwynn, E.J. & W.J. Purton (1911-12) 'The monastery of Tallaght', *Proceedings of the Royal Irish Academy* 29C, 115-180.

He, Sheng, Petros Samara, Jan Burgers, and Lambert Schomaker (2016) 'A Multiple-Label Guided Clustering Algorithm for Historical Document Dating and Localization', *IEEE Transactions On Image Processing* 25.11, 5252-65.

Hemprich, Gisbert (2009) 'Die frühen Fassungen von *Éri óg inis na náem*', in *Festgabe für Hildegard L.C. Tristram überreicht von Studenten, Kollegen und Freunden des ehemaligen Faches Keltologie der Albert-Lugwigs-Universität in Freiburg*, ed. Gisbert Hemprich (Berlin), 289-383.

Hennessy, W. M. & Brian Mac Carthy (1887-1901) *Annala Uladh: Annals of Ulster otherwise Annala Senait, Annals of Senat: a chronicle of Irish affairs from A.D. 431 to A.D. 1540*, 4 vols, (Dublin).

Hennessy, W. M. (1871) *The Annals of Loch Cé* (2 vols) (London; repr. Dublin, 1939).

Herbert, Máire & Pádraig Ó Riain (1988) *Betha Adamnáin: The Irish Life of Adamnán* (London).

Herbert, Máire (2015) 'Three texts from *Lebor na hUidre*, and their testimony', in Ó hUiginn, 79-99.

Hillers, Barbara (1992) 'The odyssey of a folktale: *Merugud Uilix Meic Leirtis*', *Proceedings of the Harvard Celtic Colloquium* 12, 63-79.

Hillers, Barbara (2014) 'The medieval Irish wandering of Ulysses between literacy and orality' in O'Connor, 83-98.

Holmstedt, Robert D. (2009) 'Dating the language of Ruth: a study in method', Paper presented at the annual meeting of the Canadian Society of Biblical Studies. Ottawa, May 23 (available online at http://individual.utoronto.ca/holmstedt/Holmstedt_DatingLangRuth_CSBSrevAug2009.pdf).

Hoyne, Mícheál (2017) 'Early Modern miscellanea', *Ériu* 67, 169-86.

Hughes, Art (1994) 'Gaeilge Uladh', in McCone et al., 611-60.

Hughes, Kathleen (1972) *Early Christian Ireland: introduction to the sources* (London).

Hull, Vernam (1958-59) 'The later version of the Expulsion of the Déssi', *Zeitschrift für celtische Philologie* 27, 14-63.

Ingridsdottir, Kicki (2009) *Aided Derbforgaill 'The violent death of Derbforgaill': a critical edition with introduction, translation and textual notes* (Uppsala).

Jackson, K.H. (1938) *Cath Maighe Léna* (Dublin).

Jackson, K.H. (1942) 'The adventure of Laeghaire mac Crimhthainn', *Speculum* 17 (3), 377-89.

Jackson, K.H. (1983) 'The historical grammar of Irish: some actualities and some desiderata', in *Proceedings of the Sixth International congress of Celtic studies: held in University College, Galway, 6-13 July 1979*, ed. Gearóid Mac Eoin, Anders Ahlqvist and Donncha Ó hAodha (Dublin) 1-18.

Jackson, K.H. (1986) 'The date of the Tripartite Life of St. Patrick', *Zeitschrift für celtische Philologie* 41, 5-45.

Jackson, K.H. (1990) *Aislinge Meic Con Glinne* (Dublin).

Josund, Kelsey, Akshay Rampuria and Aashna Shroff (n.d.) 'Dating text from Google NGrams', https://web.stanford.edu/class/cs224n/reports/2761173.pdf.

Kaelbling, L.P., M.L. Littman and A.W. Moore (1996) 'Reinforcement learning: a survey', *Journal of Articial Intelligence Research* 4, 237-85.

Kanhabua, Nattiya and Kjetil Norvag (2008) 'Improving temporal language models for determining time of non-timestamped documents', *Proceedings of ECDL'2008*.

Kanhabua, Nattiya and Kjetil Norvag (2009) 'Using temporal language models for document dating', in *Machine Learning and Knowledge Discovery in Databases*, ed. W. Buntine, M. Grobelnik, D. Mladenić, J. Shawe-Taylor (Berlin) 738-41.

Kelly, Fergus (1998) *Early Irish farming: a study based mainly on the law-texts of the 7th and 8th centuries AD* (Dublin).

Kelly, Fergus (2002) 'Texts and transmissions: the law-texts', in *Ireland and Europe in the early Middle Ages: texts and transmission. Irland und Europa im früheren Mittelalter: Texte und Überlieferung*, ed. Próinséas Ní Chatháin and Michael Richter (Dublin), 230-42.

Kelly, Patricia (1982) 'Dialekte im Altirschen?' in *Sprachwissenschaft in Innsbruck*, ed. Wolfgang Meid et al., 85-9.

Kelly, Patricia (n.d.) 'Echtra Loegairi meic Crimthainn', Thesaurus Linguae Hibernicae, Online: University College Dublin. http://www.ucd.ie/tlh/text/pk.tlh.001.text.html.

Kitchin, Rob (2014) 'Big Data, New Epistemologies and Paradigm Shifts', *Big Data & Society* 1 (1).

Kofoed, Jens Bruun (2006) 'Using linguistic difference in relative text dating: insights from other historical linguistic case studies', *Hebrew Studies* 47, 93-114.

Kohavi, Ron and Foster Provost (1998) 'Glossary of terms', *Machine Learning* 30, 271-74.

Kotsakos, Dimitrios, Theodoros Lappas, Dimitrios Kotzias, Dimitrios Gunopulos, Nattiya Kanhabua, and Kjetil Nørvåg (2014) 'A burstiness-aware approach for document dating', *Proceedings of SIGIR'14*, ACM (New York), 1003-6.

Koza, J.R., F.H. Bennett, David Andre and M.A. Keane (1996) 'Automated design of both the topology and sizing of analog electrical circuits using genetic programming', *Artificial Intelligence in Design* (Dordrecht), 151-70.

Kraaij, W. (2004) *Variations on language modelling for information retrieval.* Ph.D. thesis (University of Twente).

Kulkarni, Vivek, Yingtao Tian, Parth Dandiwala and Steven Skiena (2018) 'Simple neologism based domain independent models to predict year of authorship', *Proceedings of the 27th International Conference on Computational Linguistics*, 202-212.

Kumar, Abhimanu, Matthew Lease, and Jason Baldridge (2011) 'Supervised language modelling for temporal resolution of texts', *Proceedings of CIKM* 2011 (Glasgow), 2069-72.

Lappas, Theodoros, Benjamin Arai, Manolis Platakis, Dimitrios Kotsaskos, and Dimitrios Gunopulos (2009) 'On burstiness-aware search for document sequences', *Proceedings of ECDL'2009*, 477-86.

Le Deuff, Olivier (2018) *Digital humanities: history and development* (London).

Lévi-Strauss, Claude (1966) *The savage mind* (Chicago).

Li, Xiaoyan and W. B. Croft (2003) 'Time-based language models', *Proceedings of CIKM'2003*, 469-75.

Lloyd, S.P. (1982) 'Least squares quantization in PCM', *IEEE Transactions on Information Theory* 28 (2), 129-37.

Mac Airt, Seán & Gearóid Mac Niocaill (1983) *The Annals of Ulster (to A.D. 1131)* (Dublin).

Mac Airt, Seán (1951) *The annals of Inisfallen* (Dublin).

Mac Cana, Proinsias (1980) *The learned tales of medieval Ireland* (Dublin).

Mac Donncha, Frederic (1976) 'Medieval Irish homilies', in *Biblical studies: the medieval Irish contribution*, ed. Mairtín McNamara (Dublin), 59-71.

Mac Donncha, Frederic (1980-83) 'Dáta *Vita Tripartita Sancti Patricii*', *Éigse* 18 (1980-81) 125-142; 19 (1982-83) 354-72.

Mac Eoin, Gearóid (1960-61) 'The date and authorship of *Saltair na Rann*', *Zeitschrift für celtische Philologie* 28, 51-67.

Mac Eoin, Gearóid (1968) 'The mysterious death of Loeghaire mac Néill', *Studia Hibernica* 8, 22-48.

Mac Eoin, Gearóid (1982a) 'The dating of Middle Irish texts', *Proceedings of the British Academy* 68, 109-37.

Mac Eoin, Gearóid (1982b) 'Observations on *Saltair na rann*', *Zeitschrift für celtische Philologie* 39, 1-28.

Mac Eoin, Gearóid (1994) 'The interpolator H in Lebor na hUidre', in *Ulidia: proceedings of the First International Conference on the Ulster Cycle of Tales, Belfast and Emain Macha, 8-12 April 1994*, ed. J.P. Mallory and Gearóid Stockman (Belfast), 39-46.

Mac Gearailt, Uáitéar (1986) 'The Edinburgh text of *Mesca Ulad*', *Ériu* 37, 133-80.

Mac Gearailt, Uáitéar (1988) 'On textual correspondences in early Irish heroic tales' in *Proceedings of the First North American Congress of Celtic Studies, Ottawa, 1986*, ed. G.W. Mac Lennan (Ottawa) 343-55.

Mac Gearailt, Uáitéar (1989) 'Zum Irischen des 12. Jahrhunderts', *Zeitschrift für celtische Philologie* 43, 11-52.

Mac Gearailt, Uáitéar (1991) '*Cath Ruis na Ríg* and twelfth-century literary and oral tradition' *Zeitschrift für celtische Philologie* 44, 128-53.

Mac Gearailt, Uáitéar (1992) 'The language of some late Middle Irish texts in the Book of Leinster', *Studia Hibernica* 26, 167-216.

Mac Gearailt, Uáitéar (1999) 'Zur literarischen Sprache des 11. Jahrhunderts', in *Akten des Zweiten Deutschen Keltologen-Symposiums*, ed. Rolf Ködderitzsch, Arndt Wigger, and Stefan Zimmer (Tübingen) 105-120.

Mac Gearailt, Uáitéar (2004) 'Scéal *Chath Rois na Ríogh*: tuilleadh faoi na foinsí', *Aistí ag iompar scéil in omós do Shéamus P. Ó Mórdha*, ed. Breandán Ó Conaire (2004) 57-85.

Mac Gearailt, Uáitéar (2006-7) 'The making of Fingal Rónáin', *Studia Hibernica* 34, 63-84.

Mac Gearailt, Uáitéar (2010) *On the date of the Middle Irish recension II Táin bó Cúailnge*. Quiggin memorial lectures, 11 (Cambridge).

Mac Gearailt, Uáitéar (2012) 'Middle Irish archaisms in early modern Irish prose', *Studia Hibernica* 38, 57-116.

Mac Mathúna, Liam (2007) 'The growth of Irish (L1) / English (L2) Literary Code-mixing, 1600-1900: contexts, genres and realisations', in *The Celtic languages in contact: Papers from the workshop within the framework of the XIII International congress of Celtic studies, Bonn, 26-27 July 2007*, ed. H.L.C. Tristram (Potsdam) 217-34.

Mac Mathúna, Séamus (1985) *Immram Brain: Bran's journey to the Land of Women* (Tübingen).

Mac Niocaill, Gearóid (1958) review of R. Meyer (1958) in *Éigse* 9, 134-6.

Mac Niocaill, Gearóid (1959) 'Annála Uladh agus Annála Locha Cé, 1014-1220', *Galvia* 6, 337-40.

Mac Niocaill, Gearóid (1968) 'The Proportional Method in Dating Irish Texts', *Studia Celtica* 3, 47-52.

Mac Niocaill, Gearóid (1975) *The medieval Irish annals* (Dublin).

McCarthy, D.P. (2008) *The Irish annals: their genesis, evolution and history* (Dublin).

McCone, Kim (1985) 'The Würzburg and Milan glosses: our earliest sources of "Middle Irish"', *Ériu* 36, 85-106.

McCone, Kim (2000) *Echtrae Chonnlai and the beginnings of vernacular narrative writing in Ireland* (Maynooth).

McCone, Kim, Damian McManus, Cathal Ó Háinle, Nicholas Williams, and Liam Breatnach (1994) (edd.) *Stair na Gaeilge in ómós do Pádraig Ó Fiannachta* (Maigh Nuad).

McManus, Damian (1983) 'A chronology of the Latin loan-words in Early Irish', *Ériu* 34, 21-71.

McManus, Damian (1994) 'An Nua-Ghaeilge Chlasaiceach' in McCone et al., 335-445.

McManus, Damian (2002) 'The language of the *Beatha*', in *Beatha Aodha Ruaidh. The life of Red Hugh O'Donnell: historical and literary contexts*, ed. Pádraig Ó Riain. ITS subsidiary series, 12 (London) 54-73.

Meid, Wolfgang (1974) *Táin Bó Fraích*, revised edition (Dublin).

Meid, Wolfgang (2017) *Die Suche nach der Traumfrau. Aislinge Óenguso: Oengus' Traum, eine altirische Sage* (Innsbruck).

Meyer, Kuno (1886) *Merugud Uilix maicc Leirtis: the Irish Odyssey* (London).

Meyer, Kuno (1890) 'The oldest version of Tochmarc Emire', *Revue Celtique* 11, 433-57.

Meyer, Kuno (1894) *Hibernica minora. Being a fragment of the Old-Irish treatise on the Psalter.* Anecdota Oxonienesia, Mediaeval and Modern Irish Series 8 (Oxford).

Meyer, Kuno (1901) 'The expulsion of the Dessi', *Y Cymmrodor* 14, 101-35.

Meyer, Kuno (1911) *Betha Colmáin maic Lúacháin: Life of Colmán son of Lúachan* (Dublin and London). Reprinted as *Life of Colmán of Lynn: Betha Colmáin Lainne* (Dublin 1999).

Meyer, Robert T. (1958) *Merugud Uilix maic Leirtis* (Dublin).

Moran, Pádraic (2015) 'Language interaction in the St Gall Priscian', *Peritia* 26, 113-42.

Murphy, Gerard (1952), 'On the date of two sources', *Ériu* 16, 151-6.

Murphy, Gerard (1955) *Saga and myth in ancient Ireland* (Dublin).

Murphy, K. P. (2012) *Machine Learning: a probabilistic perspective* (Cambridge, MA).

Murray, Kevin (2004) *Baile in Scáil: The Phantom's Frenzy*, Irish Texts Society 58 (London).

Murray, Kevin (2005) 'Dialect in medieval Irish? Evidence from placenames', *Studia Celtica Fennica* 2, 97-109.

Murray, Kevin (2012a) "*Ticfa didiu rí aile forœ*': prophecy, sovereignty narratives and medieval Irish hagiography', in *The medieval imagination: Mirabile Dictu. Essays in honour of Yolande de Pontfarcy Sexton*, ed. Phyllis Gaffney & Jean Michel Picard (Dublin), 111-122.

Murray, Kevin (2012b) 'Interpreting the evidence: problems with dating the early *fianaigecht* corpus', *The Gaelic Finn Tradition*, ed. S.J. Arbuthnot and Geraldine Parsons (Dublin), 31-49.

Murray, Kevin (2014) 'The reworking of old Irish narrative texts in the Middle Irish period: contexts and motivations', in Boyle and Hayden, 291-306.

Murray, Kevin (2017) *The early Finn cycle* (Dublin).

Nagy, J.F. (1997) *Conversing with angels and ancients: literary myths in medieval Ireland* (Dublin).

Neidorf, Leonard (2013) 'The dating of Widsið and the study of Germanic antiquity', *Neophilologus* 97, 165-183.

Neidorf, Leonard (2015) 'On the Epistemology of Old English Scholarship' *Neophilologus* 99.4, 631-46.

Nelson, R. D. (2014) *Historical Roots of the Old Testament (1200-63 BCE)* (Atlanta, GA).

Ní Dhonnchadha, Máirín (1982) 'The guarantor list of Cáin Adomnáin, 697', *Peritia* 1, 178-215.

Ní Mhaonaigh, Máire (1992) 'Breifne bias in *Cogad Gáedel re Gallaib*', *Ériu* 43, 135-59.

Ní Mhaonaigh, Máire (1995) 'Cogad Gáedel re Gallaib: some dating considerations', *Peritia* 9, 354-77.

Ní Mhaonaigh, Máire (2014), 'Poetic authority in Middle Irish narrative: a case study' in Boyle & Hayden, 263-289.

Niculae, Vlad, Marcos Zampieri, Liviu P. Dinu, and Alina Ciobanu (2014) 'Temporal text ranking and automatic dating of texts' *Proceedings of EACL'14*, 17-21.

Nuner, R.D. (1958-59) 'The verbal system of the *Agallamh na Senórach*', *Zeitschrift für celtische Philologie* 27, 231-310.

Ó Briain, Máirtín (1993) review of Herbert & Ó Riain 1986, *Studia Hibernica* 27 (1993) 157-8.

Ó Catháin, Seán (1933) 'Some studies in the development from Middle to Modern Irish, based on the Annals of Ulster', *Zeitschrift für celtische Philologie* 19, 1-47.

Ó Cathasaigh, Tomás (1976) 'On the LU version of "The expulsion of the Dési"', *Celtica* 11, 150-57.

Ó Cathasaigh, Tomás (1990) 'On the *Cín Dromma Snechta* version of *Togail Brudne Uí Dergae*', *Ériu* 41, 103-114.

Ó Ceithearnaigh, Séamus (1942) *Regimen na Sláinte*. 3 vols, Leabhair o Láimhsgríbhnibh 9 (Dublin).

Ó Concheanainn, Tomás (1973-74) 'The reviser of Leabhar na hUidhre', *Éigse* 15, 277-88.

Ó Concheanainn, Tomás (1975-76) '"Aided Nath Í" and the scribes of Leabhar na Huidhre', *Éigse* 16, 146-62.

Ó Concheanainn, Tomás (1987) 'The manuscript tradition of *Mesca Ulad*', *Celtica* 19, 13-30.

Ó Concheanainn, Tomás (1991) 'Aided Nath Í and Uí Fhiachrach geneaologies', *Éigse* 25, 1-27.

Ó Concheanainn, Tomás (1996) 'Textual and historical associations of Leabhar na hUidhre', *Éigse* 29, 65-120.

Ó Corráin, Donncha (1987) 'The semantic development of Old Norse *Jarl* in Old and Middle Irish', *Proceedings of the 10th Viking Congress* (Oslo) 287-93.

Ó Corráin, Donncha (1994) 'Early Ireland: directions and re-directions', *Bullán: an Irish Studies journal* 1.2, 1-15.

Ó Corráin, Donnchadh (2015) 'Máel Muire, the scribe: family and background', in Ó hUiginn, 1-28.

Ó Corráin, Donnchadh (2017) *Clavis litterarum Hibernensium: medieval Irish books & texts* (*c.400-c.1600*) 3 vols. (Turnhout).

Ó Cróinín, Dáibhí (2013) '*Eól dam seiser cloinne Cuinn*: the fortunes of twelfth-century Irish syncretistic poem', in *Gablánach in scélaigecht: Celtic studies in honour of Ann*

Dooley, ed. Sarah Sheehan, Joanne Findon and Westley Follett (Dublin), 198-219.

Ó Cuív, Brian (1967-68) 'Some developments in Irish metrics', *Éigse* 12, 273-90.

Ó Cuív, Brian (1988) 'Personal names as an indicator of relations between native Irish and settlers in the Viking period', in *Settlement and Society in Medieval Ireland: studies presented to F.X. Martin*, ed. John Bradley (Kilkenny) 79-88.

Ó Cuív, Brian (2001) *Catalogue of Irish language manuscripts in the Bodleian Library at Oxford and Oxford College libraries*. Part 1: Descriptions (Dublin).

Ó hAodha, Donncha (1978) *Bethu Brigte* (Dublin).

Ó hUiginn, Ruairí (1996) 'Cú Chulainn and Connla', in *(Re)Oralisierung*, ed. H.L.C. Tristram, *ScriptOralia* 84 (Tübingen 1996) 223-46.

Ó hUiginn, Ruairí (2013) 'Transmitting the text: some linguistics issues in the work of the Franciscans', in *Irish Europe, 1600-1650: Writing and Learning*, ed. Raymond Gillespie and Ruairí Ó hUiginn (Dublin) 85-104.

Ó hUiginn, Ruairí (2015) *Lebor na hUidre: Codices Hibernenses Eximii 1* (Dublin).

Ó Máille, Tomás (1910) *The language of the Annals of Ulster* (Manchester).

Ó Muirchertaigh, Peadar (2015) *Gaelic dialects present and past: a study of modern and medieval dialect relationships in the Gaelic languages*, unpublished Ph.D. thesis (Edinburgh).

Ó Néill, Pádraig P. (1979) 'The Old-Irish treatise on the psalter and its Hiberno-Latin background', *Ériu* 30, 148-64.

Ó Néill, Pádraig P. (1981) 'The background to the Cambrai Homily', *Ériu* 32, 137-147.

Ó Néill, Pádraig P. (2000) 'Irish observance of the three Lents and the date of the St Gall Priscian' *Ériu* 51, 159-80.

Ó Néill, Pádraig P. (2002) 'The Old-Irish glosses of the *prima manus* in Würzburg, m.p.th.f.12: text and context reconsidered', in *Ogma: essays in Celtic Studies in honour of Próinséas Ní Chatháin*, ed. Michael Richter & Jean-Michel Picard (Dublin), 230-41.

Ó Néill, Pádraig P. (2014) 'Old wine in new bottles: the reprise of early Irish psalter exegesis in Airbertach mac Cosse's poem on the psalter', in Boyle and Hayden, 121-40.

Ó Riain, Gordon (2012) 'The language of *Caithréim Thoirdhealbhaigh*' in *Caithréim Thoirdhealbhaigh: reassessments*, ed. Liam P. Ó Murchú, Irish Texts Society Subsidiary series 24, 54-76.

Ó Riain, Pádraig (1978) *Cath Almaine*, Medieval and Modern Irish Series 25 (Dublin 1978).

Ó Riain, Pádraig (2011) *A dictionary of Irish saints* (Dublin).

O'Brien, M.A. (1938-39) 'The Old Irish Life of St. Brigit', *Irish Historical Studies* 1, 119-134, 343-353.

O'Brien, M.A. (1955) 'A Middle-Irish poem on the Christian kings of Leinster', *Ériu* 17, 35-51.

O'Connor, Ralph (2014) *Classical literature and learning in medieval Irish narrative* (Cambridge).

O'Grady, S.H. (1929) *Caithréim Thoirdhealbhaigh: The triumphs of Turlough*, 2 vols, (London).

O'Grady, S.H. (1992) *Catalogue of the Irish Manuscripts in the British Library*, vol. 1 (reprint) (Dublin).

O'Rahilly, Cecile (1966) 'Marcach = "messenger"?', *Celtica* 7 (1966), 32.

O'Rahilly, Cecile (1976) *Táin Bó Cúailnge Recension I* (Dublin).

O'Rahilly, Cecile (1984) *Táin Bó Cúalnge from the Book of Leinster* (Dublin).

O'Sullivan, William (1966) 'Notes on the scripts and make-up of the Book of Leinster', *Celtica* 7, 1-31.

Oskamp, H. P. A. (1966-67) 'Notes on the history of Lebor na hUidre', *Proceedings of the Royal Irish Academy* (C) 65, 117-37.

Oskamp, H. P. A. (1975-76) 'Mael Muire: compiler or reviser?', *Éigse* 16, 177-82.

Parsons, Geraldine (2009) '*Acallam na senórach* as prosimetrum', *Proceedings of the Harvard Celtic Colloquium*, 24/25, 86-100.

Pedregosa, Fabian, Elodie Cauvet, Gael Varoquaux, Christophe Pallier, Bertrang Thirion, and Alexandre Gramfort (2012) 'Learning to rank from medical imaging data', *CoRR*, abs/1207.3598.

Platt, John (1998) 'Fast training of support vector machines using sequential minimal optimization', in *Advances in Kernel Methods – Support Vector Learning*, ed. B. Schoelkopf, C. Burges and A. Smola (Cambridge, MA) 41-65.

Pokorny, Julius (1921) 'Germanisch-Irisches', *Zeitschrift für celtische Philologie* 13, 111-29.

Ponte, J.M. and W.B. Croft (1998) 'A language modeling approach to information retrieval', *Proceedings of SIGIR'1998*.

Popescu, Octavian and Carlo Strapparava (2013) 'Behind the times: detecting epoch changes using large corpora', *Proceedings of IJCNLP-2013*, Nagoya, Japan, October.

Popescu, Octavian and Carlo Strapparava (2014) 'Time corpora: epochs, opinions and changes', *Knowledge-Based Systems* 69, 3-13.

Popescu, Octavian and Carlo Strapparava (2015) 'SemEval 2015, Task 7: Diachronic Text Evaluation', *Proceedings of the 9th International Workshop on Semantic Evaluation* (*SemEval 2015*), 870-78.

Poppe, Erich (1992) 'The Early Modern Irish version of Beves of Hamtoun', *Cambridge Medieval Celtic Studies* 23, 77-98.

Qiu, Fangzhe (2016) 'A note on *comaccomol*', *Celtica* 28, 201-207.

Quin, Gordon (1939) *Stair Ercuil ocus a bás* (London).

Quinlan, Ross (1993) *C4.5: Programs for Machine Learning* (San Mateo, CA).

Ramsay, Stephen (2011) *Reading machines: towards an algorithmic criticism* (University of Illinois, Urbana).

Ramsay, Stephen and Geoffrey Rockwell (2012) 'Developing things: notes toward an epistemology of building in the digital humanities', in Gold 2012, 75-84.

Rezetko, Robert (2003) 'Dating Biblical Hebrew: evidence from Samuel-Kings and Chronicles' in I. Young (ed.), *Biblical Hebrew: Studies in Chronology and Typology* (London) 215-50.

Rieder, Bernhard and Theo Röhle (2012) 'Digital methods: five challenges' in Berry 2012, 67-84.

Rieder, Bernhard and Theo Röhle (2017) 'Digital Methods: From Challenges to Bildung', in Schäfer & van Es 2017, 109-24.

Risk, Henry (1968-69) 'French loan-words in Irish', *Études celtiques* 12, 585-655.

Risk, Henry (1974-75) 'French loan-words in Irish' (cont.), *Études celtiques* 14, 67-98.

Robinson, F. N. (1908) *'The Irish Lives of Guy of Warwick and Bevis of Hampton', Zeitschrift für celtische Philologie* 6, 9-180, 273-338.

Rodway, Simon (2013) *Dating medieval Welsh literature: evidence from the verbal system* (Aberystwyth).

Rowland, Jenny (2014) *A selection of early Welsh saga poems* (London).

Russell, Paul (2005) 'What was best of every language: the early history of the Irish language', in *A new history of Ireland* vol. 1, ed. Dáibhí Ó Cróinín (Oxford) 439-50.

Samuel, Arthur (1959) 'Some studies in machine learning using the game of checkers', *IBM Journal of Research and Development*, 3 (3), 210-29.

Schäfer, M.T. & Karin van Es (2017) *The datafied society: studying culture through data* (Amsterdam).

Schlüter, Dagmar (2010) *History of Fable? The Book of Leinster as a document of cultural memory in twelfth-century Ireland* (Münster).

Sharpe, Richard (1982) 'Palaeographical considerations in the study of the Patrician documents in the Book of Armagh', *Scriptorium: revue internationale des études rel atives aux manuscrits* 36.1, 3-28.

Sharpe, Richard (1990), review of Herbert & Ó Riain 1988, *Cambridge Medieval Celtic Studies* 19, 75-6.

Shaw, Francis (1934) *The dream of Óengus: Aislinge Óenguso* (Dublin).

Sheahan, Shawn (1938) *An Irish Version of Gualterus de Dosibus* (Washington D.C.).

Simms, Katharine (2009) *Medieval Gaelic sources* (Dublin).

Smith, P.J. (2007) *Three historical poems ascribed to Gilla Cóemáin: a critical edition of the work of an eleventh-century Irish scholar* (Münster).

Sommerfelt, Alf (1915-21) 'Le système verbal dan *In cath catharda*', *Revue celtiques* 36 (1915-16) 23-62, 295-334, 37 (1917-19) 230-46, 353-7, 38 (1920-21) 25-47.

Sommerfelt, Alf (1922) 'Recherches sur l'histoire de vieux-norrois en Irlande', *Revue celtiques* 39, 175-98.

Stajner, Sanja and Marcos Zampieri (2013) 'Stylistic changes for temporal text classification', *Text, Speech, and Dialogue. TSD 2013*, ed. I. Habernal & V. Matoušek (Berlin)

519–26.

Stamou, Constantina (2005) *Dating Victorians: an experimental approach to stylochronometry* Ph.D. thesis (University of Bedfordshire).

Stifter, David (2013) 'Towards the linguistic dating of early Irish law texts', in *Medieval Irish Law: Text and Context*. Sydney Series in Celtic Studies 12 (Sydney) 163-208.

Stifter, David (2015) 'The language of the poems of Blathmac', in *The poems of Blathmac son of Cú Brettan: reassessments*, ed. Pádraig Ó Riain. Irish Texts Society subsidiary series 27 (London) 47-103.

Stokes, Whitley & John Strachan (1901) *Thesaurus Paleohibernicus: a collection of Old-Irish glosses, scholia, prose and verse*. Vol. 1 (Cambridge). Reprinted Dublin 1975.

Stokes, Whitley & John Strachan (1903) *Thesaurus Paleohibernicus: a collection of Old-Irish glosses, scholia, prose and verse*. Vol. 2 (Cambridge). Reprinted with supplement, Dublin 1975.

Stokes, Whitley (1883) *The Saltair na Rann: a collection of early Middle Irish poems edited from MS. Rawl. B. 502, in the Bodleian Library* (Oxford).

Stokes, Whitley (1893) 'The violent deaths of Goll and Garb', *Revue celtique* 14, 396-449

Stokes, Whitley (1897) 'Cuimmín's poem on the saints of Ireland', *Zeitschrift für celtische Philologie* 1, 59-73.

Stokes, Whitley (1898) 'The Gaelic Maundeville', *Zeitschrift für celtische Philologie* 2, 1-62, 226-312.

Stokes, Whitley (1902) 'On the deaths of some Irish heroes', *Revue celtique* 23, 302-22; 27, 202-3.

Stokes, Whitley (1909) 'In cath catharda: The civil war of the Romans: an Irish version of Lucan's Pharsalia', in *Irische Texte mit Wörterbuch*, 4 (2), 1-581.

Stokes, Whitley (1993) *The Annals of Tigernach*, 2 vols (Felinfach), repr. from *Revue Celtique* 16 (1895) 374-419; 17 (1896) 6-33, 116-263, 337-420; 18 (1897) 9-59, 150-303.

Stolcke, Andreas (2002) 'SRILM – An Extensible Language Modeling Toolkit', *Proceedings of the International Conference on Spoken Language Processing* 2, 901-4.

Stolcke, Andreas, Jing Zheng, Wen Wang, and Victor Abrash (2011) 'SRILM at sixteen: update and outlook', *Proceedings of IEEE Automatic Speech Recognition and Understanding Workshop*, 5.

Studer, Patrick (2008) *Historical corpus stylistics: media, technology and change* (Bloomsbury Publishing).

Swanton, Michael (1997) *Beowulf: Revised Edition* (Manchester: Manchester University Press).

Szymanski, Terrence and Gerard Lynch (2015) 'UCD: Diachronic Text Classification with Character, Word, and Syntactic N-grams', *Proceedings of the 9th International Workshop on Semantic Evaluation (SemEval 2015)* 879-83.

Theuerkauf, Marie-Luise (2017) 'The death of Boand and the recensions of Dindṡenchas Érenn', *Ériu* 67, 49-97.

Thurneysen, Rudolf (1921) *Die irische Helden und Königsage bis zum siebzehnten Jahrhundert* (Halle).

Thurneysen, Rudolf (1935) *Scéla Mucce Meic Dathó* (Dublin).

Thurneysen, Rudolf (1946) *A grammar of Old Irish*, trans. and revised by D.A. Binchy & Osborn Bergin (Dublin).

Tilahun, Gelila, Andrey Feuerverger and Michael Gervers (2012) 'Dating medieval English charters', *The annals of applied statistics* 6.4, 1615-40.

Toner, Gregory (1998) 'The transmission of *Tochmarc Emire*', *Ériu* 49, 71-88.

Toner, Gregory (2000) 'Reconstructing the earliest Irish tale lists', *Éigse* 32, 88-120.

Toner, Gregory (2005) 'Authority, verse and the transmission of *senchas*', *Ériu* 55, 59-84.

Toner, Gregory (2007) *Bruiden Da Choca* (London).

Tristram, H.L.C. (1992) 'Feis und fled: Wirklichkeit un Darstellung in mittelalterlichen irischen Gastmahlserzählungen', *ScriptOralia* 43, 182-220.

Tsoumakas, Grigorios and Ioannis Katakis (2007) 'Multi-label classification: an overview', *International Journal of Data Warehousing & Mining* 3 (3), 1-13.

Uhlich, Jürgen (2006) 'Some textual problems in Rónán's lament I: two quatrains concerning Echaid's daughter', *Ériu* 56, 13-62.

Uricchio, William (2017) 'Data, culture and the ambivalence of algorithms' in Schäfer & van Es 2017, 125-137.

Van Es, Karin, Nicolás López Coombs & Thomas Boeschoten (2017) 'Towards a reflexive digital data analysis', in Schäfer & van Es 2017, 171-80.

Vendryes, Joseph, Édouard Bachellery, and Pierre-Yves Lambert (1987) *Lexique étymologique de l'Irlandais ancien: Lettre C* (Dublin).

Wahlberg, Fredrik, Lasse Mårtensson, and Anders Brun (2016) 'Large scale continuous dating of medieval scribes using a combined image and language model', *12th IAPR Workshop on Document Analysis Systems* (DAS), 48-53.

Walsh, Paul (1912) 'The topography of *Betha Colmáin*', *Zeitschrift für celtische Philologie* 8, 568-82.

Wan, X. (2007) 'TimedTextRank: adding the temporal dimension to multi-document summarization', *Proceedings of SIGIR'2007*, 867-8.

Wang, Chong, David Blei, and David Heckerman (2008) 'Continuous time dynamic topic models', *Proceedings of Uncertainty in Artificial Intelligence*.

Watson, J. C. (1941) *Mesca Ulad* (Dublin).

West, Máire (1990) 'Leabhar na hUidhre's position in the manuscript history of *Togail Bruidne Da Derga* and *Orgain Brudne Uí Dergae*', *Cambridge Medieval Celtic Studies* 20, 61-98.

West, Máire (1999) 'The genesis of *Togail Bruidne da Derga*: a reappraisal of the two-source theory', *Celtica* 23, 413-35.

Witten, I.H., Eibe Frank and M.A. Hall (2011) *Data Mining: Practical machine learning tools and techniques*. Morgan Kaufmann, Third edition.

Young, Ian, Robert Rezetko, and Martin Ehrensvärd (2009) *Linguistic Dating of Biblical Texts*. 2 vols. (London).

Zampieri, Marcos, A.M. Ciobanu, Vlad Niculae, and L.P. Dinu (2015) 'AMBRA: a ranking approach to temporal text classification', *Proceedings of the 9th International Workshop on Semantic Evaluation* (*SemEval 2015*), 851-5.

Index

10-fold cross-validation 58, 62-63, 70-71, 73-76, 81-82, 84, 86, 88, 97, 163
5-gram 6, 49. *See also* n-gram

absolute chronology 138. *See also* relative chronology, chronometrics, calendrical dating
  absolute date 3, 6, 23, 38, 98, 137
ancient texts 2, 6, 9, 11, 94, 132, 141
Anglo-Norman 34-36, 78, 148
Anglo-Saxon 11, 35
Annals of Connacht 79
Annals of Inisfallen 77-83, 90-93, 95-96, 129
Annals of Loch Cé 77, 79-81, 83, 86-87, 91, 93, 95-96
Annals of the Four Masters 32, 34
Annals of Tigernach 35, 130, 139, 144
Annals of Ulster 30, 33, 77-81, 83-85, 91-93, 95-96, 132, 134-135, 145, 159
Arabic 6, 39, 49, 101-102
archaisation 9, 21-22, 28, 31-33, 37
  archaism 29-33, 37-38, 103, 117, 134, 154-155, 159
Artificial Intelligence 3, 141
attribution 1-2, 9, 11-13, 138
authenticity 12, 31, 39
authority 12, 18, 31
authorship 1, 6, 11-14, 16, 18, 20, 24, 26, 28, 30-31, 128, 138, 145, 147, 150, 152, 156-157
autograph manuscript 11, 39

bias compensation 102-116, 120-121, 123-127, 131, 137. *See also* Reinforcement and Adaptive Learning
biblical texts 11, 36. *See also* Hebrew
black boxing 7, 133
Book of Leinster 13-14, 17-18, 25, 34, 117-118, 144-147, 150, 152-155, 157-159
Book of the Dun Cow (*Lebor na hUidre*) 17, 23, 25, 32, 35, 117-118, 143-144, 146-147, 154, 157-158, 160-161
Brownian motion 42
BurstySimDater 44, 48

calendrical dating 3, 132. *See also* absolute dating
Chi-squared feature selection 43
chronometrics 6, 109, 116, 119, 124, 132, 137-140. *See also* absolute dating
closure (*dúnad*) 13
cluster analysis 57-58, 162
Column Subset Selection (CSS) 60-61
conservatism 2, 9, 22, 24, 27-30, 92, 103, 119, 147
corpus analysis 41
Corpus of Electronic Texts (CELT) 79-80, 98-99

datability 64-65, 90-92
diachronic text evaluation (DTE) 41, 43, 46-47, 50-51, 53, 59-60, 67-75, 80-81, 83, 85-87, 91-92. *See also* chronometrics
dialect 2, 9, 22-23, 26-27, 29-30, 36-37, 39-40, 102, 129
digital humanities 7-9, 141
digital literary criticism 141
document dating 6, 41
domain adaptation 104-105

English
  Middle English 34-35, 148
  Old English 35
event detection 41, 48

feature selection 9, 41, 43, 50, 65, 68, 81, 163. *See also* Chi-squared feature selection
flexible time intervals (FTI) 41, 52-54, 63-64, 70-77, 81-92, 95, 97, 100, 105
focussed dating 119-26
forgery 32
Freecycle 67-68, 70, 74-77, 85, 87-88, 90-91, 134-136
Frobenius norm 44

Gaelic 9, 12, 17, 26, 34, 77, 134-135. *See also* Irish, Scottish Gaelic
genre 5-6, 11, 19, 49, 98, 103, 105, 116, 132-133, 136, 141
Google Books 5

Google syntactic database 72, 92
granularity 2, 44, 47, 56, 69, 71-72, 81, 83, 119, 123, 131
Greedy Grouping (GG) 42, 52, 56-58, 72
Greedy Grouping via Mutual Information (GG_{MI}) 56, 58
guarantor 14. *See also* witness

Hebrew 36, 40. *See also* biblical texts

information diffusion 41, 48
internal evidence 2, 9, 12-17, 19, 98, 112, 144-145, 149-150, 152
intertextuality 17-18
Irish
  Middle Irish 17, 22, 24-25, 30, 33, 35, 38, 111-112, 116, 119, 123, 125-128, 133, 135-137, 140, 148-149, 151-153, 155-156, 159-161
  Old Irish 12, 16-17, 21-28, 30-31, 35, 38-39, 111, 116, 119, 123-127, 133, 135-137, 139, 143, 148, 153, 155, 159, 160-161
  Early Modern Irish 19, 30, 33, 39, 111, 114, 116, 119, 124, 125-127, 130-131, 135-137, 139-140
  Classical Modern Irish 19, 31, 39

J48 69

K-means clustering 57-58, 162
K-nearest neighbour 49

landmark selection 41, 52, 57-63, 73. *See also* Temporal Landmark Selection
language modelling 5, 9, 41-43, 46-51, 65. *See also* temporal model
law tracts 15, 18, 20, 23, 26, 32
lazy method 44
lemmatisation 5, 133, 135
lexical dating 11, 33-36
linguistic dating 2-3, 9, 11, 21-26, 31-33, 36-40, 48, 98, 150
loanwords 34-36, 149, 154
loss function 46-47

machine learning 3-5, 7-11, 21, 40, 42-44, 46, 48-51, 103-104, 132, 162-164
metrics/verse 9, 12-13, 17, 19-21, 30-31, 39, 98, 112, 123, 139-140, 146, 150, 153-154, 156

Moore-Penrose 44
multi-class classification 41, 51-54, 56, 62-63, 65-66, 72, 83

Naïve Bayes (NB) 69, 162-163
Naïve Bayes Multinomial (NBM) 53, 55, 68-74, 80
Natural Language Processing (NLP) 41-42, 48
neologism 32, 36
n-grams 44, 51, 54, 68-69, 72, 80-81, 92, 132-134, 163
non-parametric memory-based distance 43
non-standardised (language/orthography) 4-5, 67, 132. *See also* standardisation
normal distribution matrix (NM) 60, 73-77, 82-90
normalised log-likelihood ration (NLLR) 42
Norse 34-35

obscurantism 31
Old Irish glosses 16, 24, 27-29, 130, 139, 143, 159-160
orthography 2, 4-6, 22, 27, 30, 78, 100, 121, 132, 134-135, 138, 143, 151, 157, 159

palimpsest 11, 23
parsing 5, 81
periodisation 125-127
Portuguese 43
probability theory 65

ranking 43, 48-49, 51-52, 56, 66
  ordinal ranking 21, 47, 49, 65
Rawlinson B 502 17, 117-118, 143-144, 156
readability 41, 43
redaction 14, 25, 128-129, 131, 151. *See also* revision
register 23-24, 26-29, 33, 37, 39-40, 129-30, 136, 140, 154
regression 43, 45-52, 65-66, 162
  regression analysis 48
  logistic regression 65, 162
  ordinal regression 43, 48-51
reinforcement and adaptive learning 102-106, 123, 125. *See also* bias compensation

relative chronology 2-3, 6, 18, 23, 38, 138, 147. *See also* absolute chronology
revision (textual) 2, 5-6, 13-14, 17, 23-26, 37, 39, 94-95, 99, 102, 109, 111-112, 114, 127, 129-131, 138, 154. *See also* redaction, transmission
Romance 34
Romanian 43
roscad 20, 31, 150

Scottish Gaelic 30. *See also* Gaelic
semantic similarity 42
SemEval-2015 43
Sequential Minimal Optimization (SMO) 69
similarity metrics 42
Singular Value Decomposition (SVD) 61
Sliding Time Intervals (STI) 41, 52-57, 70-77, 80, 82-90, 92
SRILM toolkit 49
St Gall glosses 16, 27-29, 159
standard multi-class SVM classification 43, 51
standardisation (linguistic/orthographic) 4-6, 27-28, 39, 132, 134, 136. *See also* non-standardised
stemmatics 25-26, 32
strata (linguistic/textual) 2, 5, 11, 14, 16, 23-26, 29, 32-33, 37, 39, 76, 94, 100-101, 109, 112-114, 127-128, 131, 133, 138, 157, 161
stratification 3, 127-128
style 12, 15, 19, 21, 28-30, 32-33, 42, 44, 50, 65, 103, 105, 109, 140, 152, 154, 157-158, 170
stylistics 51
supervised classification 43
supervised learning 4, 162. *See also* unsupervised learning
Support Vector Machine (SVM) 43, 51, 68-73, 80, 162

tale lists 18
temporal distribution 51-53, 63-66, 69, 83-84, 87-88, 105
Temporal Landmark Selection (TLS) 57-64, 70-77, 81-91
temporal model 33, 42, 44, 46, 48-49, 125, 129-130, 132-37. *See also* language modelling
temporal text classification 41
term burstiness 44, 48
term frequency-inverse document frequency (tf-idf) 42
Text Encoding Initiative (TEI) 99
text summarisation 41
topic modelling 4, 42, 44, 134-137, 139, 162-163
Trained Distribution Matrix (TM) 60, 73-77, 82-89
Trained Normal Distribution Matrix (TNM) 60, 73-77, 82-89
transmission (textual) 5, 17, 23, 26, 38-39, 67, 92-94, 100, 113, 117-19, 129-132. *See also* revision

UCD system 43, 51, 62, 67, 69, 71-77, 81-89, 95, 97
Uniform Distribution Matrix (UM) 60, 73-77, 82-90
unigram 42-43. *See also* n-gram
unsupervised learning 4, 162. *See also* supervised learning

vector quantification 57
verse. *See* metrics

Weka 3.7 Java Library 67
Wiener process 42
witness 12, 14
Würzburg glosses 16, 27, 29, 159

Yellow Book of Lecan 32, 118, 147, 151, 158-159